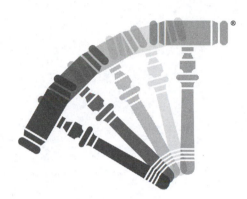

Casenote® Legal Briefs

TAXATION

Keyed to Courses Using

Burke and Friel's
Taxation of Individual Income

Tenth Edition

Wolters Kluwer
Law & Business

Copyright © 2013 CCH Incorporated. All Rights Reserved.

Published by Wolters Kluwer Law & Business in New York.

Wolters Kluwer Law & Business serves customers worldwide with CCH, Aspen Publishers, and Kluwer Law International products. (www.wolterskluwerlb.com)

No part of this publication may be reproduced or transmitted in any form or by any means, electronic or mechanical, including photocopy, recording, or utilized by any information storage and retrieval system, without written permission from the publisher. For information about permissions or to request permission online, visit us at wolterskluwerlb.com or a written request may be faxed to our permissions department at 212-771-0803.

To contact Customer Service, e-mail customer.service@wolterskluwer.com, call 1-800-234-1660, fax 1-800-901-9075, or mail correspondence to:

Wolters Kluwer Law & Business
Attn: Order Department
P.O. Box 990
Frederick, MD 21705

Printed in the United States of America.

1 2 3 4 5 6 7 8 9 0

ISBN 978-1-4548-3285-0

Certified Chain of Custody
Product Line Contains At Least
20% Certified Forest Content
www.sfiprogram.org
SFI-00756

About Wolters Kluwer Law & Business

Wolters Kluwer Law & Business is a leading global provider of intelligent information and digital solutions for legal and business professionals in key specialty areas, and respected educational resources for professors and law students. Wolters Kluwer Law & Business connects legal and business professionals as well as those in the education market with timely, specialized authoritative content and information-enabled solutions to support success through productivity, accuracy and mobility.

Serving customers worldwide, Wolters Kluwer Law & Business products include those under the Aspen Publishers, CCH, Kluwer Law International, Loislaw, Best Case, ftwilliam.com and MediRegs family of products.

CCH products have been a trusted resource since 1913, and are highly regarded resources for legal, securities, antitrust and trade regulation, government contracting, banking, pension, payroll, employment and labor, and healthcare reimbursement and compliance professionals.

Aspen Publishers products provide essential information to attorneys, business professionals and law students. Written by preeminent authorities, the product line offers analytical and practical information in a range of specialty practice areas from securities law and intellectual property to mergers and acquisitions and pension/benefits. Aspen's trusted legal education resources provide professors and students with high-quality, up-to-date and effective resources for successful instruction and study in all areas of the law.

Kluwer Law International products provide the global business community with reliable international legal information in English. Legal practitioners, corporate counsel and business executives around the world rely on Kluwer Law journals, looseleafs, books, and electronic products for comprehensive information in many areas of international legal practice.

Loislaw is a comprehensive online legal research product providing legal content to law firm practitioners of various specializations. Loislaw provides attorneys with the ability to quickly and efficiently find the necessary legal information they need, when and where they need it, by facilitating access to primary law as well as state-specific law, records, forms and treatises.

Best Case Solutions is the leading bankruptcy software product to the bankruptcy industry. It provides software and workflow tools to flawlessly streamline petition preparation and the electronic filing process, while timely incorporating ever-changing court requirements.

ftwilliam.com offers employee benefits professionals the highest quality plan documents (retirement, welfare and non-qualified) and government forms (5500/PBGC, 1099 and IRS) software at highly competitive prices.

MediRegs products provide integrated health care compliance content and software solutions for professionals in healthcare, higher education and life sciences, including professionals in accounting, law and consulting.

Wolters Kluwer Law & Business, a division of Wolters Kluwer, is head-quartered in New York. Wolters Kluwer is a market-leading global information services company focused on professionals.

Format for the Casenote® Legal Brief

Nature of Case: This section identifies the form of action (e.g., breach of contract, negligence, battery), the type of proceeding (e.g., demurrer, appeal from trial court's jury instructions),or the relief sought (e.g., damages, injunction, criminal sanctions).

Fact Summary: This is included to refresh your memory and can be used as a quick reminder of the facts.

Rule of Law: Summarizes the general principle of law that the case illustrates. It may be used for instant recall of the court's holding and for classroom discussion or home review.

Facts: This section contains all relevant facts of the case, including the contentions of the parties and the lower court holdings. It is written in a logical order to give the student a clear understanding of the case. The plaintiff and defendant are identified by their proper names throughout and are always labeled with a (P) or (D).

Party ID: Quick identification of the relationship between the parties.

Concurrence/Dissent: All concurrences and dissents are briefed whenever they are included by the casebook editor.

Analysis: This last paragraph gives you a broad understanding of where the case "fits in" with other cases in the section of the book and with the entire course. It is a hornbook-style discussion indicating whether the case is a majority or minority opinion and comparing the principal case with other cases in the casebook. It may also provide analysis from restatements, uniform codes, and law review articles. The analysis will prove to be invaluable to classroom discussion.

Palsgraf v. Long Island R.R. Co.
Injured bystander (P) v. Railroad company (D)

N.Y. Ct. App., 248 N.Y. 339, 162 N.E. 99 (1928).

NATURE OF CASE: Appeal from judgment affirming verdict for plaintiff seeking damages for personal injury.

FACT SUMMARY: Helen Palsgraf (P) was injured on R.R.'s (D) train platform when R.R.'s (D) guard helped a passenger aboard a moving train, causing his package to fall on the tracks. The package contained fireworks which exploded, creating a shock that tipped a scale onto Palsgraf (P).

⚖ RULE OF LAW
The risk reasonably to be perceived defines the duty to be obeyed.

FACTS: Helen Palsgraf (P) purchased a ticket to Rockaway Beach from R.R. (D) and was waiting on the train platform. As she waited, two men ran to catch a train that was pulling out from the platform. The first man jumped aboard, but the second man, who appeared as if he might fall, was helped aboard by the guard on the train who had kept the door open so they could jump aboard. A guard on the platform also helped by pushing him onto the train. The man was carrying a package wrapped in newspaper. In the process, the man dropped his package, which fell on the tracks. The package contained fireworks and exploded. The shock of the explosion was apparently of great enough strength to tip over some scales at the other end of the platform, which fell on Palsgraf (P) and injured her. A jury awarded her damages, and R.R. (D) appealed.

ISSUE: Does the risk reasonably to be perceived define the duty to be obeyed?

HOLDING AND DECISION: (Cardozo, C.J.) Yes. The risk reasonably to be perceived defines the duty to be obeyed. If there is no foreseeable hazard to the injured party as the result of a seemingly innocent act, the act does not become a tort because it happened to be a wrong as to another. If the wrong was not willful, the plaintiff must show that the act as to her had such great and apparent possibilities of danger as to entitle her to protection. Negligence in the abstract is not enough upon which to base liability. Negligence is a relative concept, evolving out of the common law doctrine of trespass on the case. To establish liability, the defendant must owe a legal duty of reasonable care to the injured party. A cause of action in tort will lie where harm, though unintended, could have been averted or avoided by observance of such a duty. The scope of the duty is limited by the range of danger that a reasonable person could foresee. In this case, there was nothing to suggest from the appearance of the parcel or otherwise that the parcel contained fireworks. The guard could not reasonably have had any warning of a threat to Palsgraf (P), and R.R. (D) therefore cannot be held liable. Judgment is reversed in favor of R.R. (D).

DISSENT: (Andrews, J.) The concept that there is no negligence unless R.R. (D) owes a legal duty to take care as to Palsgraf (P) herself is too narrow. Everyone owes to the world at large the duty of refraining from those acts that may unreasonably threaten the safety of others. If the guard's action was negligent as to those nearby, it was also negligent as to those outside what might be termed the "danger zone." For Palsgraf (P) to recover, R.R.'s (D) negligence must have been the proximate cause of her injury, a question of fact for the jury.

▶ ANALYSIS
The majority defined the limit of the defendant's liability in terms of the danger that a reasonable person in defendant's situation would have perceived. The dissent argued that the limitation should not be placed on liability, but rather on damages. Judge Andrews suggested that only injuries that would not have happened but for R.R.'s (D) negligence should be compensable. Both the majority and dissent recognized the policy-driven need to limit liability for negligent acts, seeking, in the words of Judge Andrews, to define a framework "that will be practical and in keeping with the general understanding of mankind." The Restatement (Second) of Torts has accepted Judge Cardozo's view.

Quicknotes

FORESEEABILITY A reasonable expectation that change is the probable result of certain acts or omissions.

NEGLIGENCE Conduct falling below the standard of care that a reasonable person would demonstrate under similar conditions.

PROXIMATE CAUSE The natural sequence of events without which an injury would not have been sustained.

Issue: The issue is a concise question that brings out the essence of the opinion as it relates to the section of the casebook in which the case appears. Both substantive and procedural issues are included if relevant to the decision.

Holding and Decision: This section offers a clear and in-depth discussion of the rule of the case and the court's rationale. It is written in easy-to-understand language and answers the issue presented by applying the law to the facts of the case. When relevant, it includes a thorough discussion of the exceptions to the case as listed by the court, any major cites to the other cases on point, and the names of the judges who wrote the decisions.

Quicknotes: Conveniently defines legal terms found in the case and summarizes the nature of any statutes, codes, or rules referred to in the text.

Note to Students

Wolters Kluwer Law & Business is proud to offer *Casenote® Legal Briefs*—continuing thirty years of publishing America's best-selling legal briefs.

Casenote® Legal Briefs are designed to help you save time when briefing assigned cases. Organized under convenient headings, they show you how to abstract the basic facts and holdings from the text of the actual opinions handed down by the courts. Used as part of a rigorous study regimen, they can help you spend more time analyzing and critiquing points of law than on copying bits and pieces of judicial opinions into your notebook or outline.

Casenote® Legal Briefs should never be used as a substitute for assigned casebook readings. They work best when read as a follow-up to reviewing the underlying opinions themselves. Students who try to avoid reading and digesting the judicial opinions in their casebooks or online sources will end up shortchanging themselves in the long run. The ability to absorb, critique, and restate the dynamic and complex elements of case law decisions is crucial to your success in law school and beyond. It cannot be developed vicariously.

Casenote® Legal Briefs represents but one of the many offerings in Legal Education's Study Aid Timeline, which includes:

- *Casenote® Legal Briefs*
- *Emanuel® Law Outlines*
- Emanuel® *Law in a Flash* Flash Cards
- Emanuel® *CrunchTime®* Series
- *Siegel's Essay and Multiple-Choice Questions and Answers Series*

Each of these series is designed to provide you with easy-to-understand explanations of complex points of law. Each volume offers guidance on the principles of legal analysis and, consulted regularly, will hone your ability to spot relevant issues. We have titles that will help you prepare for class, prepare for your exams, and enhance your general comprehension of the law along the way.

To find out more about Wolters Kluwer Law & Business' study aid publications, visit us online at *www.wolterskluwerlb.com* or email us at *legaledu@wolterskluwer.com*. We'll be happy to assist you.

A. Decide on a Format and Stick to It

Structure is essential to a good brief. It enables you to arrange systematically the related parts that are scattered throughout most cases, thus making manageable and understandable what might otherwise seem to be an endless and unfathomable sea of information. There are, of course, an unlimited number of formats that can be utilized. However, it is best to find one that suits your needs and stick to it. Consistency breeds both efficiency and the security that when called upon you will know where to look in your brief for the information you are asked to give.

Any format, as long as it presents the essential elements of a case in an organized fashion, can be used. Experience, however, has led *Casenote*® *Legal Briefs* to develop and utilize the following format because of its logical flow and universal applicability.

NATURE OF CASE: This is a brief statement of the legal character and procedural status of the case (e.g., "Appeal of a burglary conviction").

There are many different alternatives open to a litigant dissatisfied with a court ruling. The key to determining which one has been used is to discover *who is asking this court for what.*

This first entry in the brief should be kept as *short as possible.* Use the court's terminology if you understand it. But since jurisdictions vary as to the titles of pleadings, the best entry is the one that addresses who wants what in this proceeding, not the one that sounds most like the court's language.

RULE OF LAW: A statement of the general principle of law that the case illustrates (e.g., "An acceptance that varies any term of the offer is considered a rejection and counteroffer").

Determining the rule of law of a case is a procedure similar to determining the issue of the case. Avoid being fooled by red herrings; there may be a few rules of law mentioned in the case excerpt, but usually only one is *the* rule with which the casebook editor is concerned. The techniques used to locate the issue, described below, may also be utilized to find the rule of law. Generally, your best guide is simply the chapter heading. It is a clue to the point the casebook editor seeks to make and should be kept in mind when reading every case in the respective section.

FACTS: A synopsis of only the essential facts of the case, i.e., those bearing upon or leading up to the issue.

The facts entry should be a short statement of the events and transactions that led one party to initiate legal proceedings against another in the first place. While some cases conveniently state the salient facts at the beginning of the decision, in other instances they will have to be culled from hiding places throughout the text, even from concurring and dissenting opinions. Some of the "facts" will often be in dispute and should be so noted. Conflicting evidence may be briefly pointed up. "Hard" facts must be included. Both must be *relevant* in order to be listed in the facts entry. It is impossible to tell what is relevant until the entire case is read, as the ultimate determination of the rights and liabilities of the parties may turn on something buried deep in the opinion.

Generally, the facts entry should not be longer than three to five *short* sentences.

It is often helpful to identify the role played by a party in a given context. For example, in a construction contract case the identification of a party as the "contractor" or "builder" alleviates the need to tell that that party was the one who was supposed to have built the house.

It is always helpful, and a good general practice, to identify the "plaintiff" and the "defendant." This may seem elementary and uncomplicated, but, especially in view of the creative editing practiced by some casebook editors, it is sometimes a difficult or even impossible task. Bear in mind that the *party presently* seeking something from this court may not be the plaintiff, and that sometimes only the cross-claim of a defendant is treated in the excerpt. Confusing or misaligning the parties can ruin your analysis and understanding of the case.

ISSUE: A statement of the general legal question answered by or illustrated in the case. For clarity, the issue is best put in the form of a question capable of a "yes" or "no" answer. In reality, the issue is simply the Rule of Law put in the form of a question (e.g., "May an offer be accepted by performance?").

The major problem presented in discerning what is *the* issue in the case is that an opinion usually purports to raise and answer several questions. However, except for rare cases, only one such question is really the issue in the case. Collateral issues not necessary to the resolution of the matter in controversy are handled by the court by language known as *"obiter dictum"* or merely *"dictum."* While dicta may be included later in the brief, they have no place under the issue heading.

To find the issue, ask *who wants what* and then go on to ask *why did that party succeed or fail in getting it.* Once this is determined, the "why" should be turned into a question.

The complexity of the issues in the cases will vary, but in all cases a single-sentence question should sum up the issue. *In a few cases*, there will be two, or even more rarely, three issues of equal importance to the resolution of the case. Each should be expressed in a single-sentence question.

Since many issues are resolved by a court in coming to a final disposition of a case, the casebook editor will reproduce the portion of the opinion containing the issue or issues most relevant to the area of law under scrutiny. A noted law professor gave this advice: "Close the book; look at the title on the cover." Chances are, if it is Property, you need not concern yourself with whether, for example, the federal government's treatment of the plaintiff's land really raises a federal question sufficient to support jurisdiction on this ground in federal court.

The same rule applies to chapter headings designating sub-areas within the subjects. They tip you off as to what the text is designed to teach. The cases are arranged in a casebook to show a progression or development of the law, so that the preceding cases may also help.

It is also most important to remember to *read the notes and questions* at the end of a case to determine what the editors wanted you to have gleaned from it.

HOLDING AND DECISION: This section should succinctly explain the rationale of the court in arriving at its decision. In capsulizing the "reasoning" of the court, it should always include an application of the general rule or rules of law to the specific facts of the case. Hidden justifications come to light in this entry: the reasons for the state of the law, the public policies, the biases and prejudices, those considerations that influence the justices' thinking and, ultimately, the outcome of the case. At the end, there should be a short indication of the disposition or procedural resolution of the case (e.g., "Decision of the trial court for Mr. Smith (P) reversed").

The foregoing format is designed to help you "digest" the reams of case material with which you will be faced in your law school career. Once mastered by practice, it will place at your fingertips the information the authors of your casebooks have sought to impart to you in case-by-case illustration and analysis.

B. Be as Economical as Possible in Briefing Cases

Once armed with a format that encourages succinctness, it is as important to be economical with regard to the time spent on the actual reading of the case as it is to be economical in the writing of the brief itself. This does not mean "skimming" a case. Rather, it means reading the case with an "eye" trained to recognize into which "section" of your brief a particular passage or line fits and having a system for quickly and precisely marking the case so that the passages fitting any one particular part of

the brief can be easily identified and brought together in a concise and accurate manner when the brief is actually written.

It is of no use to simply repeat everything in the opinion of the court; record only enough information to trigger your recollection of what the court said. Nevertheless, an accurate statement of the "law of the case," i.e., the legal principle applied to the facts, is absolutely essential to class preparation and to learning the law under the case method.

To that end, it is important to develop a "shorthand" that you can use to make marginal notations. These notations will tell you at a glance in which section of the brief you will be placing that particular passage or portion of the opinion.

Some students prefer to underline all the salient portions of the opinion (with a pencil or colored underliner marker), making marginal notations as they go along. Others prefer the color-coded method of underlining, utilizing different colors of markers to underline the salient portions of the case, each separate color being used to represent a different section of the brief. For example, blue underlining could be used for passages relating to the rule of law, yellow for those relating to the issue, and green for those relating to the holding and decision, etc. While it has its advocates, the color-coded method can be confusing and time-consuming (all that time spent on changing colored markers). Furthermore, it can interfere with the continuity and concentration many students deem essential to the reading of a case for maximum comprehension. In the end, however, it is a matter of personal preference and style. Just remember, whatever method you use, underlining must be used sparingly or its value is lost.

If you take the marginal notation route, an efficient and easy method is to go along underlining the key portions of the case and placing in the margin alongside them the following "markers" to indicate where a particular passage or line "belongs" in the brief you will write:

N   (NATURE OF CASE)
RL   (RULE OF LAW)
I   (ISSUE)
HL   (HOLDING AND DECISION, relates to the RULE OF LAW behind the decision)
HR   (HOLDING AND DECISION, gives the RATIONALE or reasoning behind the decision)
HA   (HOLDING AND DECISION, applies the general principle(s) of law to the facts of the case to arrive at the decision)

Remember that a particular passage may well contain information necessary to more than one part of your brief, in which case you simply note that in the margin. If you are using the color-coded underlining method instead of marginal notation, simply make asterisks or checks in the margin next to the passage in question in the colors that indicate the additional sections of the brief where it might be utilized.

The economy of utilizing "shorthand" in marking cases for briefing can be maintained in the actual brief writing process itself by utilizing "law student shorthand" within the brief. There are many commonly used words and phrases for which abbreviations can be substituted in your briefs (and in your class notes also). You can develop abbreviations that are personal to you and which will save you a lot of time. A reference list of briefing abbreviations can be found on page x of this book.

C. Use Both the Briefing Process and the Brief as a Learning Tool

Now that you have a format and the tools for briefing cases efficiently, the most important thing is to make the time spent in briefing profitable to you and to make the most advantageous use of the briefs you create. Of course, the briefs are invaluable for classroom reference when you are called upon to explain or analyze a particular case. However, they are also useful in reviewing for exams. A quick glance at the fact summary should bring the case to mind, and a rereading of the rule of law should enable you to go over the underlying legal concept in your mind, how it was applied in that particular case, and how it might apply in other factual settings.

As to the value to be derived from engaging in the briefing process itself, there is an immediate benefit that arises from being forced to sift through the essential facts and reasoning from the court's opinion and to succinctly express them in your own words in your brief. The process ensures that you understand the case and the point that it illustrates, and that means you will be ready to absorb further analysis and information brought forth in class. It also ensures you will have something to say when called upon in class. The briefing process helps develop a mental agility for getting to the *gist* of a case and for identifying, expounding on, and applying the legal concepts and issues found there. The briefing process is the mental process on which you must rely in taking law school examinations; it is also the mental process upon which a lawyer relies in serving his clients and in making his living.

Abbreviations for Briefs

acceptance	acp	offer	O
affirmed	aff	offeree	OE
answer	ans	offeror	OR
assumption of risk	a/r	ordinance	ord
attorney	atty	pain and suffering	p/s
beyond a reasonable doubt	b/r/d	parol evidence	p/e
bona fide purchaser	BFP	plaintiff	P
breach of contract	br/k	prima facie	p/f
cause of action	c/a	probable cause	p/c
common law	c/l	proximate cause	px/c
Constitution	Con	real property	r/p
constitutional	con	reasonable doubt	r/d
contract	K	reasonable man	r/m
contributory negligence	c/n	rebuttable presumption	rb/p
cross	x	remanded	rem
cross-complaint	x/c	res ipsa loquitur	RIL
cross-examination	x/ex	respondeat superior	r/s
cruel and unusual punishment	c/u/p	Restatement	RS
defendant	D	reversed	rev
dismissed	dis	Rule Against Perpetuities	RAP
double jeopardy	d/j	search and seizure	s/s
due process	d/p	search warrant	s/w
equal protection	e/p	self-defense	s/d
equity	eq	specific performance	s/p
evidence	ev	statute	S
exclude	exc	statute of frauds	S/F
exclusionary rule	exc/r	statute of limitations	S/L
felony	f/n	summary judgment	s/j
freedom of speech	f/s	tenancy at will	t/w
good faith	g/f	tenancy in common	t/c
habeas corpus	h/c	tenant	t
hearsay	hr	third party	TP
husband	H	third party beneficiary	TPB
injunction	inj	transferred intent	TI
in loco parentis	ILP	unconscionable	uncon
inter vivos	I/v	unconstitutional	unconst
joint tenancy	j/t	undue influence	u/e
judgment	judgt	Uniform Commercial Code	UCC
jurisdiction	jur	unilateral	uni
last clear chance	LCC	vendee	VE
long-arm statute	LAS	vendor	VR
majority view	maj	versus	v
meeting of minds	MOM	void for vagueness	VFV
minority view	min	weight of authority	w/a
Miranda rule	Mir/r	weight of the evidence	w/e
Miranda warnings	Mir/w	wife	W
negligence	neg	with	w/
notice	ntc	within	w/i
nuisance	nus	without	w/o
obligation	ob	without prejudice	w/o/p
obscene	obs	wrongful death	wr/d

Table of Cases

Note: There are no principal cases in Chapter 1 of the casebook.

CHAPTER **2**

Gross Income: Concepts and Limitations

Quick Reference Rules of Law

Commissioner v. Glenshaw Glass Co.

Internal Revenue Service (D) v. Punitive damages recipient (P)

348 U.S. 426 (1955).

NATURE OF CASE: Appeal by the Commissioner (D) of a tax court ruling in favor of a taxpayer.

FACT SUMMARY: Glenshaw Glass Co. (Glenshaw) (P) settled a lawsuit for $800,000, a portion of which it sought to exclude from gross income as punitive damages for fraud.

RULE OF LAW

Money received as punitive damages must be included as gross income.

FACTS: Glenshaw (P) was involved in protracted litigation with Hartford-Empire Company. Glenshaw (P) sought exemplary damages for fraud and treble damages due to antitrust violations. The suit was settled, and Glenshaw (P) received roughly $800,000. A method of allocation determined that $324,529.94 represented payment for punitive damages for fraud and antitrust violations. Glenshaw (P) did not report this amount on its taxes. The Commissioner (D) noticed a deficiency and Glenshaw (P) filed suit in tax court on the matter, where it prevailed. On appeal, the court of appeals upheld the decision for the taxpayer. The Commissioner (D) appealed to the U.S. Supreme Court.

ISSUE: Must money received as punitive damages recovery be reported as gross income?

HOLDING AND DECISION: (Warren, C.J.) Yes. Money received as punitive damages must be included as gross income. The definition of gross income, promulgated by Congress in I.R.C. § 22(a), begins from an all-inclusive standpoint. Receipts are assumed to be gross income unless an exclusion removes them from the category. In this case, Glenshaw (P) has an undeniable accession to wealth. The fact that the payments were extracted from wrongdoers as punishment for unlawful conduct does not detract from the characterization as gross income. Reversed.

▶ ANALYSIS

This case provides a simple example of how courts analyze gross income. The very broad statutory definition is given full effect and deference. Essentially, a rough starting point is that everything is gross income unless explicitly excluded.

■▬■

Quicknotes

GROSS INCOME The total income earned by an individual or business.

■▬■

Cesarini v. United States

Money finders (P) v. Federal government (D)

296 F. Supp. 3 (1969), *aff'd*, 482 F.2d 812 (6th Cir. 1970).

NATURE OF CASE: Action by taxpayers for recovery of income tax payments.

FACT SUMMARY: The Cesarinis (P), after finding money in a piano and declaring it on their taxes, filed an amended tax return that removed the funds in question from gross income.

RULE OF LAW

Unless expressly excluded by law, gross income includes all income from whatever source derived.

FACTS: In 1957, Mr. and Mrs. Cesarini (P) purchased a used piano. In 1964, while cleaning the piano, they discovered $4,467 in old currency. The original owner of the money was unascertainable, and the Cesarinis (P) exchanged the old currency for new. They then declared the money as ordinary income from other sources on their 1964 joint income tax return. On October 18, 1965, the Cesarinis (P) filed an amended return eliminating the sum of $4,467 from the gross income computation and requesting a refund in the amount of $836.51, the tax paid on the discovered funds. On January 18, 1966, the Commissioner of Internal Serivce (D) rejected the refund claim in its entirety. The Cesarinis (P) filed an action in U.S. District Court to recover the taxes paid on the discovered funds.

ISSUE: Unless expressly excluded by law, does gross income include all income from whatever source derived?

HOLDING AND DECISION: (Young, J.) Yes. Unless expressly excluded by law, gross income includes all income from whatever source derived. Section 61(a) of Title 26 U.S.C. is the starting point for determining what should be included in gross income. The definition of gross income is expansive, limited only by express exclusion of specific items. The Supreme Court has frequently held that such all-inclusive language defining gross income was intended by Congress to reach the full measure of its taxing power under the Sixteenth Amendment. In this case, the Cesarinis (P) increased their wealth by the discovery of treasure trove. They argue that since Congress recently enacted code sections that expressly included the value of prizes and awards in gross income computation, and specifically exempted gifts, the intent was to place treasure trove in the category of gift, making treasure trove nontaxable. But this argument overlooks the basic principle that unless an explicit exemption can be identified, income from any source is included in gross income calculation. The Cesarinis' (P) claim is denied.

ANALYSIS

Finding a comprehensive definition of income has proven nearly impossible. The solution has generally been to start with the proposition that any benefit received is income, and then remove specific circumstances from the definition. In this case, discovered wealth is not exempted from the definition of gross income, thus becoming taxable. And since there is not a compelling reason, such as misplaced economic incentives, to exempt treasure trove, it is unlikely to ever be exempted from the definition.

Quicknotes

GROSS INCOME The total income earned by an individual or business.

Old Colony Trust Company v. Commissioner

Salaried employee (D) v. Internal Revenue Service (P)

279 U.S. 716 (1929).

NATURE OF CASE: Appeal from a finding of tax deficiency.

FACT SUMMARY: The Commissioner (P) sought to tax, as additional income to the employee, the amount of his federal income taxes that were paid on his behalf by his employer.

RULE OF LAW

The payment by an employer of the income taxes assessed against his employee constitutes additional taxable income to the employee.

FACTS: The American Woolen Company's board of directors resolved that the company should pay the federal income taxes assessed upon the incomes of certain of its officers including its president, Wood. Wood's taxes for the years 1918 and 1919 totaled slightly more than $1,000,000, and were paid by the company. The Commissioner (P) argued that that payment amounted to additional income to Wood and was taxable as income to him. The Board of Tax Appeals upheld the Commissioner's (P) position, and this appeal followed. [The status of Old Colony Trust Company (D) was not explained in the casebook excerpt.]

ISSUE: Does the payment by an employer of the income taxes assessed against his employee constitute additional taxable income to the employee?

HOLDING AND DECISION: (Taft, C.J.) Yes. The payment by an employer of the income taxes assessed against his employee constitutes additional taxable income to the employee. The payment of the tax by the employer was in consideration of the services rendered by the employee and was a gain derived by the employee from his labor. The form of payment is irrelevant. The discharge by a third person of an obligation to him is equivalent to receipt by the person taxed. Further, the taxes were paid upon a valuable consideration, namely, the services rendered by the employee and as part of the consideration for such services. Nor was the payment of taxes a gift. Even though the payment was entirely voluntary, it was nevertheless compensation. Affirmed.

▶ ANALYSIS

The same result was reached in the following cases: (1) *United States v. Boston and Maine Railroad*, 279 U.S. 732 (1929), where the lessee railroad paid the taxes on its lessor's income; (2) *Ethel S. Amey*, 22 T.C. 756 (1954), where a lease provided that the lessee, in addition to paying rent directly to the lessor, should make mortgage payments on the property; and (3) *Sachs v. Commissioner*,

277 F.2d 879 (8th Cir. 1960), where a corporation paid fines levied on its president. In Rev. Rule, 68-507, 1968-z C.B. 485, the Internal Revenue Service held that payments made to a minister by his church in order to help him to pay his self-employment tax were taxable income to him.

■=■

McCann v. United States

Income-receiving vacationers (P) v. Federal government (D)

Ct. Cl., 81-2 U.S.T.C. § 9689 (1981), *aff'd*, 696 F.2d 1386 (Fed. Cir. 1983).

NATURE OF CASE: Review of judgment denying claim for refund.

FACT SUMMARY: The McCanns (P) received an all-expenses-paid trip as a reward for Mrs. McCann's job performance, but they did not include the value of the trip in their gross income calculation on their joint income tax returns.

🏛 RULE OF LAW
When services are paid for in a form other than money, the fair market value of the thing received must be included in gross income.

FACTS: Mrs. McCann (P) was employed by Security Industrial Insurance Company (Security). In 1973, she was awarded an all-expenses-paid trip to Las Vegas, based upon her exceptional job performance for Security. Only 47 of 400 Security employees met the target sales goals to qualify for the trip. While the trip was referred to as a sales seminar, the trip was almost entirely for leisure. Roughly two hours of the three-day trip were substantively related to any aspect of work. The remaining time was spent sightseeing, attending shows and banquets, and independently enjoying resort activities. The McCanns (P) did not include the value of the trip on their joint tax return for 1973. They were subsequently audited and found to be deficient in the amount of $199.16, plus accrued interest of $64.97. The deficiency was calculated based upon the tax on the cost of the trip to Security. The McCanns (P) paid the amount and then filed a claim for refund. The claim was denied. They then took their claim before the U.S. Claims Court where the court ruled against them, and finally the case was appealed to the U.S. Court of Appeals.

ISSUE: When services are paid for in a form other than money, must the fair market value of the thing received be included in gross income?

HOLDING AND DECISION: (White, J.) Yes. When services are paid for in a form other than money, the fair market value of the thing received must be included in gross income. It is already settled that income need not be in the form of money to be included in gross income for tax purposes. When a company rewards an employee for exceptional performance by providing an all-expenses-paid vacation, then clearly the employee has received some benefit. The only difficulty in such a circumstance is determining the value of the noncash payment to the employee. Certainly, different employees would value a trip differently. But since a subjective valuation would be impossible to determine, the cost of supplying the trip stands adequately for the value of the trip. In this case, Security spent over $68,000 on the trip for employees. The tax on the McCanns' (P) portion was calculated to be $199.16. The McCanns (P) never disputed this method of calculation at trial. Since the trip was effectively a bonus payment, and the value was not disputed, the Internal Revenue Service is affirmed.

▶ ANALYSIS

The issues in this case point toward characterization and valuation. The court took great pains to point out how many of the shows the employees attended were "topless" shows. If the trip were required for business, then the value of the trip would not be included in gross income. And absent any stipulated value for the noncash payment, courts will usually rely upon the actual monetary cost of providing the payment to the employees.

■≡■

Quicknotes

GROSS INCOME The total income earned by an individual or business.

■≡■

Pellar v. Commissioner

House builder (P) v. Internal Revenue Service (D)

U.S. Tax Ct., 25 T.C. 299 (1955), *acq.*, 1956-2 C.B. 7.

NATURE OF CASE: Suit contesting Internal Revenue Service's calculation of gross income.

FACT SUMMARY: The Pellars (P) paid $55,000 for a house fairly valued at $70,000, but paid no taxes on the $15,000 difference that they realized.

🏛 RULE OF LAW
The purchase of property for less than its fair market value does not, of itself, give rise to the realization of taxable income.

FACTS: The Pellars (P) entered into an agreement with a construction company for the building of a dwelling. The price was fixed in advance at $40,000. After adding extras for the Pellars (P) and correcting construction errors, the actual cost of construction was substantially higher than the set price. However, the contractor was content to take a small loss on the job since Sam Briskin, father of Rosalie Pellar (P), was involved with several corporations that had employed the contractor for well over one million dollars in work. The contractor stuck with the arranged price in the hopes of keeping and extending the goodwill of Sam Briskin. The completed house was valued on the market at $70,000. The Pellars (P) spent $15,000 on preparing the land for construction. Added to the $40,000 construction costs, the Pellars (P) spent only $55,000 on the house. The Internal Revenue Service (D) assessed the Pellars (P) with a deficiency in taxes on the $15,000 not included in their gross income. The Pellars (P) then sought to have the deficiency notice overturned in tax court.

ISSUE: Does the purchase of property for less than its fair market value, of itself, give rise to the realization of taxable income?

HOLDING AND DECISION: (Fisher, J.) No. The purchase of property for less than its fair market value does not, of itself, give rise to the realization of taxable income. A realization of income normally arises and is taxed upon sale or other disposition of a piece of property. Thus, if a property is purchased for less than market value and then is sold later at market value, the difference will be taxed as profit, and the property owner has not avoided taxation on the extra profit. The only exception arises if the purchase price is so unreasonably low as to indicate a sham exchange or the inclusion of other consideration. In this case, however, there are no clear facts to suggest that the Pellars (P) realized any income. While the contractor did hope to maintain goodwill with Sam Briskin, there was no guarantee of future work or referrals. The contractor merely made the business decision to accept a small loss for potential future business.

The Pellars (P) will be responsible for taxes on the extra potential profits at any time in the future that they choose to sell the property. Decision entered for the Pellars (P).

▶ ANALYSIS

Part of what underlies the general rule in this case is the need to determine when to apply a tax on realized profits on real property. Allowing the buyer to defer any tax burden until the time of sale appeals to common sense. Given the generally high cost of real property, the buyer would be dissuaded from purchasing if a tax payment had to be made in full at the time of purchase. Money received at the time of sale reduces the burden of paying tax on the realized profit.

■=■

Roco v. Commissioner

Payment-receiving accountant (P) v. Internal Revenue Service (D)

U.S. Tax Ct., 121 T.C. 160 (2003).

NATURE OF CASE: Challenge to income tax deficiency and accuracy-related penalty.

FACT SUMMARY: Roco (P) claimed that a $1,568,087 qui tam payment should not have been included in his gross income and that an accuracy-related penalty for failing to report this amount was unwarranted.

RULE OF LAW
A qui tam payment made under the False Claims Act (FCA) is includable in gross income.

FACTS: Roco (P), an accountant, received a payment from the United States of $1,568,087 in 1997 as his relator's (i.e., informant's) share of the settlement proceeds in a qui tam action under the FCA. The Department of Justice issued a Form 1099-MISC showing that it had paid him this amount. Roco (P) researched the issue and correctly determined that the specific issue of whether a qui tam payment to a relator was includable in gross income had not been addressed by tax authorities (e.g., cases, Internal Revenue Code (I.R.C.), regulations, etc.). Roco (P) requested a private letter ruling on the issue, but withdrew his request when he was told that the Internal Revenue Service (IRS) (D) would rule that the payment was includable in income. Roco (P) failed to include the payment as income on his 1997 return. The IRS (D) audited his return, determined a deficiency, and assessed a 20 percent accuracy-related penalty.

ISSUE: Is a qui tam payment made under the FCA includable in gross income?

HOLDING AND DECISION: (Colvin, J.) Yes. A qui tam payment made under the FCA is includable in gross income. The qui tam payment is a reward to the relator, and rewards are generally includable in gross income. There is no exclusion from gross income in the I.R.C. for proceeds received by a relator in a qui tam proceeding. Punitive damages, like qui tam payments, are not intended to compensate the recipient for actual damages, and punitive damages are also includable in gross income. The qui tam payment is not a penalty, but an incentive for someone like Roco (P) to provide information and prosecute claims. Therefore, Roco's (P) qui tam payment is includable in gross income.

▶ ANALYSIS

The court rejected the taxpayer's argument that if qui tam payments are includable in gross income, taxpayers will be discouraged from bringing actions under the FCA, reasoning that such an argument could also be made with respect to the taxing of any reward. Thus, it seems that Congress has made the policy decision that qui tam compensation for relators by itself is a sufficient incentive, and that providing an additional tax break for such compensations is not necessary to promote qui tam actions.

Quicknotes

GROSS INCOME The total income earned by an individual or business.

QUI TAM An action brought before the court in which the plaintiff sues on behalf of the state as well as for himself; a statute that provides that part of the penalty imposed as the result of such action will go to the plaintiff and the remainder to the state or some other institution.

CHAPTER 3

The Effect of an Obligation to Repay

Quick Reference Rules of Law

North American Oil Consolidated v. Burnet

Oil company (P) v. Commissioner, Internal Revenue Service (D)

286 U.S. 417 (1932).

NATURE OF CASE: Appeal from assessment of tax liability for income allegedly earned in 1917.

FACT SUMMARY: Income earned in 1916 from property in the hands of a receiver was not reported or given to North American Oil (North American) (P) until 1917.

🏛 RULE OF LAW
Funds impounded by a receiver who is in control of only a portion of a corporation's property may be taxed to the corporation only when the corporation finally has an unqualified right to receive them.

FACTS: North American (P) held oil property owned by the United States. A suit was begun to oust North American (P), and a receiver was appointed to manage the property and retain the income until the suit was decided. In 1917, the court decided in favor of North American (P), and income earned in 1916 was turned over to it. The government appealed, and the case was finally decided in favor of North American (P) in 1922. The Commissioner determined that the income earned in 1916 should be included in North American's (P) 1917 income, and assessed a deficiency tax on this amount. The Board of Tax Appeals found that the income was taxable to the receiver in 1916, but was overturned by the court of appeals. The United States Supreme Court granted certiorari.

ISSUE: May funds impounded by a receiver who is in control of only a portion of a corporation's property be taxed to the corporation only when the corporation finally has an unqualified right to receive them?

HOLDING AND DECISION: (Brandeis, J.) Yes. Funds impounded by a receiver who is in control of only a portion of a corporation's property may be taxed to the corporation only when the corporation finally has an unqualified right to receive them. First, the income was not taxable to the receiver in 1916 because he was only in control of a portion of North American's (P) property. This is consistent with long-standing treasury regulations. Next, the income could not be taxed to North American (P) in 1916, because it might never receive the funds. The first time North American (P) had an unqualified right to the funds was after the district court awarded them to it in 1917. At the time the receivership was vacated, North American (P) had a claim for the money and actually received it. The fact that the case was not ultimately settled until 1922 is immaterial. If North American (P) had lost, it would have repaid the funds out of current assets and taken a deduction for that amount for the 1922 tax year. The funds received in 1917 should have been reported as income for that year. The decision of the court of appeals is affirmed.

▶ ANALYSIS

This case demonstrates, among other things, that a taxpayer who reports income under the claim of right doctrine would be entitled to a deduction if subsequently required to refund the money, but that the money is reported as income in the year it was received, and a deduction, if any, would be taken for the year in which the money is required to be refunded. This accords with the principle that money received under a claim of right, without any restrictions as to the money's disposition, is income, rather than a loan.

■=■

Quicknotes

RECEIVER An individual who is appointed by the court to maintain the holdings of a corporation, individual or other entity involved in a legal proceeding.

■=■

James v. United States

Embezzler (D) v. Federal government (P)

366 U.S. 213 (1961).

NATURE OF CASE: Review of court of appeals decision affirming a conviction for tax evasion.

FACT SUMMARY: James (D) embezzled in excess of $738,000 during the years 1951 through 1954, but he did not report these amounts in gross income.

RULE OF LAW
All unlawful gains, including embezzled funds, are to be included in gross income in the year in which the funds or other property are misappropriated.

FACTS: James (D) was a union official who embezzled over $738,000 during the years 1951 through 1954 from his employer union and an insurance company. James (D) did not report the embezzled funds on his tax returns as gross income received in those years. He was indicted in federal court and convicted for willfully attempting to evade the federal income tax due in the respective years. James (D) appealed, and the conviction was affirmed by the court of appeals. He then petitioned the United States Supreme Court for certiorari.

ISSUE: Are all unlawful gains, including embezzled funds, to be included in gross income in the year in which the funds or other property are misappropriated?

HOLDING AND DECISION: (Warren, C.J.) Yes. All unlawful gains, including embezzled funds, are to be included in gross income in the year in which the funds or other property are misappropriated. This ruling expressly overrules the holding of *Commissioner v. Wilcox*, 327 U.S. 404 (1946). Congress has extensive powers to levy taxes. Nowhere in the expansive tax code has there been a suggestion that the Congress intended to treat the law-breaking taxpayer any differently from the honest one. At one time, this Court held in *Wilcox* that embezzled money did not fall into the category of gross income since the embezzler was under an unqualified duty to repay the money to his employer. But the same can be said of any misappropriation. Whether the transfer of legal title occurs or not, the individual has increased his or her wealth. Loans are distinguishable since they must be repaid over a certain period; misappropriated funds might never be detected and recovered. In this case, James (D) gained control over the embezzled funds. Thus, in the applicable years, he should have reported this income on his taxes. However, James's (D) conviction was a felony for willfully failing to account for his taxes or willfully attempting to evade his obligation to pay taxes. Since the Wilcox exception for embezzled funds was in effect at the time of the embezzlement, the element of willfulness could

not be proved. Reversed and remanded for dismissal of the indictment.

CONCURRENCE AND DISSENT: (Black, J.) The embezzler has the same funds he was entrusted with as an employee. He has gained no title through the embezzlement. By allowing the funds to be subjected to a tax, the United States is taking a preferential claim on money that ought to be restored to the rightful owner. It seems that there is no answer to this argument. It appears that the only result of the holding in this case, which erroneously overrules *Wilcox*, is to place the federal government in the business of prosecuting embezzlers under the guise of tax evasion. However, the Constitution does not permit the federal government to prosecute local crimes, such as embezzlement or theft.

▶ ANALYSIS

The corollary rule to the one handed down in this case is that repayment of illegal income entitles the criminal taxpayer to a deduction. See Rev. Rul. 65-254, 1965-2 C.B. 50.

Quicknotes

EMBEZZLEMENT The fraudulent appropriation of property lawfully in one's possession.

Commissioner v. Indianapolis Power & Light Company

Internal Revenue Service (P) v. Public utility (D)

493 U.S. 203 (1990).

NATURE OF CASE: Appeal from affirmance of denial of Commissioner deficiency.

FACT SUMMARY: The Internal Revenue Service (IRS) Commissioner (P) asserted deficiencies against Indianapolis Power & Light Company (IPL) (D), after it required certain customers to make deposits with it to assure future payment of their electric bills.

> ## RULE OF LAW
> Customer deposits are not income where the taxpayer receiving the deposits has an express or implied obligation to repay the deposits and lacks complete dominion over their disposition.

FACTS: Indianapolis Power & Light Company (IPL) (D), a public utility, required its electric customers to make deposits to assure prompt payment. The amount of the required deposit was twice the customer's estimated monthly bill. IPL (D) paid interest on the deposits. A customer could get a refund of the deposit by demonstrating acceptable credit. The customer could choose to have the refund applied against subsequent bills. IPL (D) did not treat the deposits as income at the time of receipt. Instead, they were treated as current liabilities. If the deposits were later used to offset a customer's bill, the utility made the necessary accounting adjustments. The IRS Commissioner (P) asserted deficiencies for IPL's (D) accounting practice on the basis that the deposits were advance payments for IPL (D) electricity, and therefore taxable as income in the year of receipt. The tax court ruled in favor of IPL (D) on the basis that only 5 percent of IPL (D) customers were required to make deposits; that the customer rather than the utility controlled the ultimate disposition of the deposit; and that IPL (D) consistently treated the payments as loans by the customers by paying the customers' interest on the payments. The court of appeals affirmed the tax court's decision. The IRS Commissioner (P) appealed, and the United States Supreme Court granted certiorari to resolve a conflict among the circuits.

ISSUE: Are customer deposits income where the taxpayer receiving the deposits has an express or implied obligation to repay the deposits and lacks complete dominion over their disposition?

HOLDING AND DECISION: (Blackmun, J.) No. Customer deposits are not income where the taxpayer receiving the deposits has an express or implied obligation to repay the deposits and lacks complete dominion over their disposition. IPL (D) asserts that the payments are similar to loans. The IRS Commissioner (P) contends that a deposit to secure payment of future income is analogous to an advance payment over the customer deposits. Rather, these deposits are acquired subject to an express "obligation to repay," either at the time service is terminated or at the time a customer establishes good credit. If the customer makes timely payments his deposit will ultimately be refunded. Both the timing and the method of that refund are largely within the customer's control. It is not dispositive that the deposits are not segregated by IPL (D) from its other funds. After all, the same might be said of commercial loan proceeds. Even though the deposits frequently will be used to pay for electricity (either because a customer defaults, or a customer chooses to apply the refund of the deposit to future bills), the individual who makes an advance payment retains no right to insist upon return of the funds; so long as the recipient of the payment fulfills the terms of the bargain, he may retain the payment. By contrast, an IPL (D) customer may insist upon repayment in cash or he may choose to apply the money to the purchase of electricity. Therefore, the utility acquires no unfettered dominion over the money at the time of receipt. Affirmed.

ANALYSIS

In an analogous case with a different outcome, a state regulatory agency allowed the taxpayer, a public utility, to increase its rates in order to finance the construction of a power plant, subject to the agency's obligation to refund the increase over a thirty-year period after the new plant began operations. The Court rejected the utility's claim that the increased rate amounts should be treated as loans. The Court reasoned that the utility's obligation to repay was only a declaration of regulatory policy, not a fixed obligation to repay, and that the funds were not segregated to be repaid to the same people from whom they had been collected (*Iowa Southern Utilities Co. v. United States*, 841 F.2d 1108 [Fed. Cir. 1988]). In a case that followed *Indianapolis Power & Light*, the Tax Court, resting its decision on the "complete dominion" theory, ruled that funds received by a funeral home pursuant to "preneed funeral contract" were nontaxable deposits, and would not be taxed until the funeral home provided funeral services and goods to the contract's buyer, reasoning that because the buyer could cancel the contract and obtain a refund, the funeral home did not have the degree of control over the funds required by *Indianapolis Power & Light* to render them taxable income. *Perry funeral Home, Inc. v. Comm'r*, T.C. Memo 2003-340.

Continued on next page.

Quicknotes

DEFICIENCY   Refers to amount of tax taxpayer owes, or is claimed to owe, the IRS.

■═■

CHAPTER 4

Gains Derived from Dealings in Property

Quick Reference Rules of Law

Philadelphia Park Amusement Co. v. United States

Loss-taking company (P) v. Federal government (D)

U.S. Ct. Cl., 126 F. Supp. 184 (1954).

NATURE OF CASE: Action to require the allowance of a deduction.

FACT SUMMARY: Philadelphia Park Amusement Co. (P) deeded its interest in a bridge to the city in exchange for a ten-year extension on a railroad franchise and later claimed a deduction for its unrecovered cost of the franchise as measured by the undepreciated cost of the bridge.

🏛 RULE OF LAW
The cost basis of property is established as of the date of a taxable exchange.

FACTS: Philadelphia Park Amusement Co. (Amusement Co.) (P) obtained a 50-year franchise to operate a railroad service to its amusement park. A bridge was constructed to operate the railroad. When the franchise was about to expire, Amusement Co. (P) offered to transfer the bridge to the city in exchange for a ten-year franchise extension. No gain or loss was reported from the transaction. Amusement Co. (P) later abandoned the railroad service in favor of bus transportation. It then attempted to take a loss deduction from its income based on the abandonment of the franchise, as measured by the undepreciated cost of the bridge. The Internal Revenue Service (D) denied the deduction on the ground that since the bridge had no value and there had been no taxable exchange, no loss could be maintained. Amusement Co. (P) maintained that the value of the franchise was equal to the value of the bridge and it was entitled to take the undepreciated basis as a loss.

ISSUE: Is the cost basis of property established as of the date of a taxable exchange?

HOLDING AND DECISION: [Judge not stated in casebook excerpt.] Yes. The cost basis of property is established as of the date of a taxable exchange. A transfer of assets, except where exempted by statute, is a taxable event. The taxpayer's basis in the new property is its fair market value as of the date of transfer plus any taxable gain to him associated with the transaction. The taxpayer is taxed on the difference between the adjusted basis of the property given in exchange (here, the bridge) and the fair market value of the property received in exchange (here, the franchise extension). Where the transfer was made at arm's length and the new asset cannot be valued, it is deemed to be equal to the value of the asset that was given up by the taxpayer. While the franchise extension cannot be valued, the bridge had some value on the date of transfer, and such value can be determined with a reasonable degree of certainty. This amount should be deemed the cost basis of

Amusement Co. (P) in the franchise. The undepreciated value of the franchise as of the date of abandonment was a proper deduction. The failure of Amusement Co. (P) to properly record the transaction originally does not prevent it from later establishing the valuations for the purpose of deducting the loss due to abandonment. Suspended and remanded for proper valuation of the bridge and, if possible, the franchise.

▶ ANALYSIS

The amount paid for an asset is its basis. If the property is later sold for more than its original price, the taxpayer has made a taxable gain. If the taxpayer depreciates the asset over a period of time, his basis is reduced to the extent of the depreciation deductions. If the property is exchanged for other than cash, the adjusted basis is the value of the property received, plus any gain that was taxed to the taxpayer as a result of the transaction. If a loss was taken, the adjusted basis is the value of the property received.

◼▬◼

Quicknotes

ADJUSTED BASIS The occurrence of events with respect to an asset that requires a corresponding increase or decrease in the value a taxpayer assigns to the costs expended in acquiring that asset, to reflect the occurrence of those events.

BASIS The value assigned to a taxpayer's costs incurred as the result of acquiring an asset, and used to compute tax amounts toward the transactions in which that asset is involved.

◼▬◼

CHAPTER 5

Gifts, Bequests, and Inheritance

Quick Reference Rules of Law

Commissioner v. Duberstein

Internal Revenue Service (D) v. Gift-receiving businessman (P)

363 U.S. 278 (1960).

NATURE OF CASE: Review of reversal of tax court decision upholding a determination of a tax deficiency.

FACT SUMMARY: Duberstein (P) was given a car by a business associate but did not declare the car as taxable income, deeming it a gift.

🏛 RULE OF LAW
In determining whether transferred property constitutes a gift, the trier of fact must analyze all relevant factors, rather than relying solely on the transferor's or transferee's subjective intent.

FACTS: Duberstein (P) was the president of Duberstein Iron and Metal Company. For many years the company had done business with Mohawk Metal Corporation, of which Berman was the president. The two presidents did extensive business together, and from time to time, Duberstein (P) would direct potential customers to Berman that were of no interest to Duberstein's (P) company. After receiving particularly useful information, Berman gave Duberstein (P) a Cadillac. Duberstein (P) later testified that he did not believe that he would have been given the car had he not provided valuable information. Duberstein (P) did not report the car as gross income, and the Commissioner (D) noticed a deficiency. Duberstein (P) filed suit in tax court, but the tax court ruled for the Internal Revenue Service (D). On appeal, the court of appeals reversed. The Commissioner (D) appealed to the United States Supreme Court.

ISSUE: In determining whether transferred property constitutes a gift, must the trier of fact analyze all relevant factors, rather than relying solely on the transferor's or transferee's subjective intent?

HOLDING AND DECISION: (Brennan, J.) Yes. In determining whether transferred property constitutes a gift, the trier of fact must analyze all relevant factors, rather than relying solely on the transferor's or transferee's subjective intent. The meaning of the term "gift," as applied to particular transfers, has always been a matter of contention. The problem is that the statute uses "gift" in a colloquial sense, rather than a common-law sense. The characterization of the donor is of little use, since the donor would have an incentive to hide business compensation in the guise of gifts. And characterization by the taxpayer is of even lesser value. But were this court to attempt to reconcile all previous decisions on the matter and promulgate a test to categorize transfers as gifts, it would be painting far too broadly. Thus, each case must be examined on the particular facts, and deference must be given to the findings of the trier of fact. Here, the tax court found that the overtone of Berman's gift was a compensation for past services. The transfer was of a sufficiently business-oriented nature to move it outside the gift exclusion. Reversed.

▶ ANALYSIS

One of the problems with the sweeping language that Congress used as it fashioned the tax Code is that courts have less guidance with which to divine the intent of Congress in specific circumstances. Courts have adopted a loose system for dealing with this problem. They expect Congress will enact clarifications or reforms if Congress finds that the courts do not interpret the Code correctly.

■■■

Quicknotes

GIFT A transfer of property to another person that is voluntary and without consideration.

■■■

Wolder v. Commissioner

Stock-receiving attorney (P) v. Internal Revenue Service (D)

493 F.2d 608 (2d Cir. 1974).

NATURE OF CASE: Appeal of tax court ruling that stocks and cash received under a will constitute taxable income.

FACT SUMMARY: Wolder (P) agreed to render legal services to a client without billing for them in exchange for money and stocks bequeathed to him in her will.

🏛 **RULE OF LAW**
While gross income will generally not include property acquired by gift, devise, or bequest, where such property is received for the purpose of payment for services performed, it becomes taxable income.

FACTS: Wolder (P) and his client, Boyce, entered into a written agreement in 1947. The essence of the agreement was that Wolder (P) would provide Boyce with any legal services she required for the entirety of her life without billing for the services. In exchange, Boyce agreed to bequeath 500 shares of stock to Wolder (P), and any other securities or funds that might come into her possession through her ownership of the original 500 shares. In 1957, Boyce received 750 shares of common stock and 500 shares of convertible preferred in exchange for her original 500 shares as a result of a corporate merger. In 1964, the convertible preferred was redeemed for $15,845. Boyce, true to her agreement, revised her will to bequeath to Wolder (P) the sum of $15,845 and the 750 shares of common stock. Over the course of Boyce's life, Wolder (P) did render legal services to her, though the services consisted largely of revising her will. After he received the legacy, Wolder (P) was found to be deficient in his tax payments for not including it in his gross income. The tax court ruled against Wolder (P) in his claim that the bequest was exempt under the tax code, and Wolder (P) appealed to the court of appeals.

ISSUE: While gross income will generally not include property acquired by gift, devise, or bequest, where such property is received for the purpose of payment for services performed, does it becomes taxable income?

HOLDING AND DECISION: (Oakes, J.) Yes. While gross income will generally not include property acquired by gift, devise, or bequest, where such property is received for the purpose of payment for services performed, it becomes taxable income. In *Commissioner v. Duberstein*, 363 U.S. 278 (1960), the United States Supreme Court held that the true test with respect to gifts was whether the gift was a bona fide gift, or simply a method for paying compensation. Here, there is no dispute that services were rendered to Boyce by Wolder (P). The bequest was, in effect, a delayed payment for the services. Following Boyce's death, the New York Surrogate Court held that Wolder (P) did in fact receive a bequest. But New York law cannot control the federal power to define what constitutes income. Payment for services falls under the category of gross income, and hiding that payment in the guise of a bequest does not change that fact. Affirmed.

▶ **ANALYSIS**

Given the decision in *Duberstein*, this case is even more clear-cut. In *Duberstein*, the transfer was made without consideration, with no moral or legal obligation. Here, services were agreed upon and performed, making the bequest very clearly a payment for services rendered.

━━■

Quicknotes

BEQUEST A transfer of property that is accomplished by means of a testamentary instrument.

━━■

Olk v. United States

Craps dealer (P) v. Federal government (D)

536 F.2d 876 (9th Cir. 1976).

NATURE OF CASE: Appeal from trial court verdict granting refund of income taxes.

FACT SUMMARY: Olk (P), a craps dealer, claimed that monies known as "tokes" given to him by players at the casino were nontaxable gifts.

🏛 RULE OF LAW
Receipts by taxpayers, who are engaged in rendering services, where the receipts are contributed by those with whom the taxpayers have some personal or functional contact, are taxable income when in conformity with the practices of the area and easily valued.

FACTS: Olk (P) was a craps dealer at two Las Vegas casinos. It was common practice for about 5 percent of the players at these casinos to voluntarily give money to the dealers or to place bets for them. These "tokes" were given to the dealers as a result of impulsive generosity or superstition on the part of players, and not as a form of compensation for services. The tokes given to the dealers were placed in a common pool and equally divided among them at the end of each shift. Olk (P) received between ten and twenty dollars a day as his share of the tokes. He claimed that the tokes qualified as nontaxable gifts. The trial court agreed, and the Commissioner (D) appealed.

ISSUE: Are receipts by taxpayers who are engaged in rendering services, where the receipts are contributed by those with whom the taxpayers have some personal or functional contact, taxable income when in conformity with the practices of the area and easily valued?

HOLDING AND DECISION: (Sneed, J.) Yes. Receipts by taxpayers, who are engaged in rendering services, where the receipts are contributed by those with whom the taxpayers have some personal or functional contact, are taxable income when in conformity with the practices of the area and easily valued. Whether a receipt qualifies as a nontaxable gift depends on the basic reason for the donor's conduct, that is, the donor's dominant motive. If the dominant motive is detached and disinterested generosity, then the receipt is considered a nontaxable gift. In this case, however, tokes by superstitious players are motivated by a desire to pay tribute to the gods of fortune, in the hopes that such tokes will be returned bounteously. This conduct can only be described as an involved and intensely interested act. Moreover, the regularity of the tokes, the equal division of them by the dealers, and the legal daily amount received indicate that a reasonable dealer would regard them like wages. Therefore,

the tokes constitute taxable income, and Olk (P) is not entitled to his refund. Reversed.

▶ ANALYSIS

Ordinary tips, like tokes, are includable in income based on the assumption that they are payments for services rendered. However, the government has long struggled with the problem of enforcement with regard to the reporting of such receipts. Section 6053 of the Internal Revenue Code requires employees who receive tips and their employers that are "large food or beverage establishments," such as restaurants and bars, and that employ more than ten people, to adhere to a stringent set of rules and filing requirements concerning actual or putative tip income.

━■━■

Quicknotes

TAXABLE INCOME Earned monies applied to the prevailing income tax rate to determine the amount of income tax that is payable.

━■━■

Goodwin v. United States

Gift-receiving minister (P) v. Federal government (D)

67 F.3d 149 (8th Cir. 1995).

NATURE OF CASE: Appeal from summary judgment that payments received were taxable income, not excludable gifts.

FACT SUMMARY: The Reverend and Mrs. Lloyd L. Goodwin (the Goodwins) (P) contended that "special occasion gifts" made to them by members of their congregation were nontaxable gifts.

🏛 RULE OF LAW
Regular, sizable payments made by persons to whom the taxpayer provides services may be regarded as a form of compensation and, therefore, as taxable income.

FACTS: For the three tax years at issue, 1987 through 1989, the Goodwins (P) received an estimated $15,000 each year in "special occasion gifts" from members of their congregation. These special occasion gifts were made in addition to an annual salary from the church, which was less than or roughly comparable with the gifts for the tax years at issue, and use of a church parsonage. The Goodwins (P) reported only the annual salary and parsonage on their joint income-tax returns; they did not report the special occasion gifts as taxable income. The Commissioner (D) assessed deficiencies for the 1987 to 1989 tax years based upon the estimated unreported special occasion gifts. The parties agreed to a stipulation that stated that church members made the special gifts out of love, admiration, and respect and not out of any sense of obligation or fear that the Goodwins (P) might otherwise leave. The parties filed cross-motions for summary judgment. The district court granted summary judgment in favor of the Commissioner (D). The Goodwins (P) appealed, and the court of appeals granted review.

ISSUE: May regular, sizable payments made by persons to whom the taxpayer provides services be regarded as a form of compensation and, therefore, as taxable income?

HOLDING AND DECISION: (Loken, J.) Yes. Regular, sizable payments made by persons to whom the taxpayer provides services may be regarded as a form of compensation and, therefore, as taxable income. No reasonable jury could conclude that these payments were excludable from the Goodwins' taxable income, and, therefore, summary judgment was appropriate. The Commissioner's (D) proposed test, that the gifts inspired by love, admiration, and respect were directly attributable to the taxpayer's services and, therefore, taxable compensation as a matter of law, sweeps too broadly, as it would include as taxable income every spontaneous, unsolicited gift.

However, the Goodwins (P) may also not prevail here as a matter of law because, from an objective perspective, the critical fact is that the special occasion gifts were made by the congregation as a whole, and the congregation leaders collected the cash payments in a routine and highly structured manner. Moreover, because the gifts were sizeable as compared to Reverend Goodwin's (P) salary, it can be inferred that the congregation knew that without the gifts, they would not be able to retain Goodwin (P). Affirmed.

▎ANALYSIS

This case demonstrates that where a payment can objectively be shown to compensate for services rendered in the past, it will be deemed taxable income, whereas if the payment is made to show goodwill, esteem, or kindliness toward the person, without thought of compensating the person for their service, the payment will not be taxable. Thus, if the congregants in this case had made gifts to the Goodwins (P) in a random, unorganized fashion—even if the gifts were substantial—the Goodwins (P) would have had a much better argument that those payments should be characterized as exempt from taxation.

◼▬◼

Quicknotes

GIFT A transfer of property to another person that is voluntary and without consideration.

◼▬◼

CHAPTER 6

Sale of a Principal Residence

Quick Reference Rules of Law

Guinan v. United States

Multiple home owner (P) v. Federal government (D)

2003-1 U.S.T.C. (CCH) P50, 475 (D. Ariz. 2003).

NATURE OF CASE: Motion for summary judgment in action for refund of income taxes paid.

FACT SUMMARY: The Guinans (P), who owned residences in Georgia, Arizona, and Wisconsin, contended that for purposes of excluding gain realized from the sale of their Wisconsin residence, the mere fact that they occupied the Wisconsin residence for more days than any other residence, during the five years from the time they bought the Wisconsin residence to the time they sold it, rendered it their "principal residence."

🏛 RULE OF LAW
Time spent in a residence is not the single determinative factor as to whether the residence is a taxpayer's "principal residence" for purposes of excluding gain realized from the sale of that residence.

FACTS: The Guinans bought their Wisconsin residence in 1993 and sold it in 1998. During that period, they also owned homes in Georgia and Arizona and occupied the Wisconsin residence for more days than they occupied the other two residences. However, they spent more time in the Wisconsin house only during the first year of the five-year period and spent more time in the Georgia and Arizona houses combined than they did in the Wisconsin house. Also, they were not registered to vote in Wisconsin, and they did not file Wisconsin tax returns. The Taxpayer Relief Act of 1997, 26 U.S.C. § 121(a), provides that "gross income shall not include gain from the sale . . . of property if, during the five-year period ending on the date of sale . . . , such property has been owned and used by the taxpayer as the taxpayer's principal residence for periods aggregating two years or more." Having satisfied that statute's time-period requirements, the Guinans (P) sought a refund of $45,009 for taxes they paid in 1998 on the gain realized from the sale of their Wisconsin residence. The Internal Revenue Service disallowed the requested refund.

ISSUE: Is time spent in a residence the single determinative factor as to whether the residence is a taxpayer's "principal residence" for purposes of excluding gain realized from the sale of that residence?

HOLDING AND DECISION: [Judge not stated in casebook excerpt.] No. Time spent in a residence is not the single determinative factor as to whether the residence is a taxpayer's "principal residence" for purposes of excluding gain realized from the sale of that residence. The fact that the Guinans (P) utilized the Wisconsin residence on more days in total during the relevant five-year period than either the Georgia residence or the Arizona residence is not determinative for purposes of § 121(a) since the governing regulation refers to the time spent in a residence during a single tax year. While time spent in a residence is a major factor, if not the most important factor, in determining whether it is the principal residence, other factors are also relevant, and in this case those other factors, taken as a whole, do not establish that the Wisconsin house was the Guinans' (P) principal residence during the relevant time period. A majority of the relevant factors do not actually favor any one of the residences as being the principal residence: The location of the Guinans' (P) recreational and other activities do not favor Wisconsin since the evidence reflects activities in both Wisconsin and Georgia; the Guinans' (P) children did not reside in any of the states; they received their mail and did their banking in each of the states; and they had cars and boats registered in each of the states. More significant factors supporting the Wisconsin house as not being the Guinans' (P) residence were that they were not Wisconsin registered voters or licensed drivers, and that they did not file Wisconsin state taxes. Finally, the one relevant factor decidedly favoring Wisconsin as the principal residence, i.e., the imposing size of the Wisconsin house, is insufficient as a matter of law to overcome the facts and circumstances establishing that Wisconsin was not the Guinans' (P) principal residence for purposes of § 121(a). Motion for summary judgment denied.

▶ ANALYSIS

In arriving at its decision, the court looked to Treasury Regulation § 1.121-1(b)(2) for guidance. That regulation states: In the case of a taxpayer using more than one property as a residence, whether property is used by the taxpayer as the taxpayer's principal residence depends upon all of the facts and circumstances. If a taxpayer alternates between two properties, using each as a residence for successive periods of time, the property that the taxpayer uses a majority of the time during the year ordinarily will be considered the taxpayer's principal residence. In addition to the taxpayer's use of the property, relevant factors in determining a taxpayer's principal residence include, but are not limited to:

(1) The taxpayer's place of employment;
(2) The principal place of abode of the address listed on the taxpayer's family members;
(3) The federal and state tax returns, driver's license, automobile registration, and voter registration card;
(4) The taxpayer's mailing address for bills and correspondence;

Continued on next page.

(5) The location of the taxpayer's banks; and
(6) The location of religious organizations and recreational clubs with which the taxpayer is affiliated.

■═■

Quicknotes

RESIDENCE The place of abode where one remains for more than a temporary period.

■═■

Gates v. Commissioner

House owner (P) v. Taxing authority (D)

U.S. Tax Ct., 135 T.C. 1 (2010).

NATURE OF CASE: Action challenging the Internal Revenue Service's determination that gain realized from a sale of a taxpayer's real property was not excludable from income under Internal Revenue Code (I.R.C.) § 121(a) as a sale of the taxpayers' principal residence.

FACT SUMMARY: The Gates (P) demolished their principal residence and built a bigger house on the property, but never resided in the new house. They contended that the gain realized from the sale of the new house should have been excluded from their income under I.R.C. § 121(a) as a sale of their principal residence.

🏛 RULE OF LAW

To qualify under I.R.C. § 121(a) for the exclusion from income of gain from the sale of property used as a taxpayer's principal residence, the taxpayer must sell not only the land on which the principal residence is located, but also the principal residence itself.

FACTS: The Gates (P) resided for at least two years in a house that was their principal residence. They wanted to enlarge the house, but after being informed of stringent building and permit restrictions enacted since the house was built, they decided to demolish the house and build a significantly bigger house on the property that was two to three times the footprint of the original house. The Gates (P) never resided in the new house after it was constructed, and sold it for a gain of $591,406. The Internal Revenue Service (IRS) (D) determined that the gain was not eligible to be excluded from the Gates' (P) income under I.R.C. § 121(a) as gain from the sale of their principal residence. The IRS (D) asserted that for property to qualify for this exemption, the property owner-taxpayer must own and occupy the dwelling as his principal residence for at least two of five consecutive years immediately preceding the sale. Because the Gates (P) never resided in the new dwelling before its sale, the IRS (D) argued that the new house was never their principal residence. The Gates (D) responded that the exclusion under § 121(a) applies to the gain on the sale of property that was used as the taxpayer's principal residence, and that, here, they used the original house as their principal residence for the requisite period and they sold the land on which the original house had been situated. The Gates (P) contended that the term "property" includes not only the dwelling but also the land on which the dwelling is situated. The Gates (P) sought review of the IRS (D) determination in U.S. Tax Court.

ISSUE: To qualify under I.R.C. § 121(a) for the exclusion from income of gain from the sale of property used as a taxpayer's principal residence, must the taxpayer sell not only the land on which the principal residence is located, but also the principal residence itself?

HOLDING AND DECISION: (Marvel, J.) Yes. To qualify under I.R.C. § 121(a) for the exclusion from income of gain from the sale of property used as a taxpayer's principal residence, the taxpayer must sell not only the land on which the principal residence is located, but also the principal residence itself. Section 121 does not define the terms "property" and "principal residence," so accepted principles of statutory construction must be applied. Because these terms have more than one possible meaning, they are ambiguous. Accordingly, the legislative history must be consulted to determine Congress's intent. The legislative history demonstrates that Congress intended the term "principal residence" to mean the primary dwelling or house that a taxpayer occupied as his principal residence. Nothing in the legislative history indicates that Congress intended § 121 to exclude gain on the sale of property that does not include a house or other structure used by the taxpayer as his principal place of abode. Although a principal residence may include land surrounding the dwelling, the legislative history supports a conclusion that Congress intended the exclusion to apply only if the dwelling the taxpayer sells was actually used as his principal residence for the period required by § 121(a). This conclusion is supported by the regulations enacted under the predecessor statute to § 121, which had as their focal point a dwelling—not just the property on which it was located, as well as case law interpreting the predecessor section. Thus, although the Gates (P) would have satisfied the requirements under § 121 had they sold or exchanged the original house instead of tearing it down, the statute must be applied as written by Congress. Decision for Commissioner.

DISSENT: (Halpern, J.) While there is adequate ground for the majority's conclusion that, to qualify for the § 121 exclusion, the taxpayer must sell not only the land on which her principal residence is located but also the principal residence itself, there is also adequate ground for concluding that the Gates's (P) sale of the new house qualified for that exclusion. As a matter of statutory construction, although the majority is correct that the Supreme Court has said that exclusions from income are to be

Continued on next page.

narrowly construed, the Supreme Court has also said that, if the meaning of a tax provision liberalizing the law from motives of public policy is doubtful, then it should not be narrowly construed. Applying this principle here, the majority's conclusion would lead to an untenable result where a taxpayer who has satisfied the property use condition of the exemption is forced to rebuild by a natural disaster that has demolished her dwelling, but then sells the rebuilt dwelling without occupying it for at least two years. If the house had been only damaged (and not demolished), and the taxpayer repaired it, she would get an exclusion. That is an untenable distinction. The appropriate approach would be to treat demolition and rebuilding of the taxpayer's house no differently from renovation. Otherwise, under the majority's approach, it will not be clear at what point remodeling is tantamount to reconstruction and resets the temporal clock to zero time elapsed. For example, where the new house is built on the old foundation, it is not clear whether that is remodeling or rebuilding. In any event, the better course is to avoid provoking such questions.

▶ *ANALYSIS*

Regulations under § 121 provide that if a taxpayer meets certain requirements, gain from the sale of land alone may qualify for the exclusion. See § 1.121-1(b)(3), Income Tax Regs. However, to qualify under this provision of the regulations, the taxpayer must still sell a "dwelling unit" that meets the requirements under 121 within 2 years before or after the sale of the land. Sec. 1.121-1(b)(3)(i)(C), Income Tax Regs. The regulations under § 121 are effective for sales on or after Dec. 24, 2002. Sec. 1.121-1(f), Income Tax Regs.

■■■

Quicknotes

RESIDENCE The place of abode where one remains for more than a temporary period.

■■■

CHAPTER 7

Scholarships and Prizes

Quick Reference Rules of Law

McCoy v. Commissioner

Car-winning employee (P) v. Internal Revenue Service (D)

U.S. Tax Ct., 38 T.C. 841 (1962), *acq.*, 1963-2 C.B. 5.

NATURE OF CASE: Action contesting the valuation of income received in the form of an automobile.

FACT SUMMARY: After McCoy (P) won a new car from his employer, which he then traded in for cash and a different vehicle, he reported the value of the cash and trade-in car on his taxes.

RULE OF LAW

When an employee receives property as part of his compensation wages, it is the fair market value of property that must be reported as gross income, rather than the cost of the property to the employer.

FACTS: During 1956, McCoy (P) worked for a division of General Electric. The company had annual sales contests, and McCoy (P) was a winner in the 1956 contest. His prize was a new 1957 Lincoln Capri two-door coupe. The cost of the vehicle to General Electric was $4,452.54. Within ten days of receiving the car, McCoy (P) traded it to a dealer for $1,000 in cash and a 1957 Ford Country Squire station wagon with a dealer price of $2,600. McCoy (P) reported $3,600—the station wagon plus $1,000—in his 1956 adjusted gross income. However, General Electric submitted to the Internal Revenue Service (IRS) (D) an information return in which it reported additional compensation to McCoy (P) in the amount of $4,452.54. This was the cost to GE for the Lincoln. A deficiency in McCoy's (P) reported taxes was assessed by the IRS (D). McCoy (P) then filed suit in tax court, contesting the deficiency.

ISSUE: When an employee receives property as part of his compensation wages, is it the fair market value of property that must be reported as gross income, rather than the cost of the property to the employer?

HOLDING AND DECISION: [Judge not stated in casebook excerpt.] Yes. When an employee receives property as part of his compensation wages, it is the fair market value of property that must be reported as gross income, rather than the cost of the property to the employer. Were an employer to pay twice the market value for property then transferred to an employee as compensation for services, the employee would not be expected to declare the inflated price as the amount by which his gross income was increased. Similarly, if property transferred to an employee loses value during the course of the transfer, it seems unreasonable to tax a gain that the employee did not realize. In this case, McCoy (P) received a car as a bonus for sales. It is well-established that cars immediately lose resale value when purchased. Even if McCoy (P), who received the car in new condition, had not driven it at all, but instead attempted to sell it immediately, he most certainly could not have sold the car for the purchase price. Driving the car to the point of sale further diminished its value. In this instance, neither the price paid by GE nor the price received by McCoy (P) determines the fair market value of the car at the time McCoy (P) received it. The value of the car was reduced when taken into possession by GE, and again when it was driven by McCoy (P). Since there is no clear evidence as to the value at each of these times, a fair market value of $3,900 will be applied, falling between the $4,452.54 purchase price and the $3,600 disposition at resale. Decision entered under Rule 50.

ANALYSIS

Regulations require that income from noncash awards be assessed at fair market value. However, determining fair market value for some goods can be difficult. Generally, the determination is an evidentiary problem, but in this case, with insufficient evidence as to fair market value, the court made a best guess by splitting the difference of the respective values presented by the parties.

━■━

Quicknotes

DEFICIENCY Refers to amount of tax taxpayer owes, or is claimed to owe, the IRS.

━■━

Bingler v. Johnson

District Director, Internal Revenue Service (D) v. Employee taxpayers (P)

394 U.S. 741 (1969).

NATURE OF CASE: Appeal from reversal of ruling denying a taxpayer claim for a refund.

FACT SUMMARY: Employees (P) at Westinghouse took part in a program whereby they would receive a portion of their regular salary while working and going to school for advanced degrees, but they took exception when Westinghouse withheld taxes from the salary paid while they were in school, and sought a refund.

> **RULE OF LAW**
> A salary received by an employee on educational leave from an employer is not excludable from gross income as a scholarship or fellowship grant.

FACTS: Westinghouse offered a program to employees (P) that promoted completion of doctoral degrees. In the first phase of the program, employees (P) would work a regular job at Westinghouse while attending classes, but they would receive eight hours a week of "release time." Tuition remuneration was provided to the employees (P). The second phase of the program offered the employees (P) an educational leave of absence to complete a doctoral dissertation. During that time, a living stipend was paid by Westinghouse to the employees (P). To receive the program benefits, employees (P) had to agree to return to work at Westinghouse for at least two years. Westinghouse withheld taxes from the amounts paid to employees (P) in the educational program. The employees (P), including Johnson (P), filed claims for refunds, but they were denied. They then filed suit in district court. The jury decided against the employee taxpayers (P), but on appeal, the court of appeals reversed the decision. The Internal Revenue Service (IRS) (D) sought certiorari from the United States Supreme Court, which granted review to resolve a conflict among the circuits.

ISSUE: Is a salary received by an employee on educational leave from an employer excludable from gross income as a scholarship or fellowship grant?

HOLDING AND DECISION: (Stewart, J.) No. A salary received by an employee on educational leave from an employer is not excludable from gross income as a scholarship or fellowship grant. Congress has not specifically defined what constitutes a scholarship for purposes of the tax code. However, it does not seem inconsistent with the code to exclude from the definition of scholarship any amounts received as compensation for services performed. The exclusion of scholarships and fellowships from gross income was merely recognition by Congress that these two categories were special, rather than an attempt by Congress

to exclude all income, regardless of the source, given to support a student. Here, the jury properly found that the amounts received by the employees (P) were compensation rather than scholarships. Such a finding is reasonable because, most importantly, Westinghouse extracted a quid pro quo—the bargained for payments were given only as a "quo" in return for the "quid" of services rendered—whether past, present, or future. The employees (P) were required to hold jobs during phase one; and they had to work for Westinghouse for two years following the completion of their education. Reversed.

ANALYSIS

In the specific case of employer-employee scholarship programs, taxpayers have had difficulty arguing that the payments were excludable. The appearance of a quid pro quo between the employer and the employee has often led to the conclusion that any amounts received by employees in these programs are more properly construed as compensation, rather than scholarships. However, note that qualified-tuition-reduction programs, which permit children of teachers at certain universities and schools to attend at a reduced cost, are not taxable, provided they do not discriminate in favor of highly compensated employees. The IRS will also grant scholarship treatment to company grants or scholarships given to children of employees where the grants are controlled and limited by substantial non-employment-related factors. See Rev. Proc. 76-47, 1976-2 C.B. 670.

Quicknotes

QUID PRO QUO What for what; in the contract context used synonymously with consideration to refer to the mutual promises between two parties rendering a contract enforceable.

Note: There are no principal cases in Chapter 8 of the casebook.

CHAPTER 9

Discharge of Indebtedness

Quick Reference Rule of Law

United States v. Kirby Lumber Co.

Federal government (D) v. Bond-issuing company (P)

284 U.S. 1 (1931).

NATURE OF CASE: Appeal from judgment for taxpayer in a suit for refund of income taxes paid. [The complete procedural posture of the case is not indicated in the decision.]

FACT SUMMARY: Kirby Lumber Co. (Kirby) (P) issued bonds at par value and then later repurchased some of them in the open market below par. The Internal Revenue Service (IRS) (D) contended the difference between the issuing price and the repurchase price was a taxable gain to Kirby (P).

🏛 RULE OF LAW
The retirement of debt by a corporation for less than face value represents a realized increase in net worth to the corporation that constitutes a taxable gain.

FACTS: Kirby (P) issued bonds having a par value of around $12,127,000 for that amount. Later in the same year it was able to repurchase a part of the bonds for a price below par. The aggregate difference in price between the par value and repurchase price was around $138,000. The IRS assessed a tax on that amount contending it was a taxable gain to Kirby (P). Kirby (P) paid the tax and sued for a refund. A court held for Kirby (P), and the United States Supreme Court granted certiorari. [The complete procedural posture of the case is not indicated in the decision.]

ISSUE: Does the retirement of debt by a corporation for less than face value represent a realized increase in net worth to the corporation that constitutes a taxable gain?

HOLDING AND DECISION: (Holmes, J.) Yes. The retirement of debt by a corporation for less than face value represents a realized increase in net worth to the corporation that constitutes a taxable gain. Section 61(a) defines gross income as gains or profits and income derived from any source whatever. The retirement of debt for less-than-face or issuing value represents a gain or income for the taxable year. Through Kirby's (P) transaction, Kirby (P) made available to itself around $138,000 previously offset by the bond obligations. This represented an accession to income within the popular meaning of those words, and, therefore, it is a taxable event. Reversed.

▶ *ANALYSIS*

The proceeds of a loan are not taxable to the borrower and the repayment of the principal is not deductible since neither transaction affects the borrower's net worth. An issue arises, however, when the liability is discharged without repayment by the borrower. Where a father relinquishes a liability from the son, for example, this can quite properly be considered a gift of that amount and not taxable to the son. Where the debt is repaid through services rather than in cash, the debt reduction would clearly be income. Where insolvency is involved, § 108 of the Internal Revenue Code governs and holds that there is no insolvency exception from the general rule that gross income includes income from the discharge of indebtedness, except as provided in that section by specific exclusions, which are rather broad: Section 108(a)(1) provides that discharge of indebtedness does not generate taxable income if the discharge occurs in a federal bankruptcy case or if the discharge occurs while the taxpayer is insolvent.

Quicknotes

BOND A written instrument evidencing a debt, issued by a party to the bondholder, providing for interest payments to be made over a specific time period and promising to repay the debt upon specified terms.

Gehl v. Commissioner

Land-transferring taxpayers (P) v. Internal Revenue Service (D)

50 F.3d 12 (8th Cir. 1995).

NATURE OF THE CASE: Appeal from tax court decision that taxpayers received a gain includable as gross income from transfers of land.

FACT SUMMARY: Gehl (P) conveyed farmland by deed in lieu of foreclosure. The tax court found that the taxpayers received a gain includable as gross income from the transfers of the farmland.

RULE OF LAW
A transfer of property by deed in lieu of foreclosure constitutes a "sale or exchange" for federal income tax purposes.

FACTS: On December 30, 1988, taxpayers Gehl (P) conveyed 60 acres of land by deed in lieu of foreclosure to the Production Credit Association of the Midlands (PCA), from whom they had originally borrowed money. The Gehls (P) were credited with the fair market value of the land, $39,000, toward the outstanding balance of a $152,260 loan (the basis in the 60 acres was $14,384). On January 4, 1989, the Gehls (P) also conveyed by deed in lieu of foreclosure an additional 141 acres of the mortgaged farmland to the PCA, in partial satisfaction of the debt. The land had a fair market value of $77,725 (the basis in the 141 acres was $32,000). The Gehls (P) also paid $6,123 in cash to PCA to be applied to their loan. The PCA then forgave the remainder of the loan, $29,412. The Commissioner determined tax deficiencies of $6,887 for 1988 and $13,643 for 1989, on the theory that the taxpayers had realized a gain on the disposition of their farmland in the amount by which the fair market value of the land exceeded their basis at the time of the transfer (gains of $24,616 on the 60-acre conveyance and $45,645 on the 141-acre conveyance). The Gehls (P) petitioned the tax court for redetermination of their tax liability, arguing that any gain realized upon the transfer of their property should not be treated as income because they remained insolvent after the transactions. The tax court found in favor of the Commissioner. The court "bifurcated" its analysis of the transactions, considering separately the transfers of land and the discharge of the debt remaining. The taxpayers contended that the entire set of transactions should be considered together and treated as income from discharge of indebtedness; as such, any income derived would be excluded, as the taxpayers remained insolvent throughout the process. With regard to the discharge of indebtedness, the court determined that the $29,412 portion of the debt forgiven should be excluded, because the Gehls (P) remained insolvent after the debt was discharged. With regard to the land transfers, however, the court found that a gain existed despite the continued insolvency, because a

gain from the sale or disposition of land is not income from the discharge of indebtedness. The Gehls (P) appealed, and the court of appeals granted review.

ISSUE: Does a transfer of property by deed in lieu of foreclosure constitute a "sale or exchange" for federal income tax purposes?

HOLDING AND DECISION: (Bogue, J.) Yes. A transfer of property by deed in lieu of foreclosure constitutes a "sale or exchange" for federal income tax purposes. The Gehls' (P) transfers by deeds in lieu of foreclosure of their land to PCA in partial satisfaction of the recourse debt were properly considered sales or exchanges for purposes of Internal Revenue Code (I.R.C.) § 1001. Even though a taxpayer does not receive any cash proceeds from the land transfers, it does not mean there was no amount realized. The Gehls (P) were given credit toward an outstanding loan through the land transfer. The tax court's bifurcation of the issues was appropriate. While I.R.C. § 108, which grants an exclusion to insolvent taxpayers only as to income from discharge of indebtedness, clearly applies to the forgiven remaining balance of the loan ($29,412), the land transfers are not within the scope of § 108 and were properly treated independently. It was also proper to consider these transfers as "gains derived from dealings in property" to the extent the fair market value in the land exceeded the taxpayer's basis in the land. Affirmed.

▶ ANALYSIS

As this case demonstrates, some transactions may generate both income and a discharge of indebtedness income excludable under I.R.C. § 108, since the general insolvency exclusion found in that section is limited to the amount by which the taxpayer is insolvent, § 108(a)(3). Also, in response to the subprime mortgage crisis, Congress enacted § 108(a)(1)(E) and (h), which provide an exclusion for "qualified principal residence indebtedness" discharged on or after January 1, 2007 and before January 1, 2013. A taxpayer taking advantage of these provisions must reduce their basis in their principal residence by the amount excluded (but not below zero).

Quicknotes

FORECLOSURE An action to recover the amount due on a mortgage of real property where the owner has failed to

Continued on next page.

meet the mortgage obligations, terminating the owner's interest in the property which must then be sold to satisfy the debt.

GAIN Refers to situation where Amount Realized exceeds the Basis of an asset.

INSOLVENT One's liabilities exceed one's assets; inability to pay one's debts.

■══■

CHAPTER 10

Compensation for Personal Injury and Sickness

Quick Reference Rules of Law

Commissioner v. Schleier

Internal Revenue Service (D) v. Back-pay-receiving taxpayer (P)

515 U.S. 323 (1995).

NATURE OF THE CASE: Appeal from decision allowing the exclusion of awards for back pay and liquidated damages under the Age Discrimination in Employment Act of 1967 (ADEA).

FACT SUMMARY: Schleier (P), a man who was laid off at the age of 60, received a settlement of a claim for back pay and liquidated damages under the ADEA. Schleier (P) contended that the amount received should be excluded from his gross income.

> 🏛 **RULE OF LAW**
> Back pay awards and liquidated damages received in settlement of a claim under the ADEA are not excludable from gross income where the taxpayer cannot demonstrate that the recoveries were on account of personal injuries or sickness.

FACTS: Schleier (P), a man who was laid off at the age of 60, received a settlement of a claim for back pay and liquidated damages under the Age Discrimination in Employment Act of 1967 (ADEA) based on age discrimination. Schleier (P) contended that the amount received should be excluded from his gross income. The Commissioner (D) disagreed. [The procedural posture of the case is not presented in the casebook extract.]

ISSUE: Are back pay awards and liquidated damages received in settlement of a claim under the ADEA excludable from gross income where the taxpayer cannot demonstrate that the recoveries were on account of personal injuries or sickness?

HOLDING AND DECISION: (Stevens, J.) No. Back pay awards and liquidated damages received in settlement of a claim under the ADEA are not excludable from gross income where the taxpayer cannot demonstrate that the recoveries were on account of personal injuries or sickness. Schleier's (P) recovery of back wages and liquidated damages do not fall within the exclusion of Internal Revenue Code (I.R.C.) § 104(a)(2) because they do not satisfy the critical requirement of being "on account of personal injury or sickness." Instead, they were on account of his having turned 60. In age discrimination, the discrimination causes both personal injury and loss of wages, but neither is linked to the other. Thus, no part of the ADEA recovery is attributable to whatever injury is suffered—regardless of whether such injury is physical or emotional. Furthermore, the ADEA provides no compensation for any of the other traditional harms associated with personal injury. The remedies are limited to back wages, which are of an economic character, and liquidated damages, which Congress intended to be punitive in nature, not compensatory. Thus the recovery under the ADEA is not one based "upon tort or tort type rights." A taxpayer must first demonstrate that the underlying cause of action giving rise to the recovery is "based upon tort or tort type rights," and, second, show that the damages were received on account of personal injuries or sickness. No part of the settlement is excludable under § 104(a)(2). Reversed.

▶ ANALYSIS

The court reasoned that "punitive damages are not covered by § 104(a)(2) because they are an element of damages not designed to compensate victims, rather they are punitive in nature." The 1996 amendments to § 104(a)(2) clearly establish that the statutory exclusion does not apply to punitive damages (with limited exception, namely, punitive damages received in a wrongful-death action). This raises the question of whether a taxpayer negotiating a settlement may request that the entire settlement amount be allocated to physical injury. Will the characterization of the entire award as compensation for physical injuries be respected? The answer is not entirely clear; nevertheless, the Internal Revenue Service is likely to scrutinize such settlements closely.

■▬■

Quicknotes

LIQUIDATED DAMAGES An amount of money specified in a contract representing the damages owed in the event of breach.

PUNITIVE DAMAGES Damages exceeding the actual injury suffered for the purposes of punishment of the defendant, deterrence of the wrongful behavior or comfort to the plaintiff.

■▬■

Domeny v. Commissioner

Physically ill taxpayer (P) v. Taxing authority (D)

U.S. Tax Ct., T.C. Memo 2010-9 (2010).

NATURE OF CASE: Action challenging determination that proceeds from a settlement agreement were not on account of the recipient's physical condition, and therefore not excludable from gross income under Internal Revenue Code (I.R.C.) § 104(a)(2).

FACT SUMMARY: Domeny (P), who had multiple sclerosis (MS), contended that a part of a settlement agreement she received from her former employer, Pacific Autism Center for Education (PACE), was on account of her physical condition—as her MS symptoms had been exacerbated by what had become a hostile work environment—and therefore should have been excludable from her gross income under I.R.C. § 104(a)(2).

RULE OF LAW

Where a settlement agreement does not expressly indicate the reason for a payment made thereunder, the payment will be excludable from the recipient's gross income under I.R.C. § 104(a)(2) where it can be inferred from all the facts and circumstances that the payment was made on account of the recipient's physical injury or sickness.

FACTS: Domeny (P), who had multiple sclerosis (MS), began working for Pacific Autism Center for Education (PACE) in 2000. Eventually, PACE appointed a new executive director, who became Domeny's (P) supervisor. Domeny (P) had a strained relationship with the supervisor, who restricted her duties, and who, it turned out, was embezzling funds. Although Domeny (P) informed the PACE board of the embezzlement in 2004, the board did nothing about it. All of this contributed to Domeny's (P) stress, and, in turn, an intensification of her MS symptoms. Domeny (P) advised her supervisors on several occasions of what had become her unhealthful work environment. At some point in 2005, Domeny's (P) symptoms became so bad that her doctor advised not to go to work for two weeks. When Domeny (P) informed PACE of this, PACE terminated her. Domeny (P) then hired an attorney, who negotiated a settlement agreement with PACE for $33,308. As part of the agreement, Domeny (P) released PACE from potential federal, state and common law claims. Of the $33,308, $8,187.50 was compensation due to Domeny (P), and she reported this amount on her 2005 Federal income tax return as wage compensation. Another $8,187.50 was paid directly to her attorney, and the remaining $16,933 was paid to her without withholding deductions and was accompanied by a Form 1099-MISC reflecting that the amount was "Nonemployee compensation." The Internal Revenue Service (IRS) (D) determined that this last amount could not be excluded

from Domeny's (P) gross income pursuant to I.R.C. § 104(a)(2) because it determined that the payment was not made on account of her physical condition, as required by that section. The IRS (D) contended that because under the settlement agreement Domeny (P) released all sorts of claims, and because the agreement was ambiguous regarding any specific reason for the payment, the agreement failed to show that PACE lacked specific intent based on Domeny's (P) physical condition when making the payment. To prevail, Domeny (P) had to show that her claim against PACE was based on tort or tort type rights, and that the damages she received were on account of physical injury or sickness.

ISSUE: Where a settlement agreement does not expressly indicate the reason for a payment made thereunder, will the payment be excludable from the recipient's gross income under I.R.C. § 104(a)(2) where it can be inferred from all the facts and circumstances that the payment was made on account of the recipient's physical injury or sickness?

HOLDING AND DECISION: [Judge not identified in casebook extract.] Yes. Where a settlement agreement does not expressly indicate the reason for a payment made thereunder, the payment will be excludable from the recipient's gross income under I.R.C. § 104(a)(2) where it can be inferred from all the facts and circumstances that the payment was made on account of the recipient's physical injury or sickness. Where, as here, the settlement agreement is ambiguous or lacks express language specifying the purpose of the compensation, courts proceed to examine the intent of the payor, which can be based on all the facts and circumstances of the case. Here, it can be inferred from the terms of the settlement agreement that PACE was making the $16,933 payment to compensate Domeny (P) for her acute physical illness caused by her hostile and stressful work environment. PACE issued a Form 1099-MISC reflecting that the $16,933 was "Nonemployee compensation," but did not do so for the other two payments. Thus, the differing tax and reporting treatments used for the three payments show that PACE was aware that at least part of Domeny's (P) recovery may not have been subject to tax; i.e., was due to physical illness. Coupled with that inference is the fact that Domeny (P) advised PACE of her illness before her employment was terminated and the likelihood that her attorney represented Domeny's (P) circumstances to PACE in the course of the settlement negotiations. Domeny (P) showed that her work environment exacerbated her existing physical illness, and that her

Continued on next page.

condition and her MS flareup caused by her working conditions was intense and long lasting. For all these reasons, she has shown that the only reason for the $16,933 payment was to compensate her for her physical injuries. Decision for Domeny (P).

▶ ANALYSIS

For many decades, the Internal Revenue Code has provided taxpayers with the benefit of exclusion from gross income of any award of damages received on account of personal injury actions. The applicable provision, I.R.C. § 104(a)(2), which was at issue in this case, provides for exclusion from gross income "the amount of any damages (other than punitive damages) received (whether by suit or agreement and whether as lump sums or as periodic payments) on account of personal injuries or sickness." As this case demonstrates, while the section seems very clear and straightforward on its face, there has been a great deal of controversy among taxpayers, the IRS (D), commentators, and courts as to the meaning of "personal injury" within section 104(a)(2). Nonetheless, it is clear that once "personal injury" has been proved as the cause of the payment, the portion of the award that represents compensatory damages may be excluded from gross income. At the time the *Domeny* decision was rendered, the taxpayer also had to prove that the payment was based on tort or tort type rights. This requirement has been eliminated; Regulation § 1.104-1(c), effective January 23, 2012, eliminated this requirement.

■━■

Quicknotes

GROSS INCOME The total income earned by an individual or business.

■━■

Fringe Benefits

Quick Reference Rules of Law

Benaglia v. Commissioner

Hotel manager (P) v. Internal Revenue Service (D)

U.S. Bd. Tax. App., 36 B.T.A. 838 (1937).

NATURE OF CASE: Review of a deficiency finding by the Commissioner (D).

FACT SUMMARY: Benaglia (P) occupied a suite of rooms in a hotel where he was constantly on duty as the manager, but he did not report the value of the lodging as gross income.

🏛 RULE OF LAW
Where meals and lodging are provided to an employee for the primary purpose of benefiting the employer, the value of the meals and lodging is properly excluded from gross income.

FACTS: Benaglia (P) was employed as the manager of several hotels in Honolulu. He was constantly on duty as the manager. For the proper performance of his duties as the full-time manager, the employer required that he occupy a suite of rooms in one of the motels. He was also provided meals on the premises. Benaglia (P) did not include the value of the meals or lodging in his gross income calculation, and the Commissioner (D) assessed a deficiency of $7,845 a year for the years in question. Benaglia (P) brought an appeal in the United States Board of Tax Appeals.

ISSUE: Where meals and lodging are provided to an employee for the primary purpose of benefiting the employer, is the value of the meals and lodging properly excluded from gross income?

HOLDING AND DECISION: (Sternhagen, J.) Yes. Where meals and lodging are provided to an employee for the primary purpose of benefiting the employer, the value of the meals and lodging is properly excluded from gross income. When an employer requires that an employee reside and eat meals at a specific location, the employee loses a measure of choice for the convenience of the employer. In forgoing freedom for the convenience of the employer, the taxpayer is given the benefit of excluding the value of the meals and lodging from the calculation of gross income. In this case it is clear that residence on the hotel premises was necessary for Benaglia (P). Without a manager available on the site, proper attention to guests' needs could not be accomplished. The only way in which the duties required of Benaglia (P) could be performed was for him to reside at the hotel. Benaglia's (P) deficiency notice is vacated. Reversed.

DISSENT: (Arnold, J.) Just because Benaglia (P) had to live in the hotel does not mean that he did not benefit. Had he not lived in the hotel, he would have had to provide for a place to live and meals to eat. The tax law should concern itself with the benefits acquired by the taxpayer, not the benefits to employers.

▶ ANALYSIS

The dissent makes a logically compelling argument, considering how broadly gross income has been defined in other cases. However, Congress has been content to let stand this interpretation of § 119 since the section has been left relatively unchanged. Congress did revise § 119 in 1954 because courts were inconsistent in applying it, and in 1978, Congress amended it to exclude meals and lodging provided to an employee's spouse and dependents where such benefits fell within the ambit of the employer's convenience.

■■■

Quicknotes

GROSS INCOME The total income earned by an individual or business.

■■■

United States v. Gotcher

Federal government (D) v. Travelling businessman (P)

401 F.2d 118 (5th Cir. 1968).

NATURE OF CASE: Appeal from a determination of tax liability under Internal Revenue Code (I.R.C.) § 61.

FACT SUMMARY: The Gotchers (P) traveled to Germany on an all-expenses-paid trip provided by Volkswagen (VW), which sought to encourage investment in VW dealerships in the United States.

> 🏛 **RULE OF LAW**
> The value of a trip that is paid by a taxpayer's employer or by the taxpayer's business that is primarily for the employer's or business's benefit may be excluded from the taxpayer's gross income.

FACTS: Mr. and Mrs. Gotcher (P) received a $1,372.30 expenses-paid, 12-day trip to Germany for the purpose of touring VW's facilities there. Mr. Gotcher's (P) employer, Economy Motors, a car dealership, paid around $350 and VW paid the rest. VW provided the trip as part of an American sales effort to encourage purchases of VW vehicles by American dealerships. Mr. Gotcher (P) eventually became president of Economy Motors, in which he came to own a 50 percent share. The Gotchers (P) did not report the value of the trip as income. The Government (D) asserted a deficiency of $356.79 plus $82.29 in interest. The Gotchers (P) paid and then sought a refund. The district court held that the value of the trip was not income to the Gotchers (P), or, alternatively, was income and deductible as an ordinary business expense. The Government (D) appealed, and the court of appeals granted review.

ISSUE: May the value of a trip that is paid by a taxpayer's employer or by the taxpayer's business that is primarily for the employer's or business's benefit be excluded from the taxpayer's gross income?

HOLDING AND DECISION: (Thornberry, J.) Yes. The value of a trip that is paid by a taxpayer's employer or by the taxpayer's business that is primarily for the employer's or business's benefit may be excluded from the taxpayer's gross income. Section 61 defines gross income as income derived from whatever source, but exclusions from gross income are not limited to those enumerated by Sections 101 through 123. The "key" to Section 61 is the concept of economic gain to the taxpayer: (1) an economic gain and (2) a gain that benefits the taxpayer personally. Expense-paid items given a taxpayer-employee will not be gross income even if incidental benefit is derived therefrom, if given primarily for the employer's convenience. The trip provided by VW was necessary in order to encourage investment and consisted mainly of twelve days of touring VW plants and German dealerships. Side trips were designed to demonstrate the post-war German economy. While the trip may have been pleasurable in part, its dominant purpose was business. While Mr. Gotcher (P) was not forced to go, in a business sense, he had no choice but to go. As income is "accessions of wealth over which the taxpayer has complete control," Gotcher (P) lacked control here. When an indirect economic gain is subordinate to an overall business purpose, the recipient is not taxed. Therefore, Mr. Gotcher (P) received no income. As for Mrs. Gotcher (P), the trip was primarily a vacation. Her presence served no bona fide business purpose for Mr. Gotcher (P); only when the wife's presence is necessary to the conduct of her husband's business are her expenses deductible. Thus, tax must be paid on half the value of the trip. Affirmed in part; reversed in part.

▶ *ANALYSIS*

It is not clear what test controls in this area. A "dominant purpose" test arguably is appropriate. However, the U.S. Tax Court has included in income an amount received by an employee to the extent that amount relieved the employee of personal expenses, 14 T.C. 66 (1950). Where an employer allows an employee to use property without charge, the value of that use is income to the employee; for example, providing a rent-free residence. Even so, many fringe benefits can escape taxation. Interestingly, when the President of the United States takes family and friends on board presidential aircraft, the value of the transportation provided those persons is considered to be income to the President based on first-class airfares.

▬■▬

Quicknotes

DEFICIENCY Refers to amount of tax taxpayer owes, or is claimed to owe, by the Internal Revenue Service.

GROSS INCOME The total income earned by an individual or business.

▬■▬

Business and Profit Seeking Expenses

Quick Reference Rules of Law

Welch v. Helvering

Debt-paying commission agent (P) v. Commissioner, Internal Revenue Service (D)

290 U.S. 111 (1933).

NATURE OF CASE: Appeal from decision of court of appeals affirming determination that repayments of bankrupt corporation's debts by a commission agent were capital expenditures.

FACT SUMMARY: A grain commission agent, Welch (P), repaid debts of the bankrupt corporation he used to work for in order to rebuild his reputation and business.

🏛 RULE OF LAW
Extraordinary expenditures may not be deducted from income as business expenses.

FACTS: Welch (P) felt that it would be to his advantage to repay the debts owed by a bankrupt company that he used to work for. Therefore, over a period of years, he took a percentage of his income and repaid these discharged debts. Welch (P) attempted to deduct these payments from his income as ordinary and necessary business expenses. The Commissioner (D) disallowed them, claiming that they were capital expenditures for reputation and goodwill. The tax court and court of appeals sustained the Commissioner's (D) decision. The United States Supreme Court granted certiorari.

ISSUE: May extraordinary expenditures be deducted from income as business expenses?

HOLDING AND DECISION: (Cardozo, J.) No. Extraordinary expenditures may not be deducted from income as business expenses. The repayment of these debts may have been helpful or even necessary for the development of Welch's (P) business. At least Welch (P) thought that they were important. However, in order to qualify as a deduction, the expense must also be "ordinary." While it is difficult to define, "ordinary" means it would be accepted practice in a given segment of the business world. The mere fact that an individual conceives of a moral duty or necessity for a given expense is not determinative. It must be the normal method, based on experience, for dealing with a given situation. Since Welch's (P) actions of repaying the debts of a bankrupt company are extraordinary, to say the least, they do not qualify as an ordinary and necessary business expense. The decision of the Commissioner (D) is sustained. Affirmed.

▌ ANALYSIS

For an example of a decision upholding a similar taxpayer claim see *Dunn and McCarthy, Inc. v. Commissioner*, 139 F.2d 242 (2d Cir. 1943). In that case a corporation repaid certain employees who had lent money to the corporation's former president. The corporation was allowed the deductions on the grounds that they were made to promote and protect the taxpayer's existing business. The court held that the payments were not extraordinary and that other corporations might well act in a similar manner. *Welch* was distinguished because it involved a new business.

Quicknotes

CAPITAL EXPENDITURE Expenditure that is not deductible currently (because it does not produce a decrease in wealth), but that creates, or adds to, basis.

Higgins v. Commissioner

Employer (P) v. Internal Revenue Service (D)

312 U.S. 212 (1941).

NATURE OF CASE: Review of denial of a business-expense deduction.

FACT SUMMARY: Higgins (P), who employed individuals and incurred substantial expenses incident to managing his personal properties and investments, sought a business deduction for salaries and expenses.

🏛 RULE OF LAW
While the determination of what constitutes "carrying on a business" requires case-by-case factual analysis, salaries and other expenses incurred in the management of personal assets are not deductible as business expenses.

FACTS: Higgins (P) devoted a substantial portion of his time to the oversight of his real estate, bond, and stock investments. He hired others to assist him in this oversight, and rented office space for that purpose. Higgins (P) claimed the salaries and expenses incident to managing his investments as business deductions. The Commissioner (D) refused the deductions. Higgins (P) petitioned the Board of Tax Appeals, which upheld the Commissioner's (D) finding. Higgins (P) appealed to the court of appeals, which also affirmed. The United States Supreme Court granted certiorari.

ISSUE: While the determination of what constitutes "carrying on a business" requires case-by-case factual analysis, are salaries and other expenses incurred in the management of personal assets deductible as business expenses?

HOLDING AND DECISION: (Reed, J.) No. While the determination of what constitutes "carrying on a business," as that phrase is used in the Tax Code, requires case-by-case factual analysis, salaries and other expenses incurred in the management of personal assets are not deductible as business expenses. Not all expenses of every business transaction are deductible. Only those expenses that relate to carrying on a business may be used to offset income. It becomes a matter for factual determination when an individual claims a deduction for business expenses. In this case, Higgins (P) spent a substantial portion of time and money managing his personal investments. However, the management of personal finances does not ordinarily fall into the category of carrying on a business. It is true that greater assets require a larger investment of time to manage them, but that is the choice of the individual investor. Nothing in the facts suggests that the Internal Revenue Service (D) finding should be disturbed. Affirmed.

▶ ANALYSIS

Surprisingly, there is nothing in the Code or the regulations that defines or sets guidelines for identifying what is and what is not a trade or business. Given that there are no guidelines, it is also surprising to find that cases that define trade or business are rare. The useful reach of this particular case may, however, be limited; it most likely stands only for the proposition that management of personal assets is not a trade or business, even if done with a substantial investment of time. In contrast, courts have distinguished between traders and investors, whereby a trader is considered to be engaged in the trade or business of selling assets for short-term profits, whereas investors—such as Higgins (P)—who are concerned primarily with generating income from interest and dividends, are not considered to be engaged in a trade or business.

Quicknotes

DEDUCTION Subtraction (from gross income) in arriving at taxable income (the tax base).

Commissioner v. Groetzinger

Internal Revenue Service (D) v. Gambler (P)

480 U.S. 23 (1987).

NATURE OF CASE: Appeal from decision affirming that expenditures were business expenses.

FACT SUMMARY: Groetzinger (P) attempted to earn a living solely through wagering on dog races, but he suffered a net loss for the year and declared no gross winnings from gambling. The Commissioner (D) determined that he was subject to a minimum tax.

🏛 RULE OF LAW
While determining what constitutes a trade or business is predominantly a case-by-case factual endeavor, an activity pursued with a full-time, good-faith intention to produce income will usually qualify as a trade or business.

FACTS: During most of 1978, Groetzinger (P) spent 60 to 80 hours a week wagering on dog races. He hoped to earn a living from the wagering and had no other employment. He gambled solely for his own account. His efforts generated gross winnings of $70,000 on bets of $72,032, for a net loss of $2,032 on the year. After an audit, the Commissioner (D) determined that Groetzinger (P) was subject to a minimum tax because part of the gambling loss deduction to which he was entitled was an item of tax preference. Groetzinger (P) challenged the finding in tax court, and the tax court determined that he was in the trade or business of gambling, so that no part of his losses were an item of tax preference subjecting him to a minimum tax in 1978. The Commissioner (D) appealed, and the court of appeals affirmed. The Commissioner (D) petitioned to the United States Supreme Court for certiorari, which the court granted.

ISSUE: While determining what constitutes a trade or business is predominantly a case-by-case factual endeavor, will an activity pursued with a full-time, good-faith intention to produce income usually qualify as a trade or business?

HOLDING AND DECISION: (Blackmun, J.) Yes. While determining what constitutes a trade or business is predominantly a case-by-case factual endeavor, an activity pursued with a full-time, good-faith intention to produce income will usually qualify as a trade or business. In *Deputy v. DuPont*, 308 U.S. 488 (1940), Justice Frankfurter suggested in his concurring opinion that an individual must hold oneself out to others as engaged in the selling of goods or services before such activity will be construed as carrying on a trade or business. However, the majority did not accept Justice Frankfurter's narrowing definition. But the search for an acceptable definition of trade or business has proved fruitless. In this instance, the Commissioner (D) argues that Justice Frankfurter's definition would add clarity to the Tax Code. But this test would apparently include virtually all activities except gambling under its umbrella. Such an expansive test is of little use in judicial proceedings. Groetzinger (P) was engaged in a diligent, regular, full-time effort to earn an income through wagering. These factors alone make a compelling case that his wagering was an attempt at earning a livelihood, not just a hobby. There seems to be no acceptable alternative to the problem of characterizing actions as trade or business related. A case-by-case, factual analysis, with certain recurring elements, shall remain the less-than-satisfactory solution until Congress sees fit to decide otherwise. Groetzinger (P), with all facts considered, was engaged in the trade of gambling, admittedly with unsuccessful results. Affirmed.

▌ *ANALYSIS*

The opinion in this case expressed great discomfort with the decision in *Higgins v. Commissioner*, 313 U.S. 212 (1941), written nearly 50 years earlier. But no better approach than a case-by-case analysis has appeared even half a century later. The Court indicated that, in the absence of definitive statutory or regulatory guidance, the Court will defer to the Code's focus on the "common-sense concept of what is a trade or business." To do otherwise, in this case at least, would have caused the taxpayer to be taxed on his losses, rather than income as required by the Code.

▬▬

Quicknotes

BUSINESS EXPENSE A cost incurred or amounts expended as "ordinary and necessary expenses" in the process of conducting an income-generating activity, currently deductible from a taxpayer's liability.

▬▬

Pevsner v. Commissioner

Clothing manager (P) v. Internal Revenue Service (D)

628 F.2d 467 (5th Cir. 1980).

NATURE OF CASE: Appeal from decision upholding a business-expense deduction for clothing cost.

FACT SUMMARY: Pevsner (P) contended that because the clothing she was required to purchase and wear in her employment was not consistent with her personal lifestyle, she could deduct their cost as a business expense.

🏛 RULE OF LAW
Clothing cost is deductible as a business expense only if the clothing is specifically required as a condition of employment, is not adaptable to general usage as ordinary clothing, and is not so worn.

FACTS: Pevsner (P) was employed as the manager of the Sakowitz Yves St. Laurent Rive Gauche Boutique, which sold only women's clothes designed by Yves St. Laurent, a famous designer. The clothing was highly fashionable and expensively priced. Pevsner (P) was required as a condition of her employment to wear Yves St. Laurent clothes while working. She purchased $1,381.91 worth of the clothes and wore them exclusively at work. At home she lived a very simple life and the clothes would not be consistent with this lifestyle. She deducted the cost of the clothes as a business expense, yet the Internal Revenue Service (IRS) (D) disallowed the deduction, contending she could have worn the clothes away from work and her choice not to wear them was irrelevant to the deductibility of the clothes. The tax court allowed the deduction, and the IRS (D) appealed. The court of appeals granted review.

ISSUE: Is clothing cost a deductible business expense only if the clothing is specifically required as a condition of employment, is not adaptable to general usage as ordinary clothing, and is not so worn?

HOLDING AND DECISION: (Johnson, J.) Yes. Clothing cost is deductible as a business expense only if the clothing is specifically required as a condition of employment, is not adaptable to general use as ordinary clothing, and is not so worn. In this case, the clothing was clearly a condition of employment. However, it was only by choice that Pevsner (P) failed to wear the clothing away from work. This element must be determined by an objective test. If a deduction were allowed on the subjective attitude of the taxpayer, no workable guidelines for the deduction could be developed. Therefore, because the clothing was adaptable to ordinary use, the deduction cannot be allowed. Reversed.

▶ ANALYSIS

The use of this objective test in determining whether clothing is deductible under § 162 and 262 avoids an unfair application of the deduction. The subjective test would allow similarly situated taxpayers to be treated differently according to their lifestyle and socio-economic level. The objective test allows the greatest level of fairness to the greatest number of taxpayers.

■■■

Quicknotes

DEDUCTION Subtraction (from gross income) in arriving at taxable income (the tax base).

■■■

CHAPTER 13

Capital Expenditures

Quick Reference Rules of Law

Commissioner v. Idaho Power Co.

Internal Revenue Service (D) v. Power company (P)

418 U.S. 1 (1974).

NATURE OF CASE: Appeal from reversal of disallowance of a depreciation deduction.

FACT SUMMARY: Idaho Power Co. (P) attempted to take a deduction for depreciation on equipment it owned and used in the construction of improvements and additions to its capital facilities.

> ## 🏛 RULE OF LAW
> Depreciation allocable to the use of taxpayer-owned equipment in the construction of capital improvements must be capitalized and recovered over the useful life of the asset constructed.

FACTS: The Idaho Power Co. (P), an accrual-basis taxpayer and public utility, used some equipment it owned in the construction of improvements and additions to its capital facilities. It claimed as a deduction from gross income all the year's depreciation on such equipment, including that portion attributable to its use in constructing capital facilities. The Commissioner (D) disallowed the deduction for the construction-related depreciation, claiming it was a nondeductible capital expenditure but allowing it to be amortized and deducted over the useful life of the related capital asset. The tax court agreed. The court of appeals held that normal depreciation rules applied and allowed depreciation to be taken over the life of the equipment. The United States Supreme Court granted certiorari.

ISSUE: Must depreciation allocable to the use of taxpayer-owned equipment in the construction of capital improvements be capitalized and recovered over the useful life of the asset constructed?

HOLDING AND DECISION: (Blackmun, J.) Yes. Depreciation allocable to the use of taxpayer-owned equipment in the construction of capital improvements must be capitalized and recovered over the useful life of the asset constructed. That part of equipment depreciation that is allocable to its use in constructing capital improvements must be capitalized and recovered over the useful life of the asset constructed. The investment in the equipment is assimilated into the cost of the capital asset it constructed and is not at an end when the equipment itself is exhausted. Such capital expenditures are not deductible from current income according to Internal Revenue Code § 263. Reversed.

▌ ANALYSIS

Among the costs of constructing capital assets is the interest paid on the construction funds and the real estate taxes. Until 1976, such costs were allowed as a current deduction even though they are as tied in to the capital asset as the depreciation in this case. In that year, Internal Revenue Code § 189 was adopted, providing that such costs be charged to capital account and amortized over ten years rather than currently deducted.

■=■

Quicknotes

ACCRUAL BASIS A method of calculating taxable income based on the time at which certain events have become fixed, including the right to receive that income, the deductions to which the taxpayer has been subject, and the obligation to pay tax owed, regardless of when the taxpayer actually earned the income.

CAPITAL EXPENDITURE Expenditure that is not deductible currently (because it does not produce a decrease in wealth), but that creates, or adds to, basis.

CAPITALIZED EXPENSE A cost expended during an event or occurrence significant for tax purposes, assigned to long-term value based on continuing expenses incurred or expected in the future.

DEDUCTION Subtraction (from gross income) in arriving at taxable income (the tax base).

DEPRECIATION An amount given to a taxpayer as an offset to gross income to account for the reduction in value of the taxpayer's income-producing property due to everyday usage.

■=■

Midland Empire Packing Company v. Commissioner

Property owner (P) v. Internal Revenue Service (D)

U.S. Tax Ct., 14 T.C. 635 (1950).

NATURE OF CASE: Appeal from Commissioner's (D) decision holding that the oilproofing of a basement was a capital improvement.

FACT SUMMARY: Midland Empire Packing (Midland) (P) oilproofed its basement to protect against oil seepage from a nearby refinery.

🏛 RULE OF LAW
A structural change that does not increase the useful life or use of a building and that is the normal method of dealing with a given problem is a deductible "repair" for tax purposes.

FACTS: Midland Empire Packing (Midland) (P) used its basement for curing hides. After using it for this purpose for 25 years, Midland (P) discovered that oil seepage was occurring from a nearby refinery. The basement was oilproofed and Midland (P) attempted to deduct the oilproofing as an ordinary and necessary business expense. The Commissioner (D) denied the deduction claiming that it was a capital improvement and should be depreciated. Midland (P) appealed to the tax court.

ISSUE: Is a structural change that does not increase the useful life or use of a building and that is the normal method of dealing with a given problem a deductible "repair" for tax purposes?

HOLDING AND DECISION: (Arundell, J.) Yes. A structural change that does not increase the useful life or use of a building and that is the normal method of dealing with a given problem is a deductible "repair" for tax purposes. A repair merely serves to keep property in an operating condition over the probable life of the property and for the purpose for which it was used. It adds nothing of value to the property, but merely maintains it. Section 162 permits deductions for ordinary and necessary business expenses. While the Commissioner (D) concedes that the oilproofing was necessary, he claimed that it was not an ordinary expense. Ordinary does not mean that an expense must be habitual. It merely requires that, based on experience, the expense would be a common and accepted means of combating a given problem. Here, neither the life nor use of the basement was changed. Certainly oilproofing is the normal means of combating oil seepage. The fact that the problem did not exist for 25 years is not determinative. Once it occurred, Midland (P) dealt with it in a normal and acceptable manner. The oilproofing was a repair rather than a capital improvement. The Commissioner's (D) decision is overturned. Judgment entered under Rule 50.

▶ ANALYSIS

Hotel Sulgrave, Inc. v. Commissioner, 21 T.C. 619 (1954), held that the addition of a sprinkler system, even though ordered by the State, was a capital improvement. The court held that while it did not extend the use or life of the hotel, it made the property more valuable for use in petitioner's business through its compliance with state requirements. This case, contrasted with *Midland Empire,* shows the difficulty that may arise in drawing the line between a repair and a capital improvement. One rule of thumb that has evolved to alleviate such difficulty is a one-year rule, whereby an expenditure should be capitalized if it brings about the acquisition of an asset having a period of useful life in excess of more than one year. This is not an absolute rule, and the issue is decided on a case-by-case basis depending on all the facts and circumstances.

Quicknotes

BUSINESS EXPENSE A cost incurred or amounts expended as "ordinary and necessary expenses" in the process of conducting an income-generating activity, currently deductible from a taxpayer's liability.

CAPITALIZED EXPENSE A cost expended during an event or occurrence significant for tax purposes, assigned to long-term value based on continuing expenses incurred or expected in the future.

Mt. Morris Drive-In Theatre Co. v. Commissioner

Theater (P) v. Internal Revenue Service (D)

U.S. Tax Ct., 25 T.C. 272 (1955).

NATURE OF CASE: Appeal from disallowance of a business-expense deduction.

FACT SUMMARY: The way in which the land was cleared in building the Mt. Morris Drive-In Theatre (Mt. Morris) (P) caused an increase in drainage, so a drainage system was installed under threat of litigation from a neighbor.

> ## 🏛 RULE OF LAW
> The decisive test in determining if an expense constitutes a business expense or a capital expenditure is the character of the transaction that gave rise to the expense.

FACTS: Knowing the land on which it was building sloped toward one particular corner of the neighboring land owned by the Nickolas, Mt. Morris Drive-In Theatre (Mt. Morris) (P) went ahead and built a drive-in theatre. In so doing, it removed the covering vegetation from the land, increased its grade, and thereby increased the water drainage onto the Nickolas' land. When it rained, there was a flooding of the Nickolas' land and trailer park, so a suit was filed for the damage and for an injunction. Seeking to end the possibility of any future suit, Mt. Morris (P) settled the suit by agreeing to construct, and by constructing, a drainage system. The Commissioner (D) disallowed the taking of a business deduction for the cost, claiming it was a capital expenditure. Mt. Morris (P) appealed to the tax court.

ISSUE: Is the decisive test in determining if an expense constitutes a business expense or a capital expenditure the character of the transaction that gave rise to the expense?

HOLDING AND DECISION: (Kern, J.) Yes. The decisive test in determining if an expense constitutes a business expense or a capital expenditure is the character of the transaction that gave rise to the expense. Here, it was obvious from the beginning that a drainage system would be required and that until this was accomplished, the capital investment was incomplete. The cost of its construction was really a part of the process of completing the initial investment in the land for its intended use, so the transaction was a capital expenditure and gave rise to no business deduction. Decision entered for the Commissioner (D).

CONCURRENCE: (Raum, J.) This expenditure for drainage would clearly have been capital in character if made when the theatre was initially built, and that does not change simply because it was made later.

DISSENT: (Rice, J.) This expenditure did not improve, better, extend, increase, or prolong the property's useful life nor cure the geological defect. It merely dealt with that defect's immediate consequences. Therefore, the expenditure was not capital in nature.

▶ ANALYSIS

In a number of cases, an undetected geological defect caused problems the taxpayer had to remedy. Courts have allowed such expenditures to be treated as business expenses. The main difference in this case is that the problem was foreseeable when construction began. This case also is consistent with the precept adopted by the majority of courts that an expenditure for an item that is part of a "general plan" of rehabilitation, modernization, or improvement of the property must be capitalized, even though, standing alone, the item would appropriately be characterized as a repair. Arguably, the drainage system here was part of such a "general plan."

━■━■

Quicknotes

BUSINESS EXPENSE A cost incurred or amounts expended as "ordinary and necessary expenses" in the process of conducting an income-generating activity, currently deductible from a taxpayer's liability.

CAPITAL EXPENDITURE Expenditure that is not deductible currently (because it does not produce a decrease in wealth), but that creates, or adds to, basis.

━■━■

Quick Reference Rules of Law

Simon v. Commissioner

Musicians (P) v. Internal Revenue Service (D)

U.S. Tax Ct., 103 T.C. 247 (1994), *aff'd*, 68 F.3d 41 (2d Cir. 1995).

NATURE OF CASE: Challenge of disallowance of depreciation deduction claimed under the Accelerated Cost Recovery System (ACRS).

FACT SUMMARY: Richard Simon (P) and Fiona Simon (P), full-time professional violinists, claimed depreciation under the ACRS on two nineteenth-century violin bows they used professionally in their employment.

🏛 RULE OF LAW
A deduction for depreciation on tangible property will be available if the property falls within the meaning of "recovery property" under the Economic Recovery Tax Act of 1981 (ERTA) by being (1) tangible, (2) placed in service after 1980, (3) of a character subject to the allowance for depreciation, and (4) used in the taxpayer's trade or business, or held for the production of income.

FACTS: Richard Simon (P) and Fiona Simon (P), full-time professional violinists, acquired two Tourte bows made in the nineteenth century for regular use in their full-time employment. Bow 1 was purchased for $30,000 on November 13, 1985, and Bow 2 for $21,500 on December 3, 1985. The Tourte bows were purchased for their ability to produce a superior sound quality and not for their monetary value as collectibles. In accordance with ACRS, which in the case of the bows applied to tangible property in a five-year class, the Simons (P) claimed a depreciation of $6,300 with respect to Bow 1 and $4,515 with respect to Bow 2 on their 1989 Form 1040. The Commissioner (D) disallowed the depreciation deduction in full and issued a notice of deficiency. The Simons (P) challenged the Commissioner's (D) decision in tax court.

ISSUE: Will a deduction for depreciation on tangible property be available if the property falls within the meaning of "recovery property" under ERTA by being (1) tangible, (2) placed in service after 1980, (3) of a character subject to the allowance for depreciation, and (4) used in the taxpayer's trade or business, or held for the production of income?

HOLDING AND DECISION: (Laro, J.) Yes. A deduction for depreciation on tangible property will be available if the property falls within the meaning of "recovery property" under ERTA by being (1) tangible, (2) placed in service after 1980, (3) of a character subject to the allowance for depreciation, and (4) used in the taxpayer's trade or business, or held for the production of income. A taxpayer may seek a depreciation deduction under ACRS with respect to assets used in the taxpayer's trade or business. Under

ERTA, Congress defined five broad classes of "recovery property" and provided the period of years over which the taxpayers could recover their costs of this "recovery property." The Tourte bows fit well within the definition of "recovery property." First, the Tourte bows are tangible property. Second, they were placed in service after 1980. Third, the Tourte bows are of a character subject to the allowance for depreciation, as they are subject to exhaustion, wear and tear, and old age. Fourth and finally, the Tourte bows were regularly used by the Simons (P) in their trade or business as professional violinists. Rejected is the Commissioner's (D) argument that the bows are nondepreciable because they have value as collectibles independent of their use in playing musical instruments, and that such value prolongs the Tourte bows' useful life forever. Because an asset may outlive a taxpayer is not dispositive of the issue of whether that asset has a useful life for depreciation purposes, and an inquiry into whether an asset has a separate, nonbusiness value would render the concept of depreciation a subjective issue, which would be contrary to Congress' intent to simplify the concept and computation of depreciation. Moreover, under ERTA, the Simons (P) do not, contrary to the Commissioner's contentions, need to prove a definite useful life of the bows, since ERTA created deemed useful life periods that taxpayers may use. Richard Simon (P) and Fiona Simon (P) may depreciate the bows. Affirmed.

CONCURRENCE: (Ruwe, J.) In a significant step toward tax simplification, the requirements that a taxpayer prove the useful life and salvage or residual value of an asset were eliminated by Section 168. While this may permit an asset to be written off over a period much shorter than its actual useful life, and might even permit the entire cost to be deducted despite there being no actual decrease in the asset's economic value, that is the price of tax simplification that Congress has legislated.

▶ ANALYSIS

Pre-ERTA, to claim depreciation a taxpayer was required to prove that an asset had determinable useful life. Congress enacted ERTA, in part, to avoid disagreements over the useful life of assets, to shorten write-off periods for assets, and to encourage investment by providing for accelerated cost recovery through the tax law. The holding in this case upholds those policies.

Continued on next page.

Quicknotes

DEPRECIATION An amount given to a taxpayer as an offset to gross income to account for the reduction in value of the taxpayer's income-producing property due to everyday usage.

■■=■

Liddle v. Commissioner

Musician (P) v. Internal Revenue Service (D)

U.S. Tax Ct., 103 T.C. 285 (1994), *aff'd*, 65 F.3d 329 (3d Cir. 1995).

NATURE OF CASE: Appeal from a tax court decision allowing a depreciation deduction under the Accelerated Cost Recovery System (ACRS).

FACT SUMMARY: Liddle (P) sought a depreciation deduction under the ACRS on a seventeenth-century Viol he used in his trade or business as a full-time professional musician.

> 🏛 **RULE OF LAW**
> A deduction for depreciation on tangible property will be available if the property falls within the meaning of "recovery property" under the Economic Recovery Tax Act of 1981 (ERTA) by being (1) tangible, (2) placed in service after 1980, (3) of a character subject to the allowance for depreciation, and (4) used in the taxpayer's trade or business, or held for the production of income.

FACTS: Liddle (P) contended that he was entitled to the 1987 depreciation deduction he claimed under ACRS for the seventeenth-century Ruggeri bass Viol that he used in his trade or business as a full-time professional musician.

ISSUE: Will a deduction for depreciation on tangible property be available if the property falls within the meaning of "recovery property" under ERTA by being (1) tangible, (2) placed in service after 1980, (3) of a character subject to the allowance for depreciation, and (4) used in the taxpayer's the trade or business, or held for the production of income?

HOLDING AND DECISION: [Judge not stated in casebook excerpt.] [Yes. A deduction for depreciation on tangible property will be available if the property falls within the meaning of "recovery property" under ERTA by being (1) tangible, (2) placed in service after 1980, (3) of a character subject to the allowance for depreciation, and (4) used in the taxpayer's the trade or business, or held for the production of income. The majority opinion of the court applied the analysis used in *Simon v. Commissioner*, 103 T.C. 247 (1994), *reversed*, 68 F.3d 41 (2d Cir. 1995), and concluded that the taxpayer was entitled to the claimed depreciation deduction.]

DISSENT: (Halpern, J.) Based on the majority's finding that Liddle's (P) use of the Viol subjected it to wear and tear that did not reduce its economic value and that there is no evidence that such wear and tear exhausts the utility and value of the instrument over definite time periods, Liddle (P) has failed to prove that the Viol qualifies as "recovery property" subject to the allowance for depreciation. No deduction is allowable under § 167 with respect to proper-ty that does not have a determinable useful life. The wear and tear suffered by the Viol is not of a kind that would force the Viol to be retired from service after a determinable period. The Viol is therefore not property subject to wear and tear that limits its life and entitles the owner to a deduction for depreciation. Furthermore, in adding § 168, Congress wished to eliminate disputes over what constitutes useful life. Congress did not intend to allow for deductions for property that was previously nondepreciable because the taxpayer could not establish useful life. The majority fails to discriminate between property with a useful life that, although undetermined, is determinable, and property with a useful life that is indeterminable. Liddle (P) is therefore not entitled to a deduction under § 168.

> ▌ *ANALYSIS*

Careful consideration should be given to the issues raised in Judge Halpern's dissenting opinion. Judge Halpern argues "if active, regular, and routine use are to replace determinable useful life as the touchstone for depreciability, then . . . the majority has opened a loophole that it is inconceivable Congress intended." Judge Halpern is concerned that as long as an asset is regularly and actively used for business purposes, the assets utility as a collectible is ignored, thus giving a "field day" to sellers of fine antiques and other dual-purpose collectibles. One answer to that concern was expressed by Judge Ruwe in his concurrence in *Simon,* where he indicated that such a potential outcome is the cost of Congress's favoring tax simplification.

━■━

Quicknotes

DEPRECIATION An amount given to a taxpayer as an offset to gross income to account for the reduction in value of the taxpayer's income-producing property due to everyday usage.

━■━

CHAPTER 15

Losses and Bad Debts

Quick Reference Rules of Law

Cowles v. Commissioner

Property sellers (P) v. Internal Revenue Service (D)

U.S. Tax Ct., T.C.M. 1970-198 (1970).

NATURE OF CASE: Action challenging the denial of a deduction for losses under § 165(c)(2) of the Tax Code.

FACT SUMMARY: The Cowleses (P) listed their personal residence for sale or rent, and then claimed a loss on the eventual sale as a tax deduction.

🏛 RULE OF LAW
Mere offers to rent as well as sell a personal residence are insufficient to provide the necessary foundation for the deduction of a loss incurred in a transaction entered into for profit, as required by § 165(c)(2).

FACTS: The Cowleses (P) acquired real property that they used as a residence from 1958 until June 1964. Mr. Cowles (P) was transferred to another city, so the Cowleses (P) contracted with real estate brokers to sell their house. On July 28, 1964, some three months later, the Cowleses (P) contracted with other real estate brokers for their services in renting as well as selling the residence. Two offers to rent were received; one was rejected as too low, and the other was withdrawn. On October 11, 1966, the residence sold for $26,000. The Cowleses' (P) cost basis in the home was $34,745. The Cowleses (P) listed the loss on the sale as a deduction under § 165(c)(2). The deduction was rejected by the Commissioner (D) of the Internal Revenue Service. The Cowleses (P) initiated an action in tax court to have their deduction reinstated.

ISSUE: Are mere offers to rent as well as sell a personal residence sufficient to provide the necessary foundation for the deduction of a loss incurred in a transaction entered into for profit, as required by § 165(c)(2)?

HOLDING AND DECISION: (Tannenwald, J.) No. Mere offers to rent as well as sell a personal residence are insufficient to provide the necessary foundation for the deduction of a loss incurred in a transaction entered into for profit, as required by § 165(c)(2). This case poses a difficult conceptual problem. The Commissioner (D) concedes that an offer to rent a property is sufficient to allow certain deductions under §§ 167 and 212, which define holding a property for the production of income. This is a long-supported position in decided cases. However, offering a property for rent is insufficient to permit a holding that the property is "otherwise appropriated to income-producing purposes" within the meaning of § 1.165-9 of the Income Tax Regulations. Essentially, the case law has established that if the property was originally procured to use as a personal residence, an offer to rent as well as sell is insufficient to hold that the transaction was entered into for profit. And such a holding is necessary if a loss on the sale is to be deductible pursuant to § 165(c)(2). While it seems odd that an offer to rent will permit the deduction of some expenses associated with holding a property for the production of income, but will not permit the deduction of a loss on the sale, that is long-established case law. The Commissioner's (D) denial of the deduction is upheld.

▶ ANALYSIS

Individuals will have trouble reconciling this inconsistent position in the Code and the Regulations in their favor. Real property acquired originally as a residence simply maintains the character of a personal expenditure, even when offered for rent. Substantial steps and a sufficient length of time would probably be necessary to change the character of a property to that of a profit-seeking business.

Quicknotes

DEDUCTION Subtraction (from gross income) in arriving at taxable income (the tax base).

United States v. Generes

Federal government (D) v. Businessman (P)

405 U.S. 93 (1971).

NATURE OF CASE: Appeal by Commissioner (D) from decisions holding that transaction was a business debt rather than a nonbusiness one.

FACT SUMMARY: Generes (P) attempted to deduct funds paid by him, under the terms of an indemnification agreement of a corporation that became insolvent, as a business bad debt.

🏛 RULE OF LAW
Where a business purpose is secondary to a nonbusiness purpose for lending funds to a corporation, a taxpayer cannot claim a business bad debt deduction when the debt later becomes worthless.

FACTS: Generes (P) and his son-in-law formed an equal partnership in a construction business. As the business became successful, they incorporated. Generes (P) owned 44 percent of the stock and was the corporation's president. He received $12,000 a year for six to eight hours a week of work. Generes (P) also held a full-time position as president of a savings and loan. His average yearly income totaled $40,000. He and his son-in-law signed a surety agreement indemnifying a lender from loss on loans made to the corporation for its construction projects. The corporation seriously underbid two projects, and Generes (P) had to pay $162,000 to the lender under the agreement. Generes (P) filed a net-operating-loss carry-back for this amount on the basis that this was a business bad debt as provided for under § 172. The Commissioner (D) denied the carry-back deduction on the basis that this was a nonbusiness bad debt on which only a short-term capital loss could be claimed. A jury trial in district court was held and the jury was instructed, over the Commissioner's (D) objection, that a debt is proximately related to a taxpayer's trade or business where a significant reason for the incurrence of the debt was business motivated. The verdict was for Generes (P), and the court of appeals affirmed. The Commissioner (D) appealed, claiming that the business motivation must have been the dominant reason for the debt. The United States Supreme Court granted certiorari to resolve a split between the circuits.

ISSUE: Where a business purpose is secondary to a nonbusiness purpose for lending funds to a corporation, can a taxpayer claim a business bad debt deduction when the debt later becomes worthless?

HOLDING AND DECISION: (Blackmun, J.) No. Where a business purpose is secondary to a nonbusiness purpose for lending funds to a corporation, a taxpayer cannot claim a business bad debt deduction when the

debt later becomes worthless. The proper test to be applied to situations in which the taxpayer may have both business and nonbusiness motives for the transaction is what was his dominant/primary reason for the loan. Here, Generes (P) was both a shareholder in the corporation (a nonbusiness purpose) and an officer in it (business purpose). It must be determined whether his actions were to primarily protect his investment or to further the business of the corporation. The Code carefully distinguishes between business and nonbusiness losses, expenses and bad debt and provides for differing tax treatment. Since this evidences a congressional intent that they be treated differently, any test applied must be meaningful. If only a "significant motive" test were applied, it would do little to differentiate between business and nonbusiness motives. The "dominant motive" test provides guidelines of certainty for the triers of fact. Based on the evidence adduced at trial, Generes's (P) dominant motivation was nonbusiness. He claimed that he signed the agreement to protect his job and gave no thought to his $38,900 capital investment. In light of Generes's (P) tax bracket, this would mean that his $12,000 salary might net him $7,000. It is less than one-fifth of his capital contribution. Thus, Generes's (P) testimony was self-serving. Moreover, it is unlikely that a taxpayer would incur the potential liability accepted by Generes (P) to protect this amount of salary, especially in light of his other income. For these reasons, on the record, reasonable minds could not find that Generes' (P) dominant motive was to preserve his salary. Accordingly, his dominant motivation was nonbusiness. Reversed and remanded.

▶ ANALYSIS

In *Whipple v. Commissioner*, 373 U.S. 193 (1963), a taxpayer made loans to several corporations in which he was a major shareholder. He also sold equipment on credit and leased property to these corporations. These debts were held to be nonbusiness. Whipple was considered to be acting as an investor. A partially worthless business debt may be deducted to the extent charged off by the business, but a nonbusiness bad debt must be totally worthless before a deduction will be allowed. § 166(a)(2).

Quicknotes

DEDUCTION Subtraction (from gross income) in arriving at taxable income (the tax base).

16

Travel Expenses

Quick Reference Rules of Law

United States v. Correll

Federal government (D) v. Traveling salesman (P)

389 U.S. 299 (1967).

NATURE OF CASE: Appeal from a determination of tax liability under Internal Revenue Code (I.R.C.) § 162(a)(2).

FACT SUMMARY: Correll (P), a traveling salesman, sought to deduct as a business expense the cost of breakfast and lunch eaten on the road, although he ate dinner every night at home.

🏛 RULE OF LAW
A taxpayer traveling on business may deduct the cost of his meals only if his trip requires him to stop for rest or sleep.

FACTS: Correll (P) was a traveling salesman for a wholesale grocery company. He would eat breakfast and lunch on the road and return home in time for dinner. Correll (P) deducted the cost of breakfast and lunch as a travel expense incurred in the pursuit of business "while away from home" under § 162(a)(2). Because his travels required neither rest nor sleep, the Government (D) disallowed the deduction, ruling it to be a personal expense under § 262. After Correll (P) paid his assessed tax deficiency and sued successfully for a refund in district court, which the Sixth Circuit Court of Appeals affirmed, the Government (D) appealed.

ISSUE: May a taxpayer traveling on business deduct the cost of his meals only if his trip requires him to stop for rest or sleep?

HOLDING AND DECISION: (Stewart, J.) Yes. A taxpayer traveling on business may deduct the cost of his meals only if his trip requires him to stop for rest or sleep. The Government (D) has long interpreted the limiting phrase "away from home" to exclude all trips not requiring rest or sleep regardless of how many cities visited or miles covered in a single day. The Government's (D) view allows for easy application by placing all-day travelers in the same position. The statute speaks of "meals and lodging" as a unit to be had "away from home," which suggests an overnight stay must be made. The court of appeals' view that the plain language of this phrase requires a different conclusion must be rejected because the language of the statute is not self-defining. Reversed.

▶ ANALYSIS

Where a taxpayer was not away from home overnight but stopped his car by the roadside for naps, his deduction for the cost of his meals was disallowed. *Barry v. Commissioner,* 435 F.2d 290 (1st Cir. 1970). Rev. Rul. 75-168, 1975-19 I.R.C. § 12 permits truck drivers to deduct meal and lodging expenses during layovers of approximately eight hours that were provided for rest or sleep. However, no deduction was allowed for short, half-hour layovers. The Court admitted that the rule in *Correll* was somewhat arbitrary but saw no reason to distinguish between the New York to Washington, D.C., commuter who eats breakfast and dinner at home and lunch in the nation's capital and the city commuter who eats breakfast and dinner at home and lunch a block down the street from his office. Arguably, the Court's interpretation is a stretch, since the plain meaning to most people of "meals and lodging away from home" means what it says—the meals and lodging are had away from home. Nothing in the plain language of the statute indicates that an overnight stay is required; arguably, if Congress had wanted to incorporate such a requirement, it could easily have done so.

Quicknotes

DEDUCTION Subtraction (from gross income) in arriving at taxable income (the tax base).

Henderson v. Commissioner

Traveling taxpayer (P) v. Internal Revenue Service (D)

143 F.3d 497 (9th Cir. 1998).

NATURE OF CASE: Appeal of denial of deductions for living expenses.

FACT SUMMARY: Henderson (P) deducted living expenses he incurred while living away from home with a traveling ice show. The Commissioner (D) denied the deductions claiming that Boise, Idaho, was not Henderson's (P) tax home.

🏛 RULE OF LAW

Where a taxpayer does not have a legal tax home because he is traveling for business most of the year, and he therefore is not duplicating his expenses, he cannot claim as a deduction living expenses incurred away from a temporary residence to which he has no business connections.

FACTS: In 1990, Henderson (P) worked on three different Walt Disney's World of Ice tours, traveling to 13 states and Japan. Between tours, Henderson (P) would stay at his parents' house in Idaho. Henderson (P) received mail at his parents' residence, kept belongings there, was registered to vote in Idaho, paid Idaho state income tax, maintained an Idaho driver's license, and kept his bank account in Idaho. During 1990, he stayed at his parents' residence for about two to three months and performed minor jobs around the home. He also worked one night in Boise as a stagehand for a concert. Henderson (P) claimed deductions, under § 162(a)(2), for living expenses incurred away from home while on tour with the ice show. The Commissioner (D) disallowed the deductions because Henderson (P) had no legal tax home; he lacked the requisite business reasons for living in Boise between ice show tours. The tax court upheld the Commissioner's (D) decision and Henderson (P) appealed.

ISSUE: Where a taxpayer does not have a legal tax home because he is traveling for business most of the year, and he therefore is not duplicating his expenses, can he claim as a deduction living expenses incurred away from a temporary residence to which he has no business connections?

HOLDING AND DECISION: (Wiggins, J.) No. Where a taxpayer does not have a legal tax home because he is traveling for business most of the year, and he therefore is not duplicating his expenses, he cannot claim as a deduction living expenses incurred away from a temporary residence to which he has no business connections. Section 162(a)(2) allows a deduction for all ordinary and necessary traveling expenses while away from home in the pursuit of a trade or business. To qualify for the deduction, Henderson's (P) expenses had to be incurred while he was away

from home. Since Henderson (P) continuously traveled for work, however, he had no tax home. Henderson (P) had no business reason for his tax home to be in any location because he constantly traveled in 1990, and his personal choice to return to Boise was not dictated by business reasons, despite his minimal employment efforts in Boise. Furthermore, Henderson (P) did not have substantial, continuing living expenses in Boise that were duplicated by his expenses on the road. He paid no rent to his parents, had no ownership interest in the home, his financial contributions in Boise were limited, and any minor expenses he incurred while living with his parents did not continue during the periods while he traveled on tour. Henderson (P) is therefore an itinerant taxpayer and is not entitled to the § 162 deduction. Affirmed.

DISSENT: (Kozinski, J.) Henderson's (P) travel expenses are fully deductible because they were incurred while he was away from his home in the pursuit of business. "Home" is not a term of art; it is a common English word meaning a permanent place where a person lives, keeps his belongings, receives his mail, etc.—just as Henderson (P) did here. That Henderson's (P) home happens to be owned by his parents and they did not charge him room and board is of no consequence; it is still his home. By going on the road in pursuit of his job he had to pay for food and lodging that he would not have had to buy had he stayed at home. The job had no fixed location; therefore, the requirement that a home is not a tax-home unless it is dictated by a business necessity has no application.

▶ ANALYSIS

The cost of producing income is deductible from a person's taxable income. However, as this case demonstrates, when no costs are incurred for maintaining a residence while one is away from it, such costs cannot be deducted. As Judge Kozinski points out in his dissent, "fast planes and automobiles have turned us into a nation of itinerants" so that the notion of "home" for many has changed and, arguably, should encompass Henderson's (P) situation—a grown child living at home with his parents part of the year and working elsewhere the rest of the year. In any event, the dissent and majority agree that where a person clearly has no fixed residence, as when they travel 365 days a year, they may not deduct their living expenses while traveling for business. See, e.g., *James v. United States,* 308 F.2d 204 (9th Cir. 1962).

■■■■

Continued on next page.

Quicknotes

BUSINESS EXPENSE   A cost incurred or amounts expended as "ordinary and necessary expenses" in the process of conducting an income-generating activity, currently deductible from a taxpayer's liability.

■▬■

Bogue v. Commissioner

Independent contractor (P) v. Taxing authority (D)

U.S. Tax Ct., T.C. Memo 2011-164 (2011).

NATURE OF CASE: Action challenging determination that transportation expenses were not deductible because they were commuting expenses.

FACT SUMMARY: Bogue (P) contended that his transportation expenses were deductible because they came within the exceptions to the general rule that expenses for traveling between one's home and one's place of business or employment constitute nondeductible personal commuting expenses.

RULE OF LAW
An independent contractor's transportation expenses between his residence and temporary worksites are nondeductible commuting expenses where the contractor cannot satisfy any of the three exceptions to the general rule that expenses for traveling between one's home and one's place of business or employment constitute nondeductible personal commuting expenses.

FACTS: Bogue (P) was an independent contractor who lived with his fiancé. In 2005 and 2006 he worked to renovate five residential properties that were between 4 and 20 miles from his residence. He worked at each of the worksites for a number of months and then, when the project at that worksite was finished, he moved to another worksite. On his returns for those years, Bogue (P) claimed deductions for a variety of expenses related to his transportation between his residence and the worksites. He claimed deductions for car and truck expenses of $9,232 and $9,657, respectively, as well as deductions of $660 and $400, respectively, for tolls he paid on the way to worksites. He further deducted auto insurance expenses of $2,028 and $1,866, respectively, and also deducted $650 in car rental expenses for the period during 2005 when he was renting a car after his vehicle became inoperable. The Internal Revenue Service (IRS) (D) contended that these expenses were nondeductible commuting expenses, and also concluded that the expenses did not fall into any of three exceptions to the general rule that expenses for traveling between one's home and one's place of business or employment constitute commuting expenses and, consequently, are nondeductible personal expenses. The first exception is that expenses incurred traveling between a taxpayer's residence and a place of business are deductible if the residence is the taxpayer's principal place of business (home office exception). The second exception is that travel expenses between a taxpayer's residence and temporary work locations outside of the metropolitan area where the taxpayer lives and normally works are deductible (temporary distant worksite

exception). The third exception is that travel expenses between a taxpayer's residence and temporary work locations, regardless of the distance, are deductible if the taxpayer also has one or more regular work locations away from the taxpayer's residence (regular work location exception). Bogue (P) challenged the IRS's (D) determination.

ISSUE: Are an independent contractor's transportation expenses between his residence and temporary worksites nondeductible commuting expenses where the contractor cannot satisfy any of the three exceptions to the general rule that expenses for traveling between one's home and one's place of business or employment constitute nondeductible personal commuting expenses?

HOLDING AND DECISION: [Judge not identified in casebook excerpt.] Yes. An independent contractor's transportation expenses between his residence and temporary worksites are nondeductible commuting expenses where the contractor cannot satisfy any of the three exceptions to the general rule that expenses for traveling between one's home and one's place of business or employment constitute nondeductible personal commuting expenses. As the Supreme Court has explained, the core reason commuting expenses are not deductible is that the taxpayer makes a personal choice about where to live. Because commuting expenses are personal, they are found in the category of nondeductible expenses governed by Internal Revenue Code (I.R.C.) § 262(a). Such personal expenses contrast with trade or business expenses, which are deductible provided they satisfy the requirements of I.R.C. § 162. Section 162(a) provides that a deduction is allowed for "all the ordinary and necessary expenses paid or incurred during the taxable year in carrying on a trade or business." Commuting expenses are nondeductible unless they fall within one of the three exceptions to the general rule. Bough (P) asserts that his expenses fall within each of the three exceptions. Bough (P), however, does not come within the first exception, the home office exception. As to the second exception, the temporary distant worksite exception, which is rooted in case law, the taxpayer must have no principal place of business during the tax year, and the temporary worksite(s) must be distant from the area where the taxpayer lives and normally works. The IRS (D) has memorialized the temporary distant worksite exception in Rev. Rul. 99-7, 1999-1 C.B. at 361. The revenue ruling defines a temporary work location as one that "is realistically expected to last (and does in fact last) for 1 year

Continued on next page.

or less." However, the IRS (D) has not defined "metropolitan area." The rationale underpinning the revenue ruling recognizes that taxpayers whose work consists of many temporary worksites might not always have a choice about the location of those worksites. Although the taxpayer's choices about where to live and where to "normally work" are personal and it is assumed the taxpayer will live near the place of employment, it is unreasonable to expect that a taxpayer will move to a distant location for a temporary job. Looking to the Office of Management and Budget (OMB) for a definition of "metropolitan" is not a good approach, because in some cases, a rigid definition would disallow the deduction of travel expenses that should be permitted, and, in other cases, it would permit the deduction of such expenses that should be disallowed. Indeed, the IRS's (D) use of the term "metropolitan area" is not helpful for answering the question of whether travel expenses are deductible under the temporary distant worksite exception. Instead, the facts and circumstances must be evaluated to decide whether the travel expenses in question were incurred in traveling to a worksite unusually distant from the area where the taxpayer lives and normally works. Such an approach is consistent with the approach historically taken by a number of other courts. Here, it was Bogue's (P) normal practice during the years in issue to travel about 15 miles from his residence to a worksite. There was nothing unusual about those trips. Even the worksite that was farthest from his residence was still within the areas where he normally worked. Accordingly, Bogue (P) was not entitled to deduct travel expenses incurred in driving between his residence and those worksites. As to the third exception, the regular work location exception, the exception is not rooted in case law but has its origins in a revenue ruling. It is, essentially, an IRS concession, and will be treated as such. Under the revenue ruling, a "regular work location" is taken to mean "any location at which the taxpayer works or performs services on a regular basis," not including his residence. Also, "regular work location" and "temporary work location" are mutually exclusive. The ruling, Rev. Rul. 99-7, 1999-1 C.B. at 362, states: "If a taxpayer has one or more regular work locations away from the taxpayer's residence, the taxpayer may deduct daily transportation expenses incurred in going between the taxpayer's residence and a temporary work location in the same trade or business, regardless of the distance." Here, Bogue's (P) only work locations during the years in issues were worksites where he performed renovations. All of those worksites were temporary as defined in Rev. Rul. 99-7, so he has not shown that he had other, regular work locations. Accordingly, Bogue (P) has not established facts that would qualify him for the IRS's (D) concession. Consequently, he is not entitled to deduct his commuting expenses under the regular work location exception. Because Bogue (P) failed to qualify under any of the three exceptions, his expenses in traveling between his worksites

and his residence were nondeductible commuting expenses. Decision for the IRS (D).

ANALYSIS

The rationale for the second exception—the temporary distant worksite exception—is that it is not reasonable to expect people to move to a distant location when a job is foreseeably of limited duration. Implicit in this exception is the requirement that the taxpayer commute to a worksite distant from his or her residence. Without such a requirement, the absurd result would obtain of permitting a taxpayer, who commuted to a succession of temporary jobs, to deduct commuting expenses, no matter how close these jobs were to his residence. As to the third exception—the regular work location exception—Rev. Rul. 90-23, 1990-1 C.B. at 29, explains that "for a taxpayer who has one or more regular places of business, daily transportation expenses paid or incurred in going between the taxpayer's residence and temporary work locations are deductible business expenses under section 162(a) of the Code regardless of the distance." The court in the instant case criticized this rationale, saying "The exception would be logical if it were limited to distant temporary work locations. However, as it stands, the regular work location exception reaches a result similar to what the Court of Appeals for the First Circuit labeled 'absurd' when it held that there was an implicit requirement that, in order for travel expenses between a taxpayer's residence and a temporary work location to be deductible, the temporary work location must be distant from the taxpayer's residence." Nonetheless, the court accepted the exception as an IRS (D) concession.

Quicknotes

TRAVEL EXPENSE A cost expended for activities attendant to travel while conducting business rather than pleasure; may be treated as a business expense, which may be deductible.

CHAPTER 17

Entertainment and Business Meals

Quick Reference Rules of Law

Walliser v. Commissioner

Traveling businessman (P) v. Internal Revenue Service (D)

U.S. Tax Ct., 72 T.C. 433 (1974).

NATURE OF CASE: Suit challenging an Internal Revenue Service (IRS) denial of certain business-expense deductions.

FACT SUMMARY: Walliser (P) went abroad on tour groups in the hopes of meeting individuals interested in borrowing funds, thus enabling him to meet loan sale quotas at the bank where he worked.

🏛 RULE OF LAW
Expenses incurred traveling in the hopes of meeting potential business clients are not deductible as business expenses.

FACTS: During the taxable years 1973 and 1974, Walliser (P) was vice president and manager of First Federal Savings & Loan Association (First Federal). First Federal had loan production quotas and offered salary-raises for loan output. Walliser (P) traveled abroad in tour groups for people in the building industry. The tours were arranged as guided vacations, with sightseeing and other recreation. But Walliser (P) went on the trips to meet potential customers. He believed that the tours would generate business in the form of loans at First Federal. Walliser (P) deducted the cost of the tours as employee business expenses. The IRS (D) denied the deductions, and Walliser (P) filed suit in tax court.

ISSUE: Are expenses incurred traveling in the hopes of meeting potential business clients deductible as business expenses?

HOLDING AND DECISION: (Tannenwald, J.) No. Expenses incurred traveling in the hopes of meeting potential business clients are not deductible as business expenses. For a permissible deduction under § 274(a)(1)(A), the item must be directly related to the taxpayer's business, or, if the item directly precedes or follows a bona fide business discussion, the item must be associated with the active conduct of the taxpayer's business. Section 162(a)(2) allows a deduction for all ordinary and necessary expenses paid or incurred in carrying on any trade or business, including travel expenses in pursuit of a trade or business. But § 274 disallows some deductions that would otherwise qualify under § 162(a)(2). In particular, expenses for entertainment must meet stricter criteria than are imposed under § 162(a)(2) to qualify for deduction. Section 1.274-2 (b)(1)(iii) of the Income Tax Regulations provides that where an expenditure might qualify as both a business travel expense and an entertainment expense, it must be construed as an expenditure for entertainment. In this case, the trips taken by Walliser (P) have elements of both business travel and entertainment. It is irrelevant that he took the trips solely to find new business; sightseeing tours, under objective standards, constitute entertainment sufficient to engage § 274(a). Walliser (P) took the trips in the hopes of finding more business. But the "directly related" requirement in § 274 disallows the mere promotion of goodwill in a social setting. There is no firm link between building tours and loan sales at First Federal. Furthermore, the "associated with" requirement of § 274 is not met by Walliser's (P) trip. This element of the test is an exception to the general rule designed to allow deductions for such activities as business dinners that occur in close proximity to substantive business negotiations. A trip cannot be said to relate with temporal proximity to business activities, even where Walliser (P) discussed the possibility of providing loans during the entire trip. The discussions were of a speculative nature only, and not the substantive type of business discussion contemplated by § 274. Decision entered for the Commissioner (D).

▌ *ANALYSIS*

The personal element of entertainment expenditures has disturbed the Congress for some time. In an effort to prevent abuse of the entertainment deduction, § 274 was fashioned to force deductions to have a strong link to actual business "deals" of a specific nature, not just discussions seeking business goodwill. The deduction remains available, but the door has been narrowed by § 274.

◼▬◼

Quicknotes

BUSINESS EXPENSE A cost incurred or amounts expended as "ordinary and necessary expenses" in the process of conducting an income-generating activity, currently deductible from a taxpayer's liability.

◼▬◼

Moss v. Commissioner

Lunch-deducting attorney (P) v. Internal Revenue Service (D)

758 F.2d 211 (7th Cir.).

NATURE OF CASE: Appeal from decision disallowing tax deductions.

FACT SUMMARY: Moss (P) appealed from a tax court decision disallowing a tax deduction on his share of his firm's daily business meeting lunch expenses, contending that the business nature of the daily lunch would qualify the lunch expense for necessary business-expense treatment.

RULE OF LAW

The expenses of daily business meeting lunches among coworkers are not deductible as necessary business expenses, even though the meetings might be necessary from a business perspective.

FACTS: Moss (P) was a partner in a small law firm specializing in trial work. The members of the firm met daily for lunch at Angelo's, a restaurant convenient for their practice. At the meeting, cases were discussed with the head of the firm, and the firm's trial schedule was worked out at these lunch meetings. These meetings were necessary as each member of the firm carried an enormous caseload, requiring the members of the firm to spend most of their day in court. Thus, lunch was the most convenient meeting time, as the courts were then in recess. There was no suggestion that the attorneys dawdled over lunch, or that the restaurant chosen was extravagant. Moss (P) sought to deduct his share of the lunch expenses as a necessary business expense. The Commissioner (D) took the position that the lunch expenses were not deductible. The tax court agreed with the Commissioner (D) and disallowed the deductions. From this decision Moss (P) appealed, and the court of appeals granted review.

ISSUE: Are the expenses of daily business meeting lunches among coworkers deductible as necessary business expenses, even though the meetings might be necessary from a business perspective?

HOLDING AND DECISION: (Posner, J.) No. The expenses of daily business meeting lunches among coworkers are not deductible as necessary business expenses, even though the meetings might be necessary from a business perspective. Given the unique nature of the firm's practice there is not much dispute that the meetings themselves were necessary for the smooth functioning of the firm, and that lunch was the most convenient time to hold such meetings. Meals are deductible when they are necessary and ordinary business expenses. There is a natural reluctance to allow deductions for expenses both business and personal in nature and because the meal

deduction is allowed, the Commissioner (D) requires that the meal expense be a real business necessity. The considerations involved with business meetings with coworkers are different than where the meetings are among coworkers. In client entertainment situations, the business objective, to be fully achieved, requires the sharing of a meal. In the present situation, the meal was not an organic part of the meeting, even though the meetings were necessary from a business perspective and lunch was the most convenient time for the meeting. In evaluating cases like this, decisions must be based on the frequency of the meetings and the individual degree and circumstance of the luncheon meetings sought to be deducted. In this case, however, the lunches, not being an organic part of the business purpose of the meetings, are not deductible. Affirmed.

ANALYSIS

The current state of deductibility for expenses so long as a plausible business connection can be demonstrated is particularly unjust to a majority of taxpayers, who cannot take advantage of such deductions by virtue of their employment. Such inequities are most apparent in connection with the deductibility of various entertainment functions, such as tickets to sporting and theatrical events, which involve a significant personal component, and allow a personal subsidy to those in a position to take advantage of business deductions.

Quicknotes

BUSINESS EXPENSE A cost incurred or amounts expended as "ordinary and necessary expenses" in the process of conducting an income-generating activity, currently deductible from a taxpayer's liability.

Churchill Downs, Inc. v. Commissioner

Race track owner (P) v. Internal Revenue Service (D)

307 F.3d 423 (6th Cir. 2002).

NATURE OF CASE: Appeal from decision that certain expenses were "entertainment" expenses, and, therefore, subject to a 50 percent limit on deductibility.

FACT SUMMARY: Churchill Downs, Inc. (P), an owner and operator of horse-race tracks, argued that several expenses of several events that it hosted, including cocktail parties, receptions, dinners, brunches, and hospitality tents, were deductible in full as ordinary business expenses spent to publicize the taxpayers' racing events, and were not, as the Internal Revenue Service (IRS) (D) claimed, "entertainment" subject to a 50 percent limit on deductibility.

RULE OF LAW

Purely social, public relations events hosted by a taxpayer for the purpose of promoting and advertising its product are "entertainment" for purposes of Internal Revenue Code (I.R.C.) § 274(n)(1), which limits the deductibility of entertainment expenses to 50 percent.

FACTS: Churchill Downs, Inc. (P) owned and operated several race tracks, at which it conducted horse races. It earned revenues from wagering, admissions, seating charges, concession commissions, sponsorship revenues, licensing rights, and broadcast fees. In connection with some of its races, it hosted several promotional events, including cocktail parties, receptions, dinners, brunches, and hospitality tents. These events were by invitation only and were generally open only to dignitaries, celebrities, and the media. No horse racing was conducted at these events, nor did the events—held away from the race tracks—offer the attendees an opportunity to learn more about the races; they were purely social events. Churchill Downs (P) made no money from the events. Churchill Downs (P) deducted the full amount of these expenses as "ordinary and necessary business expenses." The IRS (D), conceding that these were "ordinary and necessary" business expenses "directly related" to the "active conduct" of Churchill Downs's (P) business, and thus that some deduction of these expenses was allowed, nevertheless argued that I.R.C. § 274(n)(1) applied to limit deduction of these expenses to 50 percent because they qualified as items associated with activity generally considered entertainment. The U.S. Tax Court agreed with the IRS (D), and the court of appeals granted review.

ISSUE: Are purely social, public relations events hosted by a taxpayer for the purpose of promoting and advertising its product "entertainment" for purposes of I.R.C. § 274(n)(1), which limits the deductibility of entertainment expenses to 50 percent?

HOLDING AND DECISION: (Siler, J.) Yes. Purely social, public relations events hosted by a taxpayer for the purpose of promoting and advertising its product are "entertainment" for purposes of I.R.C. § 274(n)(1), which limits the deductibility of entertainment expenses to 50 percent. Churchill Downs (P) argues that its events showcased its races in the manner of a product introduction. The IRS (D) countered that the fact that these events publicized the races does not save them from being "entertainment." These arguments expose an inherent tension in 26 C.F.R. § 1.274-2(b)(1)(ii). On the one hand, § 1.274-2(b)(1)(ii) states that an item generally considered to be entertainment is subject to the 50 percent limitation even if it may be described otherwise, in particular as advertising or public relations. At the same time, the regulation suggests that certain expenses generally considered entertainment but somehow instrumental to the conduct of a taxpayer's business do not qualify as "entertainment" for purposes of I.R.C. § 274(n). Here, the purpose of the parties and galas and dinners was not to make Churchill Downs's (P) product directly available to its customers or to provide them with specific information about it, but rather to create an aura of glamour in connection with the upcoming races and generally to arouse public interest in them. In this regard, the dinners, brunches, and receptions at issue are best characterized not as a product introduction event used to conduct the taxpayer's business, but as pure advertising or public relations expenses. Therefore, the expenses at issue qualify as "entertainment" under § 1.274-2(b)(1)(ii)'s objective standard.

Alternatively, Churchill Downs (P) contends that, under the objective test, an event generally considered entertainment should not be deemed "entertainment" for purposes of § 274 where the event itself is the product the taxpayer is selling. It argues that the events held in connection with its races were integral parts of a unified entertainment experience. This argument is unavailing because Churchill Downs (P) did not make any money from hosting the events. Indeed, these events were easily separable from Churchill Downs's (P) business because its primary customers, the gaming public, were not permitted to attend them, either by purchasing tickets or otherwise. Because Churchill Downs (P) was not in the business of throwing parties, it is inappropriate to characterize these non-race events as Churchill Downs's (P) "product." Also rejected is Churchill Downs's (P) argument that these events were exempt from the § 274(n)(1) limitations as "goods, services, and facilities made available to the general public" because the

Continued on next page.

events were by invitation only, those invited were not Churchill Downs's (P) regular customers, and the dinners and galas at issue were not the products that members of the general public routinely purchase from Churchill Downs (P), namely, admission to horse races or wagers. Affirmed.

▎ ANALYSIS

An issue that the court did not decide was whether, even assuming that the events at issue did not constitute "entertainment," I.R.C. § 274(n)(1)(A) would preclude full deduction of many of the expenses. That section provides that "the amount allowable as a deduction under this Chapter for . . . any expense for food or beverages . . . shall not exceed 50 percent of the amount of such expense or item which would (but for this paragraph) be allowable as a deduction under this." This limitation does not appear to be contingent on a classification of the expenses as "entertainment." Given that the events at issue were mainly dinners, brunches, breakfasts, and receptions, it seems likely that a significant portion of the expenses for which Churchill Downs (P) sought deductions could have been limited as food and beverage expenses.

■═■

Quicknotes

BUSINESS EXPENSE A cost incurred or amounts expended as "ordinary and necessary expenses" in the process of conducting an income-generating activity, currently deductible from a taxpayer's liability.

DEDUCTION Subtraction (from gross income) in arriving at taxable income (the tax base).

■═■

CHAPTER 18

Education Expenses

Quick Reference Rules of Law

Takahashi v. Commissioner

Teacher (P) v. Internal Revenue Service (D)

U.S. Tax Ct., 87 T.C. 126 (1986).

NATURE OF CASE: Suit challenging an Internal Revenue Service (IRS) denial of a deduction for educational expenses.

FACT SUMMARY: Takahashi (P), a teacher, attended a seminar on cultural diversity in Hawaii in an effort to comply with the discretionary multicultural education requirements of the employing school district.

🏛 RULE OF LAW
Educational expenses are deductible as ordinary and necessary business expenses if the education enhances skills required by the individual in his trade, or if the education meets the express requirements of the individual's employer.

FACTS: The Takahashis (P) were employed as science teachers in the Los Angeles Unified School District. The California State Education Code required teachers to complete a minimum of two semester units in a course dealing with multiculturalism to receive promotions and raises. In 1981, the Takahashis (P) attended a seminar in Hawaii entitled "The Hawaiian Cultural Transition in a Diverse Society." They attended the seminar on nine of ten days spent in Hawaii. The program lasted from one to six hours a day. The Takahashis (P) spent $2,373 on the trip. They claimed the expenses incurred on the trip as an educational expense. In a deficiency notice, the Commissioner (D) denied the expense in full. The Takahashis (P) filed suit in tax court challenging the Commissioner's (D) denial.

ISSUE: Are educational expenses deductible as ordinary and necessary business expenses if the education enhances skills required by the individual in his trade, or if the education meets the express requirements of the individual's employer?

HOLDING AND DECISION: (Nims, J.) Yes. Educational expenses are deductible as ordinary and necessary business expenses if the education enhances skills required by the individual in his trade, or if the education meets the express requirements of the individual's employer. In this case, the application of the tax regulations is fairly straightforward. There is no contention in the record that attendance of the Hawaii seminar was required by the school district. Rather, it is argued that the seminar improved teaching skills. But it is a stretch to believe that learning about multiculturalism in Hawaii aided the teaching of science classes in Los Angeles. The Commissioner (D) argues, and the point is well taken, that the burden is upon the taxpayer to show that a reasonable allocation exists between business education expenses on the trip and personal vacation expenditures; no such offering has

been made by the Takahashis (P). Since it is conceded that the trip was not required, and the content of the seminar does not seem rationally linked to the teaching of science, the threshold tests of § 1.162-5(a) of the regulations have not been met. Decision entered for the Commissioner (D).

▶ ANALYSIS

The 1986 Tax Reform Act expressed great concern over the possibility that teachers could deduct expenses that were primarily personal vacation expenses under the guise of educational expenses. An allocation of costs between personal and business can be made, but the burden is on the taxpayer to prove the allocation is reasonable.

■=■

Quicknotes

BUSINESS EXPENSE A cost incurred or amounts expended as "ordinary and necessary expenses" in the process of conducting an income-generating activity, currently deductible from a taxpayer's liability.

■=■

Wassenaar v. Commissioner

Course-taking attorney (P) v. Internal Revenue Service (D)

U.S. Tax Ct., 72 T.C. 1195 (1979).

NATURE OF CASE: Suit seeking to overturn an Internal Revenue Service (IRS) denial of educational expense deductions.

FACT SUMMARY: An attorney attempted to deduct the cost of obtaining a master's degree in taxation as an employee business expense.

🏛 RULE OF LAW
In order for educational expenses to be properly deducted, they must be incurred in maintaining or improving skills of a profession in which the taxpayer is already firmly established.

FACTS: Wassenaar (P) graduated from Wayne State University Law School in 1972. He took the bar exam in July 1972 and was notified of a passing score in October 1972. However, he was not formally admitted to the Michigan bar until May 1973. In September 1972, Wassenaar (P) entered the graduate law program in taxation at New York University (NYU). He graduated with a master's degree in taxation in May 1973. He incurred expenses of $2,781 completing the master's program. Wassenaar (P) then took his first position as an attorney. On his 1973 taxes, Wassenaar (P) sought to deduct the expenses at NYU as an employee business expense. He received a deficiency notice denying the entire deduction, and he then filed suit in tax court.

ISSUE: In order for educational expenses to be properly deducted, must they be incurred in maintaining or improving skills of a profession in which the taxpayer is already firmly established?

HOLDING AND DECISION: [Judge not stated in casebook excerpt.] Yes. In order for educational expenses to be properly deducted, they must be incurred in maintaining or improving skills of a profession in which the taxpayer is already firmly established. Generally, the cost of learning a trade or profession is not deductible if the taxpayer is learning a new trade or profession. In this case, Wassenaar (P) argued that his education at NYU helped to maintain and improve his skills as an attorney. However, it is a well-established principle that being a member in good standing of a profession is not tantamount to carrying on that profession. Wassenaar (P) had never practiced as an attorney when he enrolled at NYU. In fact, he was not even permitted to practice law as a member of the bar until he was in the process of finishing his coursework at NYU. Thus it cannot be said that he was "improving" his ability to practice a trade or business. His was an ongoing educational endeavor to become a tax-law specialist. Accordingly, Wassenaar's (P) educational expenses are not deductible. Decision entered for the Commissioner (D).

▶ ANALYSIS

The most interesting aspect of this case is that law school graduates invariably assume that a clever characterization of facts is all that is necessary to turn the law on its head. Wassenaar (P) lost because common sense is all that is required to determine that taxpayers cannot maintain and improve skills in a profession in which they do not yet engage. Furthermore, the general approach in the area of tax law has been to narrowly define a trade or business. For example, a pharmacist intern has been held to have a different trade from a licensed pharmacist.

Quicknotes

BUSINESS EXPENSE A cost incurred or amounts expended as "ordinary and necessary expenses" in the process of conducting an income-generating activity, currently deductible from a taxpayer's liability.

DEFICIENCY Refers to amount of tax taxpayer owes, or is claimed to owe, the IRS.

Furner v. Commissioner

Teacher (P) v. Internal Revenue Service (D)

393 F.2d 292 (7th Cir. 1968).

NATURE OF CASE: Appeal of tax court decision upholding Internal Revenue Service (IRS) denial of educational expense deductions.

FACT SUMMARY: Furner (P), a schoolteacher, left her position and returned to graduate school in order to be more fully versed in relevant subject matter.

RULE OF LAW
If the course of study is such that the expense thereof can reasonably be considered ordinary and necessary in carrying on the business of teaching, costs incurred in graduate study are deductible as educational expenses.

FACTS: Furner (P) majored in social studies at a teachers' college, and received a bachelor's degree in 1957. She taught in a Minnesota school, grades seven through twelve, between 1957 and 1960. She primarily taught history, a subject falling under her educational background. However, she felt that her teaching required a greater depth of knowledge than she possessed. Furner (P) arranged to enter a graduate program at Northwestern University as a full-time graduate student during the 1960–1961 school year. Because her school system did not readily grant leaves of absence, she resigned in June 1960. Furner (P) sought to deduct the cost of her graduate education, but she received a deficiency notice that denied the deduction. In her tax-court suit, the court ruled that she was not carrying on a trade or business of teaching while attending graduate school. She appealed to the court of appeals.

ISSUE: If the course of study is such that the expense thereof can reasonably be considered ordinary and necessary in carrying on the business of teaching, are costs incurred in graduate study deductible as educational expenses?

HOLDING AND DECISION: (Fairchild, J.) Yes. If the course of study is such that the expense thereof can reasonably be considered ordinary and necessary in carrying on the business of teaching, costs incurred in graduate study are deductible as educational expenses. Gaining additional education in a trade or business can be deducted as a business expense where the education maintains or improves on skills necessary to perform in the trade or business. The permissibility of this deduction is not contingent upon whether or not the attainment of additional relevant skills interrupts the carrying on of the trade or business. Certainly, education takes time to accomplish. In this case, the Commissioner (D) focused too much on

Furner's (P) year away from teaching. It is becoming usual for teachers to further their professional options by deepening their knowledge in a specific subject. Certainly, Furner (P) might have achieved her graduate degree in part-time studies, but there are factors that make finishing in a single year very attractive. It seems that her enrollment in a graduate program is a normal incident of carrying on the business of teaching. Reversed.

ANALYSIS

Whether an educational expense deduction will be permitted depends in part on the conventions in the particular trade or business. In this case, the trend in teaching was to return to graduate school if additional skills in a subject were required for advancement and job security. The education must be analyzed in the context of the business or trade in question.

Quicknotes

BUSINESS EXPENSE A cost incurred or amounts expended as "ordinary and necessary expenses" in the process of conducting an income-generating activity, currently deductible from a taxpayer's liability.

DEFICIENCY Refers to amount of tax taxpayer owes, or is claimed to owe, the IRS.

Sharon v. Commissioner

Attorney (P) v. Internal Revenue Service (D)

U.S. Tax Ct., 66 T.C. 515 (1976), *aff'd*, 591 F.2d 1273 (9th Cir. 1978).

NATURE OF CASE: Challenge to Internal Revenue Service (IRS) denial of numerous deductions for educational expenses.

FACT SUMMARY: Sharon (P), an attorney, attempted to deduct various bar admission fees and educational expenses incurred in completing licensing requirements.

> **RULE OF LAW**
> (1) All costs of minimum educational requirements for qualification in employment are personal expenditures or constitute an inseparable aggregate of personal and capital expenditures.
> (2) Capital costs incurred in obtaining a new professional license are amortizable, but educational expenses that qualify an individual for a new trade or business, by virtue of new professional certifications, are not deductible.

FACTS: Sharon (P) obtained a law degree from Columbia University in 1964. He then took the New York State bar exam, expending $175.20 for bar review courses and materials, and $25 for the bar exam fee. Sharon (P) was admitted to practice in the State of New York on December 22, 1964. He worked there in a law firm until 1967. In 1967, he accepted a position in the Office of Regional Counsel, IRS, and moved to California. Although not required by his employer, Sharon (P) decided to become a member of the California State Bar. He spent $801 on California bar review materials and fees for admission. He also spent $11 in order to be admitted to practice before the U.S. District Court and the U.S. Court of Appeals. His employer required only that he be admitted to practice before the U.S. Tax Court. Finally, in 1970, he incurred $313.35 in connection with his admission to the U.S. Supreme Court. Sharon (P) was assessed deficiencies in his tax returns for 1969 and 1970, where he deducted various educational expenses and took amortization deductions on others. The Commissioner (D) generally denied his deductions, with certain minor exceptions, and Sharon (P) petitioned the tax court for review of the disallowed deductions. The tax court granted review.

ISSUE:
(1) May the costs of obtaining a license to practice law be amortized over expected work life?
(2) Are capital costs incurred in obtaining a new professional license amortizable?

HOLDING AND DECISION: (Simpson, J.)
(1) No. All costs of minimum educational requirements for qualification in employment are personal expenditures

or constitute an inseparable aggregate of personal and capital expenditures. Educational expenses intended to qualify an individual for a trade or business cannot be capitalized. In this case, Sharon (P) attempts to characterize his legal education as an expense incident to obtaining his license to practice law, an amortizable expense. But his clever characterization is not compelling. A law school education provides benefits in numerous ways; he is not limited to the practice of law in New York, and many individuals with law degrees never practice law. The $25 fee for his license could in theory have been amortized as a capital expenditure and deducted in one year due to its minimal value. But the year in question is well passed, and all he may now do is include the remaining portion of that fee in his capital deductions for his California license. The educational amortization is denied. Affirmed.

(2) Yes. Capital costs incurred in obtaining a new professional license are amortizable, but educational expenses that qualify an individual for a new trade or business, by virtue of new professional certifications, are not deductible. Where the useful life of a license extends beyond one year, it cannot be deducted as an expense, but rather, it must be treated as a capital expenditure. In this case, the $812 spent by Sharon (P) in acquiring a California license must be divided into two parts: the cost of the review course, an educational expense, and the license fees, a capital expenditure. The bar review course is indeed an educational expense, but if it qualifies Sharon (P) for a new trade, then it is not deductible. The education aided Sharon (P) in receiving his license to practice law in California. Since he could not practice without the license, the bar review course qualified him for a new trade, the practice of law in California. It is not deductible as an educational business expense but rather is a nondeductible personal expense. The remaining $582 dollars, conferring a professional license, is a capital expenditure with a life expectancy equal to Sharon's (P) projected life expectancy. He may amortize the cost over that period. Similarly, the license to practice before the Supreme Court is an intangible asset with a useful life beyond 1 year. Therefore, Sharon (P) may not deduct the cost of obtaining the license. Because membership in the Supreme Court bar may be useful to an attorney in the practice of law, this intangible was used by Sharon (P) in 1970 when he obtained it, and he may amortize the cost of acquiring it over his life expectancy. Affirmed. Both decisions entered under Rule 155.

Continued on next page.

DISSENT: (Scott, J.) The license fees should not be amortizable over the life span of Sharon (P). While they are indeed capital expenditures, there is nothing in the record to indicate the useful life of those expenditures. The life span of the asset acquired must be ascertained with fair certainty.

DISSENT: (Irwin, J.) It seems an odd conclusion that an attorney, licensed to practice in New York, has qualified for a new trade or business by virtue of being licensed in California, since he performs the same types of tasks and activities before and after acquiring the new bar membership. The California bar exam ought to be treated as part of the cost of acquiring the license to practice in California, rather than education leading to qualification for a new trade or business.

▶ ANALYSIS

This case provides an excellent example of the difficulty in characterizing expended funds as either capital investments or expenses. The primary factor that determines the characterization is the useful life of the asset.

■▬■

Quicknotes

AMORTIZATION The satisfaction of a debt by the tendering of regular, equal payments over a period of time.

BUSINESS EXPENSE A cost incurred or amounts expended as "ordinary and necessary expenses" in the process of conducting an income-generating activity, currently deductible from a taxpayer's liability.

CAPITAL EXPENDITURE Expenditure that is not deductible currently (because it does not produce a decrease in wealth), but that creates, or adds to, basis.

■▬■

Note: There are no principal cases in Chapter 19 of the casebook.

CHAPTER

20

Hobby Losses

Quick Reference Rules of Law

Dreicer v. Commissioner

Dilettante writer (P) v. Internal Revenue Service (D)

U.S. Tax Ct., 78 T.C. 642 (1982).

NATURE OF CASE: Remand from court of appeals' reversal of tax court decision upholding notice of deficiency.

FACT SUMMARY: Dreicer (P) claimed deductible losses for expenses related to his alleged profession as a writer.

🏛 RULE OF LAW
Deductible losses under § 183 of the Internal Revenue Code (I.R.C.) are allowed if the taxpayer entered into the activity with the actual and honest objective of making a profit.

FACTS: Dreicer (P), an independently wealthy man, spent many years traveling around the world in fine style, ostensibly for the purpose of writing a travel book. His manuscript was rejected by the two publishing companies to which he submitted it. Dreicer (P) claimed deductible losses of approximately $50,000 in 1972 and 1973 for travel expenses. The Commissioner (D) disallowed the deductions on the ground that the expenses arose from activities not pursued for profit. The tax court upheld the notice of deficiency, holding that Dreicer (P) had no reasonable expectation of profits from his writings. The court of appeals reversed and remanded, ruling that the tax court had not used the proper legal standard.

ISSUE: Are deductible losses under § 183 of the I.R.C. allowed if the taxpayer entered into the activity with the actual and honest objective of making a profit?

HOLDING AND DECISION: (Simpson, J.) Yes. Deductible losses under § 183 of the I.R.C. are allowed if the taxpayer entered into the activity with the actual and honest objective of making a profit. Deductions for business expenses under § 183 must be allowed where the taxpayer has an honest objective of profits even though there may be no reasonable expectation of profits. Thus, the taxpayer's motive is the ultimate question. This motive must be determined by a careful analysis of all the surrounding objective facts. The taxpayer's statement of intent should be only one of the relevant factors. In the present case, Dreicer (P) sustained large losses for many years. Thus, the objective facts of the case show that there was no realistic possibility that he could ever earn sufficient income to offset the losses. The expenses arose from activities that were not conducted in a businesslike manner calculated to earn a profit. Accordingly, the prior decision affirming the Commissioner (D) is re-entered.

▶ ANALYSIS

Dreicer (P) wanted to be treated in the same manner as an inventor or wildcat driller would be treated; those examples are mentioned in the applicable regulations to § 183. These types of endeavors are continued in the face of large losses in the hope of a giant payoff. Ultimately, the tax court simply did not believe that Dreicer's (P) travels were actually undertaken to make money, especially since it found that he did not conduct his activities in a business-like manner calculated to earn a profit.

Quicknotes

DEDUCTION Subtraction (from gross income) in arriving at taxable income (the tax base).

LOSS Situation where amount realized (if any) exceeds the basis upon the sale or other disposition of an asset. Also refers to fact of sustained decline in value of asset (not disposed of) which gives rise to a deduction. There is also said to be a loss in a year where deductions exceed gross income.

Remuzzi v. Commissioner

Farmer surgeon (P) v. Internal Revenue Service (D)

U.S. Tax Ct., T.C.M. 1988-8 (1988).

NATURE OF CASE: Challenge to disallowance of deductions.

FACT SUMMARY: Remuzzi (P), a surgeon, claimed losses from operating a farm where his family lived.

> 🏛 **RULE OF LAW**
> In determining whether an activity is engaged in for profit, objective facts regarding the manner, success, and history of the taxpayer's efforts are given greater weight than the taxpayer's stated intent.

FACTS: Remuzzi (P), a surgeon, bought a large piece of property in 1978. The property, Farleigh Farm, contained old farm buildings but had not been operated as a farm for ten years. Remuzzi (P) made an agreement with Payne, one of his patients, whereby Payne was to raise cattle on the farm as a tenant. However, shortly thereafter, Payne was not able to work and Remuzzi (P) made some efforts to operate Farleigh Farm using his family and hired help. Remuzzi (P) reported revenues and expenses from the farm from 1978 to 1982. The revenues were extremely minimal while the losses were significant. The Commissioner (D) disallowed much of the claimed losses on the basis that Farleigh Farm was not operated for profit. Remuzzi (P) challenged the disallowance before the tax court.

ISSUE: In determining whether an activity is engaged in for profit, are objective facts regarding the manner, success, and history of the taxpayer's efforts given greater weight than the taxpayer's stated intent?

HOLDING AND DECISION: (Korner, J.) Yes. In determining whether an activity is engaged in for profit, objective facts regarding the manner, success, and history of the taxpayer's efforts are given greater weight than the taxpayer's stated intent. Section 183 of the I.R.C. allows for deductible expenses if an activity is engaged in for profit. Whether a taxpayer's objective is bona fide is a question of fact to be determined from all of the facts and circumstances and not just from the taxpayer's stated intent. Section 183's regulations list nine factors that should be taken into account: (1) the manner in which the taxpayer conducts the activity; (2) the expertise of the taxpayer; (3) the time and effort expended; (4) the expectation of asset appreciation; (5) the success of similar operations; (6) the history of the taxpayer; (7) the amount of profits; (8) the financial status of the taxpayer; and (9) the personal pleasure gained by the taxpayer. These factors create an objective standard for making the determination. In the instant case the most important factors are that Remuzzi

(P) had substantial income from his primary profession and the claimed losses reduced his tax burden. Also, there is no evidence that Remuzzi (P) treated Farleigh Farm as a business by trying to reduce expenses and maximize revenues. Remuzzi (P) had no expertise and spent little time operating the farm. Finally, it is evident that Remuzzi (P) and his family moved to the farm for personal enjoyment and pleasure. Accordingly, Remuzzi (P) failed to prove that Farleigh Farm was engaged in for profit. Decision entered for the Commissioner (D).

▶ **ANALYSIS**

Another key factor in this case was that Farleigh Farm suffered such large and consistent losses. The case also dealt with Remuzzi's (P) claim that an unpaid loan to Payne was a bad business debt. The tax court found that since the farm was not a business, a bad debt related to the farm could not be a bad business debt.

Quicknotes

DEDUCTION Subtraction (from gross income) in arriving at taxable income (the tax base).

LOSS Situation where amount realized (if any) exceeds the basis upon the sale or other disposition of an asset. Also refers to fact of sustained decline in value of asset (not disposed of) which gives rise to a deduction. There is also said to be a loss in a year where deductions exceed gross income.

Home Offices, Vacation Homes, and Other Dual-Use Property

Quick Reference Rules of Law

Popov v. Commissioner

Home-practicing musician (P) v. Internal Revenue Service (D)

246 F.3d 1190 (9th Cir. 2001).

NATURE OF CASE: Appeal from decision disallowing home office deduction.

FACT SUMMARY: Popov (P) was a professional violinist who sought to obtain a home office deduction for the space she used in her home to practice for orchestra performances and studio recordings.

🏛 RULE OF LAW
A professional musician is entitled to deduct the expenses from the portion of her home used exclusively for musical practice when the activities performed and the time spent at each business location are considered and weighed in favor of the musician.

FACTS: Popov (P) was a professional violinist who performed regularly with two orchestras and contracted with various studios to record music for the motion picture industry. The recording sessions required that Popov (P) be able to read scores quickly as the musicians did not receive their sheet music in advance of the recording sessions. None of Popov's (P) employers provided her with a place to practice. Popov (P) lived with her husband and their four-year-old daughter in a one-bedroom apartment. The apartment's living room served as her home office and she used this area to practice the violin and make recordings, which she used for practice purposes and as demonstration tapes for orchestras. No one slept in the living room and her daughter was not allowed to play in it. Popov (P) spent four to five hours a day practicing in the living room. In their 1993 tax return, the Popovs (P) claimed a home office deduction for the living room and deducted 40 percent of their annual rent and 20 percent of their annual electricity bill. The Internal Revenue Service (IRS) disallowed these deductions. Upon petition for redetermination in tax court, the court concluded that the Popovs (P) were not entitled to a home office deduction. The court of appeals granted review.

ISSUE: Is a professional musician entitled to deduct the expenses from the portion of her home used exclusively for musical practice when the activities performed and the time spent at each business location are considered and weighed in favor of the musician?

HOLDING AND DECISION: (Hawkins, J.) Yes. A professional musician is entitled to deduct the expenses from the portion of her home used exclusively for musical practice when the activities performed and the time spent at each business location are considered and weighed in favor of the musician. Based on these considerations, the Popovs (P) are entitled to a home office deduction. The Internal Revenue Code (I.R.C.) allows a deduction for a home office that is exclusively used as the "principal place of business for any trade or business of the taxpayer." Section 280A(c)(1)(A). In determining whether the space is the taxpayer's principal place of business, the relative importance of the activities performed at each business location and the time spent at each place are to be considered. In regard to the first criteria, the importance of daily practice to Mrs. Popov's (P) profession is undeniable because regular practice is essential to playing a musical instrument at a high level of ability. Without four to five hours of daily practice, she would be unable to perform in professional orchestras and would not be equipped for the peculiar demands of studio recording. Although it is in the concert halls and studios where she performs, musical performance does not fit easily into being defined as a delivery of service, whereas, for example, an anesthesiologist who delivers the service of anesthesia to patients at hospitals would fit into such a framework and a home office deduction would be denied for the anesthesiologist in that case. The other inquiry focuses on the amount of time spent at home versus the time spent at other places where business activities occur. In this case, Mrs. Popov (P) spends significantly more time practicing the violin at home than she does performing or recording. The Popovs (P) are, therefore, entitled to a home office deduction for Mrs. Popov's (P) practice space because it was exclusively used as her principal place of business. Reversed.

▌ *ANALYSIS*

The court's decision in this case was governed by *Commissioner v. Soliman,* 506 U.S. 168 (1993), in which the United States Supreme Court ruled that a home-office deduction is not permitted whenever a home office may be characterized as legitimate, and that the inquiry must instead focus on whether the home office is the taxpayer's principal place of business. In *Soliman,* the Court denied the home-office deduction to an anesthesiologist who spent around 35 hours each week with patients at three different hospitals, none of which provided him with an office, and who used a spare bedroom for contacting patients and surgeons, maintaining billing records and patient logs, preparing for treatments, and reading medical journals. The Court reasoned that his principal place of business was the hospitals, not his home. Although the Court did not develop an objective formula that yields a clear answer in every case, it did indicate that the two

Continued on next page.

primary considerations are "the relative importance of the activities performed at each business location and the time spent at each place"—the formulation used by the court of appeals in *Popov*.

■━■

Quicknotes

DEDUCTION Subtraction (from gross income) in arriving at taxable income (the tax base).

■━■

The Interest Deduction

Quick Reference Rules of Law

Davison v. Commissioner

Interest-paying borrower (P) v. Internal Revenue Service (D)

U.S. Tax Ct., 107 T.C. 35 (1996), *aff'd per curiam*, 141 F.3d 403 (2d Cir. 1998).

NATURE OF CASE: Suit contesting the denial of a claimed interest deduction.

FACT SUMMARY: Davison (P) claimed deductions for interest paid on a loan, even though the same lender provided the additional money that enabled Davison (P) to make the interest payment.

> **RULE OF LAW**
> Interest deductions are not allowed if the funds used to satisfy the interest obligations were borrowed by a cash basis borrower from the same lender to whom the interest was owed.

FACTS: Davison (P) and his two partners, Esposito and Vitale, formed a partnership known as White Tail. Through White Tail, Davison (P) and his partners borrowed a significant amount of money from John Hancock Mutual Life Insurance Company (John Hancock). The credit arrangement required White Tail to make an interest payment of $1,587,310.46 and a principal payment of $7,707.50. Both amounts were due on January 1, 1981. Due to financial difficulties, White Tail negotiated an arrangement with John Hancock whereby John Hancock loaned White Tail the money needed to make the January 1981 payments. White Tail claimed an interest deduction for the amount it claimed it "paid" to John Hancock. The Commissioner (D) issued a notice of deficiency, disallowing the deduction. Whit Tail challenged the disallowance in tax court.

ISSUE: Are interest deductions allowed if the funds used to satisfy the interest obligations were borrowed by a cash basis borrower from the same lender to whom the interest was owed?

HOLDING AND DECISION: [Judge not stated in casebook excerpt.] No. Interest deductions are not allowed if the funds used to satisfy the interest obligations were borrowed by a cash basis borrower from the same lender to whom the interest was owed. When a borrower simply increases his debt to the lender by the amount of the interest, the interest deduction is not allowed. The purpose of the $1,587,310.46 advance, made on December 30, 1980, by John Hancock to White Tail was to provide White Tail with the funds necessary to satisfy its interest obligation to John Hancock. The fact that the loan proceeds went through White Tail's bank account does not affect the substance of the transaction. Unlike previous cases that used the "unrestricted control" test that looked at whether the borrower had acquired possession or control over the proceeds of the second loan, looking at the substance of the transaction is consistent with the traditional approach of characterizing transactions

on a substance-over-form basis by looking at the economic realties of the transaction. Here, looking at the economic realities of the transaction, White Tail simply increased its debt to John Hancock, and the effect was postponement rather than payment of interest. Therefore, White Tail is not entitled to a deduction for the interest paid.

▶ ANALYSIS

The court in *Battlestein v. Commissioner*, 631 F.2d 1182 (5th Cir. 1980) (en banc) reached the same conclusion, in that the check exchanges between the lender and the borrower were plainly for no purpose other than to finance the current interest obligations; the interest deduction was therefore denied. On the other hand, where a taxpayer discharges interest payable to one lender with funds obtained from a different lender, the interest on the first loan is considered paid when the funds are transferred to the first lender.

■━■

Quicknotes

INTEREST DEDUCTION An offset to gross income based on a taxpayer's payment of interest, using money or other value that could have been used elsewhere but was instead allocated to repay the taxpayer's interest debt.

■━■

Note: There are no principal cases in Chapter 23 of the casebook.

CHAPTER

24

Casualty Losses

Quick Reference Rules of Law

Popa v. Commissioner

Businessman (P) v. Internal Revenue Service (D)

U.S. Tax Ct., 73 T.C. 130 (1979).

NATURE OF CASE: Appeal from Commissioner's denial of a § 165 casualty loss.

FACT SUMMARY: Popa (P), an executive of a U.S. company who resided in Vietnam, lost his possessions when the government collapsed and Americans were ordered evacuated.

🏛 RULE OF LAW
In unusual circumstances where it would be unfair or unreasonable to require a taxpayer to eliminate all possible noncasualty causes of a loss, a taxpayer will be entitled to claim a § 165 deduction without eliminating all possible noncasualty causes of the loss.

FACTS: Popa (P) was a vice president with Transworld Services Corp. residing in Saigon, Vietnam, in 1975. Days after Popa (P) took a business trip to Thailand, the South Vietnamese government collapsed and Americans were evacuated from the country. Popa (P) was unable to return for his possessions at his home in Saigon. Popa (P) claimed a casualty-loss deduction pursuant to § 165(c)(3) of the Internal Revenue Code (I.R.C.) for the loss of his possessions. The Commissioner (D) disallowed the deduction based on the fact that Popa (P) could not prove how the possessions were lost. Popa (P) challenged the disallowance in tax court.

ISSUE: In unusual circumstances where it would be unfair or unreasonable to require a taxpayer to eliminate all possible noncasualty causes of a loss, will a taxpayer be entitled to claim a § 165 deduction without eliminating all possible noncasualty causes of the loss?

HOLDING AND DECISION: (Sterrett, J.) Yes. In unusual circumstances where it would be unfair or unreasonable to require a taxpayer to eliminate all possible noncasualty causes of a loss, a taxpayer will be entitled to claim a § 165 deduction without eliminating all possible noncasualty causes of the loss. Section 165(c)(3) of the I.R.C. allows for a deduction under the category of "other casualty" losses. This section was designed to address sudden, cataclysmic, and devastating losses. The principle of ejusdem generis provides that unexpected, accidental forces exerted against property that are similar to the enumerated causes in § 165 also qualify for casualty losses. In unusual circumstances such as the one faced by Popa (P), it is not fair or reasonable to require the taxpayer to eliminate all possible noncasualty causes of the loss. It is clear that the only conceivable circumstances that would deny Popa (P) a casualty loss would be if his property were confiscated under the authority of some hastily enacted local law. All of the other possibilities would entitle him to the deduction. Accordingly, the most reasonable conclusion is that Popa (P) suffered a qualifying casualty loss. Decision entered under Rule 155.

DISSENT: (Fay, J.) The taxpayer has the burden of proof for alleged casualty losses. Popa (P) cannot prove the cause of his loss, and cannot prove that his loss was not caused by government confiscation. Therefore, he has failed to meet his burden of proof. The taxpayer must bear the misfortune when there is an impossibility of proving the essential facts.

▌ *ANALYSIS*

Although the dissent's position is harsh, it is well supported by the United States Supreme Court's decision in *Burnet v. Houston*, 283 U.S. 223 (1931). In *Burnet*, the taxpayer contended that it was impossible for him to prove his 1913 basis for stock that became worthless in 1920. The Court held that, therefore, his claim was unenforceable. The majority decision in *Popa* does not persuasively distinguish *Popa* from *Burnet*. However, it appears that the majority was simply ruling that there was an overwhelming likelihood that Popa's (P) possessions were stolen or destroyed in the war, rather than confiscated by the Communist regime, given what evidence was available.

■═■

Quicknotes

EJUSDEM GENERIS Belonging to the same class or type; rule of construction applied when general words follow a specified class of persons or items, then the words are not to be applied in their broad meaning but are to apply only to those persons or items listed.

■═■

Chamales v. Commissioner

Property owner (P) v. Internal Revenue Service (D)

U.S. Tax Ct., T.C.M. 2000-33 (2000).

NATURE OF CASE: Review of decision disallowing deduction.

FACT SUMMARY: The Chamaleses (P) appealed a decision of the Commissioner (D) disallowing the casualty-loss deduction they had claimed for the depreciation in the value of their property.

> ## RULE OF LAW
> (1) A horrific crime that receives national attention, and the ensuing media presence and public attention that occur in the neighborhood in which the crime was committed, do not constitute a "casualty" as that term is used in Internal Revenue Code (I.R.C.) § 165(c)(3).
> (2) Where the only damage to a taxpayer's property is a temporary market value decline, the taxpayer is not entitled to a casualty-loss deduction.

FACTS: In 1994, the Chamaleses (P) opened escrow on a property located in Brentwood Park in Los Angeles that they were interested in purchasing. They were attracted to the beautiful, parklike setting and the peacefulness of the area. At the time, O.J. Simpson (Simpson) owned a property directly west of and adjacent to that being purchased by the Chamaleses (P). During the escrow period, Nicole Simpson and Ronald Goldman were murdered, Simpson was arrested for the murders, and the neighborhood around Simpson's home became inundated with people blocking the streets and trespassing and with helicopters flying overhead. Police presence had little effect and the area continued to be inundated with onlookers until 1999 when the commotion subsided substantially. Notwithstanding the murders and ensuing mayhem, the Chamaleses (P) closed escrow and purchased the property for $2,849,000. At the time they purchased the property in 1994, the Chamaleses (P) were aware that the existing home required remodeling and repair, and, in 1995, the Chamaleses (P) began a reconstruction project costing approximately $2 million. Similar reconstruction projects in the area were undertaken by other property owners. Due to the events surrounding the murders, the Chamaleses' (P) broker estimated the decline in property value to be 20 to 30 percent. The Chamaleses' (P) 1994 tax return claimed a deduction for a casualty loss of 30 percent based on their (P) certified public accountant's discussions with two area real estate agents regarding the amount by which the Chamaleses' (P) property had decreased in value, which was estimated to be 30 to 40 percent. An expert appraisal was not obtained at this time as the accountant felt that a typical appraisal based on values throughout the Brentwood Park area would be inconclusive as to the loss suffered by the few properties closest to the Simpson home. An explanatory supplemental statement labeled "Casualty Loss" was attached to the return and stated that the loss was premised on "the calamity of the murder & trial, which was sudden & unavoidable & which resulted in a permanent loss to value of property." The Commissioner (D) disallowed the deduction, and the Chamaleses (P) challenged the disallowance in tax court.

ISSUE:
(1) Do a horrific crime that receives national attention, and the ensuing media presence and public attention that occur in the neighborhood in which the crime was committed, constitute a "casualty" as that term is used in I.R.C. § 165(c)(3)?
(2) Where the only damage to a taxpayer's property is a temporary market value decline, is the taxpayer entitled to a casualty-loss deduction?

HOLDING AND DECISION: (Nimms, J.)
(1) No. A horrific crime that receives national attention, and the ensuing media presence and public attention that occur in the neighborhood in which the crime was committed, do not constitute a "casualty" as that term is used in I.R.C. § 165(c)(3). A casualty loss arises when the nature of the occurrence precipitating the damage to the property qualifies as a casualty and the nature of the damage sustained is such that is deductible for purposes of § 165. Thus, the first issue is whether the Chamaleses (P) suffered a "casualty." Although the stabbing of Nicole Simpson and Ronald Goldman was a sudden and unexpected exertion of force, this force was not exerted upon and did not damage the Chamaleses' (P) property. Similarly, the initial influx of onlookers was not a force exerted on the Chamaleses' (P) property and was not the source of the decrease in the home's market value. Press and media attention for months bears little similarity to a fire, storm, or shipwreck and is not properly classified therewith as an "other casualty." Instead, the source of the decline in value was due to a steadily operating cause—the constant ongoing public and media attention—rather than to a "casualty." Because the Code excludes from the term "casualty" the "progressive deterioration of property through a steadily operating cause," the Chamaleses (P) did not suffer a casualty qualifying for the casualty-loss deduction.

Continued on next page.

(2) No. Where the only damage to a taxpayer's property is a temporary market value decline, the taxpayer is not entitled to a casualty-loss deduction. Even if the Chamaleses (P) had suffered a "casualty" as that term is defined in the Code, the nature of any damage caused by that casualty is not recognized as deductible. The difficulties suffered by the Chamaleses (P) as a consequence of their proximity to the Simpson residence do not constitute the type of damage contemplated by § 165(c)(3). Only physical damage to or physically necessitated permanent abandonment of property will be recognized as deductible under § 165, and a casualty-loss deduction based upon a temporary decline in market value is not permitted. The Chamaleses' (P) claimed casualty loss is thus not of a type recognized as a deductible for purposes of § 165 (c)(3). Accordingly, the Chamaleses (P) are not entitled to a casualty loss deduction based upon a postulated decline in the value of their residential property. Affirmed.

▶ ANALYSIS

On occasion, permanent devaluation of property or buyer resistance absent physical damage will support a casualty-loss deduction. In *Finkbohner v. United States,* 788 F.2d 723 (11th Cir. 1986), the Finkbohners lived on a cul-de-sac with 12 homes, and after flooding damaged several of the houses, municipal authorities ordered seven of the residences demolished and the lots maintained as permanent open space. Such irreversible changes in the character of the neighborhood were found to effect a permanent devaluation and to constitute a casualty within the meaning of § 165(c)(3). Here, by contrast, the Chamaleses (P) damages were, if at all, temporary, rather than permanent.

■=■

Medical Expenses

Quick Reference Rules of Law

Montgomery v. Commissioner

Traveling taxpayer (P) v. Internal Revenue Service (D)

428 F.2d 243 (6th Cir. 1970).

NATURE OF CASE: Appeal from reversal of disallowance of medical-expense deductions.

FACT SUMMARY: Montgomery (P) claimed that food and lodging expenses incurred while driving to the Mayo Clinic were deductible medical expenses.

> ### 🏛 RULE OF LAW
> Food and lodging expenses incurred while transporting a patient to the place of medication are deductible.

FACTS: Montgomery (P) and his wife made three round trips from their home in Kentucky to the Mayo Clinic in Minnesota for required medical treatment. During these trips, Montgomery (P) incurred a total expense for meals and lodging of $162. Montgomery (P) deducted this amount pursuant to § 213 of the Internal Revenue Code (I.R.C.) as medical expenses. The Commissioner (D) disallowed the deductions but the tax court ruled for Montgomery (P). The Commissioner (D) appealed.

ISSUE: Are food and lodging expenses incurred while transporting a patient to the place of medication deductible?

HOLDING AND DECISION: (Celebrezze, J.) Yes. Food and lodging expenses incurred while transporting a patient to the place of medication are deductible. Under the Internal Revenue Code (I.R.C.) of 1939, all food and lodging expenses of a patient on the way to, and at, the place of medication were deductible. These liberal provisions led to significant abuses as taxpayers would travel on doctors' orders to resort areas and deduct all of their expenses. The revised I.R.C. of 1954 sought to eliminate resort-area medication abuse. Thus, Congress eliminated the deductibility of food and lodging expenses at the actual place of medication but kept the transportation costs. The legislative history of the revised statute shows that Congress aimed to curb only the resort abuses and sought to continue the deductibility of traveling and transportation costs to the place of medication. Therefore, Montgomery's (P) expenses should have been allowed as proper medical expense deductions under § 213. Affirmed.

▌ ANALYSIS

Revenue Ruling 78-266 deals with the cost of child care while parents seek medical treatment. It follows court decisions that have held that these expenses are not deductible. Only expenditures that are essential for medical care qualify. While child care costs might have some relation to the medical care, they are not critical to receiving such care. Section 213(d)(2) is intended to equalize the tax treatment of inpatient and outpatient care for taxpayers required to seek medical care away from home; arguably, child care costs would be incurred regardless of whether the parents were seeking medical care away from, or at, home.

■■■

Quicknotes

DEDUCTION Subtraction (from gross income) in arriving at taxable income (the tax base).

■■■

Charitable Deductions

Quick Reference Rules of Law

Davis v. United States

Funds-providing taxpayer (P) v. Federal government (D)

495 U.S. 472 (1990).

NATURE OF CASE: Appeal from affirmance of disallowance of deductions for charitable contributions.

FACT SUMMARY: The Davises (P) provided their sons with funds that allowed the young men to work as missionaries for the Mormon Church and then sought to claim a charitable contribution deduction for those funds.

RULE OF LAW
The transfer of funds by parents to their children serving as full-time, unpaid missionaries for a church is not deductible as a charitable contribution "to or for the use of" the church under Internal Revenue Code (I.R.C.) § 170.

FACTS: The Davises (P) and their sons, Benjamin and Cecil, belonged to the Church of Jesus Christ of Latter-day Saints (the Church). The Church operates a worldwide missionary program, mostly of young men. The individual missionary's parents generally provide the necessary funds to support their children during the period of service. Missionaries receive some supervision over their use of funds but are not required to obtain advance approval of their expenditures. When Benjamin and Cecil were called as missionaries, the Davises (P) provided a total of $6,000 to their sons for their expenses while on their missions. The Davises (P) then claimed this money as a deductible charitable contribution on their tax return. The Internal Revenue Service (IRS) (D) disallowed the deductions and the Davises (P) filed suit in district court challenging the disallowance. The district court rejected their claim and granted summary judgment to the Government (D), finding that the Davises (P) themselves were not performing donated services and that their payments to their sons were not "for the use of" the Church because the Church lacked sufficient control and possession of the funds. The court of appeals affirmed, and the United States Supreme Court granted certiorari to resolve a conflict among the circuits.

ISSUE: Is the transfer of funds by parents to their children serving as full-time, unpaid missionaries for a church deductible as a charitable contribution "to or for the use of" the church under I.R.C. § 170?

HOLDING AND DECISION: (O'Connor, J.) No. The transfer of funds by parents to their children serving as full-time, unpaid missionaries for a church is not deductible as a charitable contribution "to or for the use of" the church under I.R.C. § 170. Taxpayers may claim deductions for charitable contributions only if the money goes directly to the organization or to trusts or foundations. Section 170 of the I.R.C. provides that taxpayers may claim a deduction for charitable contribution only if the

contribution is made "to or for the use of" a qualified organization. The Davises (P) contended that the funds given to their sons were "for the use of" the Church. This term could support many meanings based on the plain language of the statute. However, the legislative history shows that Congress had a specific meaning in mind. The original version of § 170 required that the contribution be given directly to the organization. Representatives of charitable foundations then requested an amendment making gifts to trust companies deductible even though the trustee held legal title to the funds. Thus, the "for the use of" language was added to allow for contributions to trusts and foundations. The IRS (D) has subsequently adopted regulations that adopt this approach to the section. In the present case, there is no suggestion that the Davises' (P) funds were used for improper purposes or for tax evasion. Still, the funds were not transferred to the Church or put in trust for the Church. The money was kept in Benjamin and Cecil's personal accounts and they had no legal obligation to spend the money for the Church. Accordingly, the deductions must be disallowed. Affirmed.

ANALYSIS

The court also rejected the Davises' (P) contention that the money could be considered unreimbursed expenditures made incident to the rendition of services. The court found that taxpayers may deduct only those expenditures incurred in connection with the taxpayer's own contributions of service, and agreed with the lower courts that here the Davises (P) had not themselves performed donated services. This holding is consistent with Treasury Regulation § 1.170.A-1(g).

Quicknotes

DEDUCTION Subtraction (from gross income) in arriving at taxable income (the tax base).

Sklar v. United States

Parents of children at private school (P) v. Federal government (D)

282 F.3d 610 (9th Cir. 2002).

NATURE OF CASE: Appeal from judgment for government in action challenging the disallowance of a claimed charitable deduction.

FACT SUMMARY: The Sklars (P) contended that they were entitled to deduct as a charitable deduction that portion of their children's private school tuition that corresponded to that part of the education that was devoted to religious instruction.

🏛 RULE OF LAW
A private school tuition that pays for some religious instruction and that does not exceed the value of the tuition for a comparable secular school is not deductible as a charitable contribution under Internal Revenue Code (I.R.C.) § 170.

FACTS: The Sklars' (P) children attended private religious school. Fifty-five percent of the school day was allocated to religious education. The Sklars (P) sought to deduct this percent of the tuition (55%) as a charitable contribution under § 170 of the I.R.C. on the theory that they received only intangible religious benefits from this part of the tuition. The Internal Revenue Service (IRS) (D) disallowed this deduction on the basis that the tuition payment was a nondeductible personal tuition expense. The Sklars (P) challenged the IRS (D) disallowance, and the tax court held for the IRS (D), finding that the expense was a nondeductible personal tuition expense rather than a charitable contribution. The Sklars (P) did not show that their purportedly charitable contribution exceeded the market value of the secular education their children received. The court of appeals granted review.

ISSUE: Is a private school tuition that pays for some religious instruction and that does not exceed the value of the tuition for a comparable secular school deductible as a charitable contribution under I.R.C. § 170?

HOLDING AND DECISION: (Reinhardt, J.) No. A private school tuition that pays for some religious instruction and that does not exceed the value of the tuition for a comparable secular school is not deductible as a charitable contribution under I.R.C. § 170. The United States Supreme Court has held that generally a payment for which one receives consideration does not constitute a contribution or gift and has expressly rejected the notion that there is an exception for payments for which one receives only religious benefits in return. Recent amendments to the Code have not changed this substantive definition of a charitable deduction, but have only enacted additional documentation requirements for claimed deduc-

tions. These amendments, through § 170(f) of the Code, provide that taxpayers claiming a charitable contribution deduction obtain from the donee an estimate of the value of any goods and services received in return for the donation, and exempts from that new estimate requirement contributions for which solely intangible religious benefits are received. The amendments also provide, through § 6115, that the donee, while generally having to provide the donor with an estimate of value of the donation, does not have to estimate such value for contributions for which solely intangible religious benefits are received. Therefore, there is no new substantive deduction to which the Sklars (P) are entitled. The Sklars (P) also contend that their tuition payments constitute partially deductible "dual payments" under Code § 6115. Such a payment is a payment made in part in consideration for goods and services and in part as a charitable contribution and a deduction is permitted for that part of the payment that is charitable. However, to qualify for the deduction, the taxpayer must establish that the dual payment exceeds the market value of the goods received in return. The Sklars (P) incorrectly assert that the market value of the secular portion of their children's education is the cost of a public school education, which is nothing. The correct market value is the cost of a comparable secular education offered by private schools. Since the Sklars (P) have presented no evidence their total payments exceeded that cost, they have not shown that their payments are dual payments, and, therefore, have not shown that any portion of their payments is entitled to be deducted. Affirmed.

▌ ANALYSIS

The court also used the constitutional argument that to permit the deductions sought by the Sklars (P) could entangle the IRS (D) and the government (D) in the affairs and beliefs of various religious faiths and organizations in violation of the constitutional principle of the separation of church and state, by possibly forcing the IRS (D) to engage in a searching inquiry of whether a particular benefit received was "religious" or "secular" in order to determine its deductibility, a process that could violate the Establishment Clause. In subsequent litigation, the Sklars (P) sought a similar deduction for tuition paid to the same private schools in later tax years—with the same result: the deduction was denied. See 125 T.C. 281 (2005), *aff'd* 549 F.3d 1252 (9th Cir. 2008).

■=■

Continued on next page.

Quicknotes

ESTABLISHMENT CLAUSE The constitutional provision prohibiting the government from favoring any one religion over others, or engaging in religious activities or advocacy.

■▬■

CHAPTER 27

Limitations on Deductions

Quick Reference Rules of Law

McWilliams v. Commissioner

Stock-swapping spouse (P) v. Internal Revenue Service (D)

331 U.S. 695 (1947).

NATURE OF CASE: Appeal from reversal of denial of Commissioner's (D) disallowance of deduction for loss incurred on the sale of stock.

FACT SUMMARY: Mr. McWilliams (P) sold shares of stock from his and his wife's estate and purchased the same number of shares of the same stock for the estate of the other spouse.

RULE OF LAW

Section 267(a)(1)'s prohibition on deductions for losses by certain related parties applies to indirect intra-family transfers that occur through a stock exchange and involve third party strangers.

FACTS: Mr. McWilliams (P) managed his and his wife's independent estates. He often sold shares from one estate or the other and then purchased the same number of shares of the same stock for the estate of the other spouse—with the intent of creating tax losses. Sales and purchases were made through the stock exchange. The spouses filed separate tax returns, and claimed the losses which he or she sustained on the sales as deductions from gross income. The Commissioner (D) disallowed the deductions based on § 267(a)(1) [formerly § 24(b)]. The McWilliams (P) challenged the disallowance in tax court, claiming that § 267(a)(1) applies only to intra-family transfers and not to legitimate sales and purchases through the exchange. The tax court held for the McWilliams (P), but the court of appeals reversed and the McWilliams (P) appealed. The United States Supreme Court granted certiorari.

ISSUE: Does Section 267(a)(1)'s prohibition on deductions for losses by certain related parties apply to indirect intra-family transfers that occur through a stock exchange and involve third party strangers?

HOLDING AND DECISION: (Vinson, C.J.) Yes. Section 267(a)(1)'s prohibition on deductions for losses by certain related parties applies to indirect intra-family transfers that occur through a stock exchange and involve third party strangers. It is true that these were bona fide sales made through a public market. However, the end result is exactly the same as that which Congress sought to prohibit under § 267(a)(1). Where a controlled group such as a family unit exists, there is a near-identity of economic interest. Transfers of property between members of these groups do not yield real economic losses. They are mere paper transactions. The loss to one is offset by a corresponding gain by the other. The introduction of a third party into the transaction does not change this result, as the statute expressly references sales made "directly or indirectly." Therefore, the transaction fits within the evil that Congress sought to eliminate. There would be no useful purpose served in limiting § 267(a)(1) in this manner. Affirmed.

▶ ANALYSIS

In *Merritt v. Commissioner*, 400 F.2d 417 (5th Cir. 1968), the court held that § 267 precluded a loss deduction where stock owned by a taxpayer was involuntarily sold on a distress sale and was purchased by the wife. Section 267 reaches many other types of related taxpayers. The statute and regulations thereunder should be consulted to determine which entities are considered "related." However, the facts of any given transaction may be determinative as to whether gains or loss will be allowed or allocated by the Commissioner.

Quicknotes

CAPITAL GAIN AND LOSS Gain or loss from the sale or exchange of a capital asset.

Miller v. Commissioner

Hostile brother deducting loss (P) v. Internal Revenue Service (D)

U.S. Tax Ct., 75 T.C. 182 (1980).

NATURE OF CASE: Appeal from disallowance of deductions for capital losses.

FACT SUMMARY: David Miller (P) was forced to sell his shares of the business he shared with his brother at a loss when their relationship became strained, but the Commissioner (D) disallowed the resulting loss deduction.

🏛 RULE OF LAW
Section 267 provides for an absolute ban on deductions for losses on transactions involving family members, so that even where family members are hostile to each other and the losses result from such hostility, the losses will be disallowed.

FACTS: Charles Miller, the sole shareholder in Charles Miller, Inc., died and left his shares and some real estate to his sons, David (P) and Marvin. Many years later, a serious dispute arose between David (P) and Marvin and arbitrators were retained to resolve the matter. The brothers refused to talk to each other and still do not. The arbitrators decided that David (P) must sell his share of the business and real estate to Marvin, which he reluctantly did. David (P) then claimed a long-term capital loss on his tax return from the sale. The Commissioner (D) disallowed the deduction on the basis of § 267. David (P) filed a petition in tax court challenging the disallowance.

ISSUE: Does § 267 provide for an absolute ban on deductions for losses on transactions involving family members, so that even where family members are hostile to each other and the losses result from such hostility, the losses will be disallowed?

HOLDING AND DECISION: (Dawson, J.) Yes. Section 267 provides for an absolute ban on deductions for losses on transactions involving family members, so that even where family members are hostile to each other and the losses result from such hostility, the losses will be disallowed. Section 267 of the Internal Revenue Code (I.R.C.) prohibits deductions for losses sustained from sales or exchanges of property between related parties. The family relationship described in § 267(c)(4) does not require a current relationship. Congress did not intend for courts to examine the intimate relationships between people. The provision was intended to provide an absolute ban without regard to the individual circumstances of some cases. Moreover, the provision does not provide for a rebuttable presumption that could be defeated by a showing of hostility between the parties or the involuntariness of the transaction. In the present case, there is no question that David (P) and Marvin were the natural children of the same parents. Therefore, they are brothers within the meaning of § 267; and the transaction at issue cannot be the basis for a capital loss deduction under any circumstances. The Commissioner (D) is affirmed. Decision entered under Rule 155.

▶ ANALYSIS

The court noted that § 267 might be seemingly unfair in certain cases but that it was fair to the great majority of taxpayers. Certainly, the court was correct in pointing out the difficulty that courts would have in looking behind the sale at the exact relationship among family members at the time of sales. The bright-line test established by this statute makes enforcement easy.

■▬■

Quicknotes

CAPITAL GAIN AND LOSS Gain or loss from the sale or exchange of a capital asset.

■▬■

CHAPTER 28

Cash-Method Accounting

Quick Reference Rules of Law

Ames v. Commissioner

Spy (P) v. Internal Revenue Service (D)

U.S. Tax Ct., 112 T.C. 304 (1999).

NATURE OF CASE: Challenge of deficiency determination.

FACT SUMMARY: Ames (P) received income from the Soviet Union for espionage activities he did for them. He claimed that he constructively received the income for tax purposes in 1985 when it was set aside for him. The Commissioner (D) argued, however, that the funds were received between the years 1989 and 1992 when they were deposited in Ames's (P) accounts.

> 🏛 **RULE OF LAW**
> A taxpayer does not constructively receive income where he does not have unfettered control or ready access to the funds constituting the putative income.

FACTS: Ames (P) held a position with the Central Intelligence Agency (CIA) from 1964 until 1994. During that time he did work involving the Soviet Union and had access to top-secret documents. During 1985, Ames (P) sold classified CIA information to the KGB (the Soviet intelligence directorate) in return for large amounts of cash. In 1985, a Soviet agent told Ames (P) that $2 million had been set aside for him in an account that he would be able to draw upon. Ames (P) received $50,000 in cash for his initial disclosure and additional cash payments at dates unknown. In 1989, Ames (P) received a document that indicated that as of May 1, 1989, about $1.8 million had been set aside for him and that some $900,000 more had been designated for him. Another document contained a discussion of arrangements for cash drop-off payments to Ames (P) and a list of information sought by the KGB. During the years 1989–1992, Ames (P) made deposits of cash totaling $1,088,000. Ames (P) filed tax returns for the years 1989–1992 that reflected income from his employment at the CIA but none of the amounts received from the KGB. He also did not report on his 1985 return any amount of unlawful income he received or that had been set aside for him. Ames's (P) returns were filed on the cash basis for reporting income.

ISSUE: Does a taxpayer constructively receive income where he does not have unfettered control or ready access to the funds constituting the putative income?

HOLDING AND DECISION: (Gerber, J.) No. A taxpayer does not constructively receive income where he does not have unfettered control or ready access to the funds constituting the putative income. Ames (P) received income from his illegal espionage activities when it was deposited in his bank accounts during taxable years 1989–1992. A taxpayer reporting income on the cash method of accounting must include an item in income for the taxable year in which the item is actually or constructively received. Constructive receipt is when a taxpayer has an unqualified, vested right to receive immediate payment. In this case, Ames (P) did not possess unregulated control over the $2 million in 1985 because he did not have ready access to it and certain conditions had to be met, or had to occur, before he could gain physical access to any funds. For instance, he had to contact the Soviets to determine whether a withdrawal could be made. The Soviets then had to arrange to have the cash transferred into the United States and have it left in a prearranged location for Ames (P). There was no certainty that these steps could be accomplished, and these conditions represented restrictions on Ames's (P) control of the money. So long as the Soviet Union retained the ability to withhold or control the funds, there was no constructive receipt and therefore Ames did not constructively receive the income before it was physically available to him. Ames (P) thus should have reported the income from his illegal espionage activities on his returns for the years 1989–1992, when he actually received the money. Decision entered for the Commissioner (D).

▶ *ANALYSIS*

In *Paul v. Commissioner*, T.C. Memo 1992-582 (1992), there was no constructive receipt where a taxpayer had to travel 68 miles in order to turn in a winning lottery ticket. Thus, it was held that the taxpayer had income in the year he received the check in payment of his lottery winning, rather than in the earlier year in which he won the lottery, even though he could have driven the 68 miles in the earlier year to have claimed his prize, but did not do so. Moreover, in general, the date when a check is received, and not the date it is mailed, determines the year of taxation.

∎▬∎

Quicknotes

CASH BASIS A system of accounting used instead of a system of accrual-basis accounting.

CONSTRUCTIVE RECEIPT OF INCOME Income determined to be taxable to the taxpayer using certain methods of accounting, whether or not the income has actually been received in cash.

∎▬∎

Cowden v. Commissioner

Oil, gas, and mineral lessor (P) v. Internal Revenue Service (D)

289 F.2d 20 (5th Cir. 1961).

NATURE OF CASE: Appeal from determination of tax liability.

FACT SUMMARY: Cowden (P), who made an oil, gas, and mineral lease to Stanolind Oil and Gas Company (Stanolind), contracted to receive "advance royalties" over a period of time from Stanolind, such royalties to be paid unconditionally and in any event.

🏛 RULE OF LAW
If a promise to pay of a solvent obligor is unconditional and assignable, not subject to setoffs, and is of a kind that is frequently transferred to lenders or investors at a discount not substantially greater than the generally prevailing premium for the use of money, such promise is the equivalent of cash and taxable in like manner as cash, if cash had been received by the taxpayer rather than the obligation.

FACTS: Cowden (P), his wife (P), and children (P) made an oil, gas, and mineral lease to Stanolind Oil and Gas Company (Stanolind) upon certain lands in Texas. By supplemental agreements, Stanolind agreed in 1951 to pay advance royalties totaling $511,192.50. The sum of $10,223.85 was payable upon execution of the instruments, $250,484.31 was due between January 5 and 10, 1952, and $250,484.34 was due between January 5 and 10, 1953. The agreement recited that payment would be made "in any event," whether or not Stanolind even continued to have its leasehold interest. Cowden (P), in 1951, assigned the payments due from Stanolind in 1952 to the bank of which he was the president. The amounts were discounted. Similarly, in 1952, he assigned Stanolind's 1953 payments to the bank, also at a discounted rate per each recipient. The taxpayers reported the amounts received by them from the assignments as long-term capital gains. The Commissioner (D) determined that the sum due from Stanolind was taxable as ordinary income in 1951, subject to depletion, to the extent of the fair market value of the obligations at the time they were created. The Commissioner (D) calculated that fair market value by applying a 4 percent discount rate. Thus, for 1951, the Commissioner determined that $487,647.46 ($511,192.50 less a 4 percent discount rate) was taxable. The tax court held that all $511,192.50 was taxable for that year on the grounds that that amount could have been paid immediately and had a cash equivalency, so that its fair market value was its face value, without discounting. Cowden (P) appealed and the court of appeals granted review.

ISSUE: If a promise to pay of a solvent obligor is unconditional and assignable, not subject to setoffs, and

is of a kind that is frequently transferred to lenders or investors at a discount not substantially greater than the generally prevailing premium for the use of money, is such promise the equivalent of cash and taxable in like manner as cash, if cash had been received by the taxpayer rather than the obligation?

HOLDING AND DECISION: (Jones, J.) Yes. If a promise to pay of a solvent obligor is unconditional and assignable, not subject to setoffs, and is of a kind that is frequently transferred to lenders or investors at a discount not substantially greater than the generally prevailing premium for the use of money, such promise is the equivalent of cash and taxable in like manner as cash, if cash had been received by the taxpayer, rather than the obligation. While parties may contract in such manner as is legal to avoid or reduce taxation, if the consideration for which one of the parties bargains is the equivalent of cash it will be subjected to taxation to the extent of its fair market value. Whether Stanolind's undertaking in this case was, when made, the equivalent of cash and, as such, taxable, is the issue. The Cowdens (P) argue that there can be no "equivalent of cash" obligation unless it is in the form of a negotiable instrument. However, that argument must be rejected, as a promissory note, negotiable in form, may not necessarily be the equivalent of cash. Substance, not form, should be looked to. As the tax court gave great weight in reaching its decision to the willingness of Stanolind to pay rather than to the substance of the transaction. The tax court should, instead, have looked at the fair market value of the obligation for which the Cowdens (P) had legally bargained for in their contracts with Stanolind. Reversed and remanded.

▶ ANALYSIS

The tax court on remand reached the same conclusion as that reached by the Commissioner (D). 20 T.C.M. 1134 (1961). The tax court said that in the light of the Fifth Circuit's opinion, it followed that, without reference to the willingness and desire of Stanolind to pay the bonus payments in their entirety in a lump sum in 1951 and at all times thereafter, the Cowdens (P), upon the execution of the oil bonus agreement in 1951, received income in the form of the equivalent of cash in the amount of the then fair market value of such agreements which value was $487,647.46, reflecting a 4 percent discount. In a subsequent case, *Warren Jones Co. v. Commissioner,* 60 T.C. 663 (1973), *rev'd on other grounds,* 524 F.2d 788 (9th Cir. 1975), the tax court applied the reasoning of *Cowden* to hold that

Continued on next page.

an interest-bearing real estate contract, with a face value of $133,000, was not the equivalent of cash where its fair market value was only around $77,000—representing a discount of around 42 percent.

■■■■

Quicknotes

CASH BASIS A system of accounting used instead of a system of accrual-basis accounting.

CONSTRUCTIVE RECEIPT OF INCOME Income determined to be taxable to the taxpayer using certain methods of accounting, whether or not the income has actually been received in cash.

■■■■

Accrual Method Accounting

Quick Reference Rules of Law

Schlude v. Commissioner

Dance-studio operator (P) v. Internal Revenue Service (D)

372 U.S. 128 (1963).

NATURE OF CASE: Appeal from judgment upholding notice of deficiency.

FACT SUMMARY: The Schludes (P), operators of a dance studio and accrual-basis taxpayers, did not include some income received in an earlier taxable year if a portion was for lessons in future years. The Commissioner (D) issued a notice of deficiency, finding that this accounting system did not clearly reflect the actual income received by the Schludes (P).

🏛 RULE OF LAW
Accrual-basis taxpayers must include in income in a particular tax year advance payments by way of cash, negotiable notes and contract installments falling due but remaining unpaid during the year.

FACTS: The Schludes (P) operated an Arthur Murray dance studio franchise. Lessons were offered under plans in which the customers made down payments and could receive the lessons at a future time. The Schludes (P) were accrual-basis taxpayers. Under this accounting system, a deferred income account was credited for the total contract price when a customer started. At the close of the fiscal year, each customer's account was analyzed for the amount of lessons he had used. If the customer was entitled to additional lessons based on his prepayment, that amount was not declared as income for that year. If there was no customer activity for over a year, any amounts in the deferred account were then recognized as gain. The Commissioner (D) issued a notice of deficiency claiming that this accounting system did not clearly reflect the actual income received by the Schludes (P) in a given year. The tax court agreed with the Commissioner (D), but the court of appeals reversed. Following its decision in *American Automobile Association v. United States*, 367 U.S. 687 (1961), the United States Supreme Court granted certiorari and vacated and remanded the court of appeals decision. On remand, the court of appeals ruled for the Commissioner (D), finding that the Schludes' (P) accounting method did not, for income tax purposes, clearly reflect income. The Schludes (P) petitioned for certiorari, and the Supreme Court granted review to consider whether the court of appeals misapprehended the scope of *American Automobile Association.*

ISSUE: Must accrual-basis taxpayers include in income in a particular tax year advance payments by way of cash, negotiable notes and contract installments falling due but remaining unpaid during the year?

HOLDING AND DECISION: (White, J.) Yes. Accrual-basis taxpayers must include in income in a particular tax year advance payments by way of cash, negotiable notes and contract installments falling due but remaining unpaid during the year. *American Automobile Association* controls this issue. In that case, the entire legislative history of the treatment of prepaid income was examined. Congress sought to grant deferral privileges to limited groups of taxpayers only. Also, *American Automobile Association* involved nearly the same practice as at issue in this case. There it was determined that where advance payments were related to services that were to be performed only upon customers' demands without relation to fixed dates, the income could not be deferred. In the present case, the Schludes (P) did not have fixed appointments for future lessons, so their accounting system is analogous to the one at issue in *American Automobile Association*. Customers could demand lessons at any time in the future under their prepaid contracts. Thus, the studio's accrual system with respect to its deferral of prepaid income was vulnerable to the Commissioner's (D) finding of a deficiency, since for accrual-basis taxpayers it is the right to receive and not the actual receipt that determines income. Therefore, these advance payments must be included as income in the taxable year they were received. However, this does not include amounts for which services had not yet been performed and which were not due and payable during the respective tax years. Affirmed in part, reversed in part, and remanded.

▶ ANALYSIS

The dissent correctly pointed out that this decision left the Schludes (P) with hardly any options under an accrual-basis method. The dissent pointed out that the most elementary principles of accrual accounting require that advances be considered reportable income only in the year they are earned by the taxpayer's rendition of the services for which the payments were made, and that the majority opinion, based primarily on resolving the issue of whether the accounting system "clearly reflects income," would force upon an accrual-basis taxpayer a cash basis for advance payments in disregard of the federal statute which explicitly authorizes income tax returns to be based upon sound accrual accounting methods. The majority also approved the Commissioner's (D) decision to include in gross income payments to the Schludes (P) by negotiable notes as well as cash. The Internal Revenue Service itself has provided some relief from the *Schlude* rule in Rev. Proc. 2004-34, which provides for a one-year deferral for

Continued on next page.

advance payments for services and certain defined items, except to the extent the taxpayer has included the advance payment in its revenues for financial accounting purposes.

■══■

Quicknotes

ACCRUAL BASIS A method of calculating taxable income based on the time at which certain events have become fixed, including the right to receive that income, the deductions to which the taxpayer has been subject, and the obligation to pay tax owed, regardless of when the taxpayer actually earned the income.

■══■

United States v. General Dynamics

Federal government (D) v. Self-insured employer (P)

481 U.S. 239 (1987).

NATURE OF CASE: Appeal from disallowance of deductions.

FACT SUMMARY: General Dynamics (P) claimed deductions for employee medical payments for services that had been rendered, but did so before the employees submitted claims forms.

🏛 RULE OF LAW
Under the accrual method, an expense is deductible for the taxable year in which all the events have occurred that determine the fact and amount of the liability.

FACTS: General Dynamics (P) became a medical care self-insurer for its employees. To receive reimbursement for covered medical services, employees submitted claims forms to General Dynamics (P) that verified and reviewed the claims before payment. Accordingly, there was a delay between the provision of medical services and payment by General Dynamics (P). Thus, General Dynamics (P) established a reserve account to reflect its liability for care received but not yet paid. For its 1972 tax return, General Dynamics (P) deducted its reserve account as an accrued expense. The Internal Revenue Service (IRS) (D) disallowed the deduction but the claims court and the court of appeals ruled for General Dynamics (P). The IRS (D) appealed. The United States Supreme Court granted certiorari.

ISSUE: Under the accrual method, is an expense deductible for the taxable year in which all the events have occurred that determine the fact and amount of the liability?

HOLDING AND DECISION: (Marshall, J.) Yes. Under the accrual method, an expense is deductible for the taxable year in which all the events have occurred that determine the fact and amount of the liability. This court has established that whether a business expense has been incurred so as to entitle an accrual-basis taxpayer to deduct it under § 162(a) is governed by the "all-events" test. This test provides that all of the events that determine the fact and amount of liability must have occurred in order for the expense to be deductible. Mere estimates of liability do not qualify; they must be firmly established. In the present case, the lower courts mistakenly found that the last event necessary to fix General Dynamics' (P) liability was the receipt of medical care by employees. Actually, General Dynamics (P) became liable only if properly documented claim forms were filed. Some employees may not have submitted forms for their services. Thus, a reserve based on the proposition

that events are likely to occur may be an appropriate conservative accounting measure, but it does not warrant a tax deduction since General Dynamics (P) could not show that its liability as to any medical care claims was firmly established as of the close of the year for which it claimed the deduction. Reversed.

▌ *ANALYSIS*

The principle outlined in this case goes back to *United States v. Anderson*, 269 U.S. 422 (1926). In that case, the Supreme Court ruled that a taxpayer had to deduct from his income a tax on profits from sales in that year. However, the tax would not be assessed and formally due until the following year. Under Rev. Rul. 2007-3, the IRS, applying the all events rule, has held that under § 461, the mere execution of a contract, without more, does not establish the fact of a taxpayer's liability for services or for insurance.

Quicknotes

ACCRUAL BASIS A method of calculating taxable income based on the time at which certain events have become fixed, including the right to receive that income, the deductions to which the taxpayer has been subject, and the obligation to pay tax owed, regardless of when the taxpayer actually earned the income.

Thor Power Tool Co. v. Commissioner

Tool company (P) v. Internal Revenue Service (D)

439 U.S. 522 (1979).

NATURE OF CASE: Appeal from disallowance of inventory write-down.

FACT SUMMARY: Thor Power Tool Co. (P) wrote down its excess inventory but did not immediately scrap the articles or sell them at reduced prices.

RULE OF LAW
Inventory accounting for tax purposes must conform to accepted practices and clearly reflect income.

FACTS: Thor Power Tool Co. (Thor) (P) manufactured and sold power tools and parts. Thor (P) used the "lower cost or market" method of valuing its inventory for financial accounting and tax purposes. In 1964, Thor (P) decided that its inventory was overvalued and wrote it all down at once. However, the excess inventory was not scrapped or sold at reduced prices. Instead, it was retained and sold at the original prices because Thor (P) found that price reductions did not help the articles sell. The write-down of the excess inventory, however, reduced the amount of income for tax purposes. The Commissioner (D) disallowed the write-down, contending that it did not serve to accurately reflect Thor's (P) 1964 income. The tax court upheld this ruling, and the court of appeals affirmed. Thor (P) appealed, and the United States Supreme Court granted certiorari.

ISSUE: Must inventory accounting for tax purposes conform to accepted practices and clearly reflect income?

HOLDING AND DECISION: (Blackmun, J.) Yes. Inventory accounting for tax purposes must conform to accepted practices and clearly reflect income. Inventory accounting is governed by §§ 446 and 471 of the Internal Revenue Code (I.R.C.), which provide that taxable income must be computed under the regular accounting method of the taxpayer and the method must clearly reflect income. These rules give the Commissioner (D) wide discretion in determining whether a particular method of inventory accounting is proper. There is no presumption that a generally accepted method is valid for tax purposes. In the present case, Thor (P) must value inventory for tax purposes at cost unless the market value is lower. Market value is defined as replacement cost unless the taxpayer can substantiate a lower valuation through evidence of actual sales or offerings. Without this type of objective evidence, a taxpayer's mere assertions as to market value are not relevant. In the present case, the excess inventory written down by Thor (P) was indistinguishable and intermingled with other inventory. Taxpayers may not write down inventory on the basis of

their own subjective valuations. Therefore, the Commissioner's disallowance must be upheld. Affirmed.

ANALYSIS

The Court also rejected Thor's (P) argument that it was impossible to offer objective evidence of the excess inventory's lower value since it could not be sold at reduced prices. The Court held that Thor (P) simply had to choose between writing off the loss and take the tax benefit or wait and hope that the article would eventually sell. The Court saw no reason why Thor (P) should be able to hedge its bets.

Quicknotes

BASIS The value assigned to a taxpayer's costs incurred as the result of acquiring an asset, and used to compute tax amounts toward the transactions in which that asset is involved.

Annual Accounting

Quick Reference Rules of Law

Burnet v. Sanford & Brooks Company

Commissioner, Internal Revenue Service (D) v. Dredging company (P)

282 U.S. 359 (1931).

NATURE OF CASE: Appeal from reversal of board of tax appeals decision sustaining Commissioner's (D) assessment of a deficiency tax for income and profits.

FACT SUMMARY: Sanford & Brooks Company (P) was paid under performance installments for a long-term dredging contract. Sanford & Brooks (P) brought suit when the contract was abandoned.

RULE OF LAW

Net income or profit is properly taxed to the accounting period in which it is received, rather than on the basis of the particular transactions of the taxpayer when they are brought to a conclusion.

FACTS: Sanford & Brooks Company (P) engaged in a long-term dredging operation. Payments were made each year by the other contracting party. Nonetheless, expenses exceeded payments by more than $176,000. A net operating loss was shown in 1913, 1915, and 1916. In 1915, the work was abandoned, and a suit was filed by Sanford and Brooks (P) in 1916 against the other contracting party. Sanford & Brooks (P) recovered their losses of more than $176,000 plus over $16,000 in interest. The Commissioner (D) assessed a delinquent tax for 1920, the year in which judgment for Sanford & Brooks (P) was affirmed by the United States Supreme Court, on the total recovery. The board of tax appeals supported the Commissioner (D), but the court of appeals held that only the interest award should have been included in income, and that the principal recovery was merely a return of losses previously incurred in 1913, 1915, and 1916. However, as part of its decision, the court of appeals required that Sanford & Brooks (P) filed amended returns for those years, from which were to be omitted the deductions of the related items of expenses paid in those years. The Commissioner (D) appealed, claiming that the entire recovery was income, and the previous expenditures could not be considered. The United States Supreme Court granted certiorari.

ISSUE: Is net income or profit properly taxed to the accounting period in which it is received, rather than on the basis of the particular transactions of the taxpayer when they are brought to a conclusion?

HOLDING AND DECISION: (Stone J.) Yes. Net income or profit is properly taxed to the accounting period in which it is received, rather than on the basis of the particular transactions of the taxpayer when they are brought to a conclusion. The recovery received by Sanford & Brooks (P) in 1920 was gross income for that year. The money received was from a contract entered into for profit.

Since no capital investments were involved, any money earned from the contract must equal gross income. The fact that no real profit was made on the contract is immaterial. The funds only become income when they are received. Net losses in previous periods have nothing to do with the current period, and the periods may not be combined. The tax must be based on a fixed taxable period, such as a fiscal year. This rationale is consistent with the meaning and purpose of the Sixteenth Amendment. It is essential that any system of taxation produces ascertainable revenue payable at a given interval. The losses sustained could only be properly taken as deductions against income in those years. Subsequent "income" must be reported in the year it was received. Reversed.

ANALYSIS

The result of this case's strict interpretation of the annual accounting rule is rather harsh. To address that harshness, Congress enacted provisions permitting net operating loss carrybacks or carryovers, now codified in Internal Revenue Code Section 172. Generally, these provisions permit a loss in one year to be used to offset income in other years so the loss does not go unused, but it applies only to business losses rather than capital losses.

Quicknotes

CAPITAL ASSET The sale or exchange of property which produces capital gain or loss.

GROSS INCOME The total income earned by an individual or business.

Alice Phelan Sullivan Corporation v. United States

Property-donating company (P) v. Federal government (D)

U.S. Ct. Cl., 381 F.2d 399 (1967).

NATURE OF CASE: Action to recover alleged overpayment of tax.

FACT SUMMARY: Two parcels of property donated to charity by Alice Phelan Sullivan Corporation (P) were returned to the company, and the Commissioner (D) taxed the recovery as income at the corporate rate for the year of recovery.

🏛 RULE OF LAW
The return of a charitable gift for which a deduction was taken in a prior tax year is treated as income in the year of its recovery and the income or gain attributable to the recovery is taxable not at the lower rates applicable at the time of the contribution and tax deduction, but at the higher rate in effect at the time of the return of the contribution to the taxpayer.

FACTS: Alice Phelan Sullivan Corporation (Alice Phelan) (P) donated two parcels of property to a charitable organization, one in 1939 and one in 1940. During each of those years, Alice Phelan (P) claimed a charitable deduction and enjoyed a total $1,877 tax benefit as the result of its contributions. In 1957, the property was returned to Alice Phelan (P). The Commissioner (D) viewed this transaction as adding $8,706 in income for 1957. Since the corporate tax rate for 1957 was 52 percent, the Commissioner (D) assessed a $4,527 deficiency. Alice Phelan (P) claimed that it should owe only the original tax benefit of $1,877 and petitioned for relief in the court of claims.

ISSUE: Is the return of a charitable gift for which a deduction was taken in a prior tax year treated as income in the year of its recovery and is the income or gain attributable to the recovery taxable not at the lower rates applicable at the time of the contribution and tax deduction, but at the higher rate in effect at the time of the return of the contribution to the taxpayer?

HOLDING AND DECISION: (Collins, J.) Yes. The return of a charitable gift for which a deduction was taken in a prior tax year is treated as income in the year of its recovery and the income or gain attributable to the recovery is taxable not at the lower rates applicable at the time of the contribution and tax deduction, but at the higher rate in effect at the time of the return of the contribution to the taxpayer. This court previously decided that in situations where prior charitable contributions are returned, the taxpayer should have to return only the amount of the original tax benefit at the time of donation. However, the principle that returned property for which a deduction was previously taken is treated as income is well ingrained in tax law. The only limitation on this principle is called the "tax benefit" rule, which permits the exclusion of recovered items from income if the initial use as a deduction did not provide a tax saving. Section 111 of the Internal Revenue Code has codified these rules. In the present case, Alice Phelan (P) obtained full tax benefits from the earlier deductions. Therefore, the returned property was properly classified as income upon its recoupment and must be taxed at the 1957 rates. The previous decision by this court to the contrary is hereby overruled, and the petition is dismissed.

▶ ANALYSIS

The decision that was overruled in this case was *Perry v. United States*, 160 F. Supp. 270 (Ct. Cl. 1958). The *Alice Phelan* court indicated that to insure the vitality of the single-year concept, it is essential not only that annual income be ascertained without reference to losses experienced in an earlier accounting period, but also that income be taxed without reference to earlier tax rates. The court found absent specific statutory authority sanctioning a departure from this principle, it could only say of *Perry* that it achieved a result that was more equitably just than legally correct.

■■■

Quicknotes

RECOUPMENT The right of a defendant to have the plaintiff's award of damages reduced because of either prior payment tendered or some unlawful action on the part of the plaintiff.

■■■

Hillsboro National Bank v. Commissioner

Refund-receiving company (P) v. Internal Revenue Service (D)

460 U.S. 370 (1983).

NATURE OF CASE: Appeal from affirmances of deficiency notice.

FACT SUMMARY: The Commissioner (D) claimed that Hillsboro National Bank (Hillsboro) (P) should have reported as income a refunded tax for which Hillsboro (P) had taken a deduction.

RULE OF LAW
The subsequent recovery of a previously deducted payment is not always necessary to invoke the tax benefit rule.

FACTS: Until 1970, Illinois imposed a property tax on shares held in banks. Banks were required to retain earnings sufficient to cover these taxes and customarily paid the taxes for the shareholders. The Internal Revenue Code (I.R.C.) allowed banks to deduct the tax amount. The shareholders were not allowed this deduction. In 1970, an amendment to the state constitution changed the law to prohibit ad valorem taxation of shares, but there was a long protracted battle over its legality. In the interim, the disputed taxes were placed in escrow. Hillsboro National Bank (Hillsboro) (P) paid the taxes for its shareholders in 1972 and took the deduction. Later, when the United States Supreme Court upheld the amendment, the county treasurer refunded the taxes directly to the individual shareholders. When Hillsboro (P) did not recognize these events on its tax return, the Commissioner (D) assessed a deficiency contending that it should have included the refunded taxes as income. The tax court and the court of appeals affirmed, and Hillsboro (P) appealed. The United States Supreme Court granted certiorari.

ISSUE: Is the subsequent recovery of a previously deducted payment always necessary to invoke the tax payment rule?

HOLDING AND DECISION: (O'Connor, J.) No. The subsequent recovery of a previously deducted payment is not always necessary to invoke the tax benefit rule. The tax benefit rule is a judicially developed principle that allays some of the inflexibilities and transactional inequities of the annual accounting system. Often, completed transactions reopen unexpectedly in subsequent tax years. In order to avoid possible distortions of income, courts have long required taxpayers to recognize repayments of past deductions as income in the subsequent year. The basic purpose of the tax benefit rule is not to simply tax recoveries but to approximate the results of a transaction-based tax system. Accordingly, the rule cancels out an earlier deduction only when a careful examination shows that the later event is inconsistent with the deduction. In the present case, the I.R.C. provision that allowed banks to take a deduction for their payments on behalf of their shareholders was focused on providing relief for the banks for their act of payment, rather than on the state's ultimate use of the tax. As long as the payment itself was not negated by a refund to the corporation, the change of character of the funds in the hands of the state does not require the corporation to recognize income. Therefore, the return of the money to the shareholders did not represent income to the banks, including Hillsboro (P). Reversed.

ANALYSIS

The tax benefit rule started in the courts but was implicitly approved by Congress when it limited the rule by enacting § 111. Its purpose is to protect the government and the taxpayer from the adverse effects of reporting a transaction based on assumptions that a subsequent event proves to have been erroneous. But not every unforeseen event will require a taxpayer to report income in the amount of this earlier deduction. Pursuant to the rule, the Commissioner may require a compensating recognition of income when an event occurs, but only if the occurrence of the event in the earlier year would have resulted in the disallowance of the deduction.

Quicknotes

AD VALOREM According to value; an ad valorem tax is imposed upon an item located within the taxing jurisdiction calculated by the value of such item.

Capital Gains and Losses

Quick Reference Rules of Law

Bynum v. Commissioner

Property seller (P) v. Internal Revenue Service (D)

U.S. Tax Ct., 46 T.C. 295 (1966).

NATURE OF CASE: Challenge to notice of deficiency.

FACT SUMMARY: Bynum (P) sold subdivided lots on his property and sought to claim the income as long-term capital gains.

🏛 **RULE OF LAW**
Capital gains treatment of real estate gains is available only to passive investors.

FACTS: Bynum (P) purchased land in 1942. Bynum (P) lived on the property and also conducted a nursery and landscaping business on the property. The business borrowed much money but was not profitable. Bynum (P), in an attempt to pay off the mortgage, improved and subdivided part of the property and advertised lots for sale as Morayshire Estates. The public was advised to contact Bynum (P) or a realtor. In 1960 and 1961, twenty lots were sold directly by Bynum (P). Bynum (P), who had continued to spend 90 percent of his time on the nursery business, then claimed the resulting income from the lot sales as capital gains profit. The Commissioner (D) asserted that the income was taxable as ordinary income since Bynum (P) was in the business of selling lots. Bynum (P) challenged the Commissioner's (D) determination in tax court.

ISSUE: Is capital gains treatment of real estate gains available only to passive investors?

HOLDING AND DECISION: (Forrester, J.) Yes. Capital gains treatment of real estate gains is available only to passive investors. Section 1221 of the I.R.C. provides that property held by the taxpayer primarily for sale to customers in the ordinary course of trade or business creates regular income. Since the long-term capital gains provisions of the Code are an exception to normal tax rates, they must be construed narrowly and the taxpayer has the burden of proving their applicability. Each determination must be considered on the basis of the particular facts of the case. In the present case, the record shows that Bynum (P) was doing more than simply trying to get out of debt. Bynum (P) was attempting to subdivide up to 233 lots, and personally conducted all of the improvement and promotional activities. This is not the posture of a passive investor. Bynum (P) was actively engaged in a second business. Thus, the property was being held primarily and principally for sale to customers in the ordinary course of this business. Therefore, income from these sales is not entitled to long-term capital gains treatment. The Commissioner (D) is affirmed.

CONCURRENCE: (Tannenwald, J.) This case shows that property profits are often partially attributable to both appreciation of value and the fruits of business. Some method of allocation should be created within an appropriate statutory framework.

▶ *ANALYSIS*

Sections 1231 and 1221 have identical language regarding property held for sale. In *Burnet v. Harmel*, 287 U.S. 103 (1932), the United States Supreme Court held that capital gains treatment was reserved for appreciations in value over a substantial period of time. Capital gains are given preferential treatment because it may sometimes be a hardship to the taxpayers when gains accruing over years of value appreciation are all taxed in one year.

■■■

Quicknotes

CAPITAL GAIN AND LOSS Gain or loss from the sale or exchange of a capital asset.

■■■

Arkansas Best Corp. v. Commissioner

Stock-losing company (P) v. Internal Revenue Service (D)

485 U.S. 212 (1988).

NATURE OF CASE: Appeal from decision reversing tax court ruling that stock loss was not capital loss.

FACT SUMMARY: Arkansas Best Corporation (P) appealed from a decision reversing the tax court's determination that a portion of its claimed stock loss was subject to ordinary loss treatment, contending that its purpose in acquiring and holding the stock was relevant to the determination of whether the stock was a capital asset.

🏛 RULE OF LAW
A taxpayer's motivation in purchasing an asset is irrelevant in determining whether the asset is a capital asset and thus subject to capital loss treatment.

FACTS: Arkansas Best Corporation (ABC) (P), a diversified holding company, began acquiring stock in the National Bank of Commerce (the Bank) in Dallas, Texas, in 1968. The Bank prospered until 1972, when it began to experience problems because of heavy real estate loans. ABC (P) continued to purchase stock in the Bank, prompted by the Bank's problems. In 1975, ABC (P) sold the bulk of its stock in the Bank and sought to take a $9,995,688 ordinary loss resulting from the sale on its 1975 tax return. The Commissioner (D) disallowed the deduction, characterizing the loss as a capital loss and not an ordinary loss. ABC (P) challenged the Commissioner's (D) decision in the U.S. Tax Court. The tax court found that ABC's (P) stock acquisitions after 1972 were made and held exclusively for business and not investment purposes, and therefore, relying on cases interpreting *Corn Products Relining Co. v. Commissioner*, 350 U.S. 46 (1955), accorded the loss realized on the sale of stock acquired after 1972 ordinary loss treatment. The court of appeals reversed the tax court, according the loss capital loss treatment, finding ABC's (P) motive in purchasing the stock irrelevant to the determination of whether the stock was a capital asset. From this decision, ABC (P) appealed, and the United States Supreme Court granted certiorari.

ISSUE: Is a taxpayer's motivation in purchasing an asset relevant in determining whether an asset is a capital asset and thus subject to capital loss treatment?

HOLDING AND DECISION: (Marshall, J.) No. A taxpayer's motivation in purchasing an asset is irrelevant in determining whether an asset is a capital asset and thus subject to capital loss treatment. It can be assumed here that the stock was acquired and held for business and not investment purposes. Section 1221 of the Internal Revenue Code does not discuss motive, however, and the language of that section does signify that the listed exceptions to the definition of "capital asset" were meant to be exclusive. To read a motive test into the § 1221 capital asset determination would render the listed exceptions superfluous. ABC's (P) reliance on *Corn Products* is too great. That decision involves an application of § 1221's inventory exception. Since ABC (P) is not a dealer in securities and has never suggested the Bank stock falls within the inventory exception, *Corn Products* has no applicability to the present case. Today's holding prevents taxpayer abuse by keeping the taxpayer from taking capital gain treatment on profits and ordinary-loss treatment on losses related to the sale of stocks, which are naturally viewed as a capital asset. Affirmed.

▶ ANALYSIS

The decision in the present case makes it clear that the nature of the asset, and not the motivation behind the asset's acquisition, determines the tax treatment of accorded losses and profits from sales of the asset. The Court's decision in the present case will restrict a trend toward expansive interpretations of the *Corn Products* decision, which resulted in any transaction integrally related to the taxpayer's business being given ordinary gain or loss treatment.

Quicknotes

CAPITAL ASSET The sale or exchange of property that produces capital gain or loss.

CAPITAL GAIN AND LOSS Gain or loss from the sale or exchange of a capital asset.

Hort v. Commissioner

Lessor (P) v. Internal Revenue Service (D)

313 U.S. 28 (1941).

NATURE OF CASE: Appeal from decisions affirming Commissioner's (D) denial of a deduction for the value of the unexpired portion of a lease.

FACT SUMMARY: Hort (P), a landlord, allowed a tenant's lease to be canceled in exchange for $140,000 and claimed a deduction for the difference between the fair rental value of the space for the unexpired term of the lease and the $140,000 he received. The Commissioner (D) disallowed the deduction.

🏛 RULE OF LAW
Where the unexpired portion of a lease is settled for cash, the payment received by the taxpayer is merely a substitute for rent that has to be reported as ordinary income.

FACTS: Hort (P) was left a building under the terms of his father's will. One of the tenants, Irving Trust Co., wished to terminate the lease prior to its expiration date. They settled the lease by paying Hort (P) $140,000 in exchange for being released from it. Hort (P) did not report the $140,000 as income and claimed a deduction for the difference between the fair rental value of the space for the unexpired term of the lease and the $140,000 he received. The Commissioner (D) disallowed the deduction and assessed a deficiency tax on the $140,000. Hort (P) claimed that the $140,000 was a capital gain and, even if it was ordinary income, he sustained a loss on the unexpired portion of the lease. The board of tax appeals and the court of appeals sustained the Commissioner (D).

ISSUE: Where the unexpired portion of a lease is settled for cash, is the payment received by the taxpayer merely a substitute for rent that has to be reported as ordinary income?

HOLDING AND DECISION: (Murphy, J.) Yes. Where the unexpired portion of a lease is settled for cash, the payment received by the taxpayer is merely a substitute for rent that has to be reported as ordinary income. Hort (P) received the money, after negotiations, as a substitute for rent. Section 61(a) would have required Hort (P) to include prepaid rent or an award for breach of contract as income. Hort (P) received an amount of money in lieu of the rental income he was entitled to under the lease. Since it was a substitute for ordinary income, it must be treated in the same manner. The consideration received by Hort (P) was not a return of capital. A lease is not considered a capital asset within the context of § 61(a). Further, the fact that Hort (P) received less than he would have under the terms of the lease does not entitle him to a deduction. No

loss was sustained. He released a legal right for a settlement sum. Hort (P) didn't have to do so, and having made the decision to settle, the amount realized by him must be deemed fair. Any injury to Hort (P) can only be fixed when the extent of the loss can be ascertained, i.e., when the property is re-rented. Until that time, no loss is deductible. The decision of the Commissioner (D) is sustained and the judgment of the court of appeals is affirmed. Affirmed.

▌ ANALYSIS

In *U.S. v. Dresser Industries, Inc.*, 324 F.2d 56 (5th Cir. 1963), the court addressed the "anticipated future income" problem. The court held that the only commercial value of any property is the present worth of future earnings or usefulness. If the government can challenge a sale based on the fact that the sales price is only a substitute for future earnings, then no asset could qualify for capital gains treatment. The question of capital gains treatment really revolves around whether the present sale represents the right to "earn" future income or the right to "earned" future income.

Quicknotes

CAPITAL ASSET The sale or exchange of property that produces capital gain or loss.

CAPITAL GAIN AND LOSS Gain or loss from the sale or exchange of a capital asset.

Davis v. Commissioner

Lottery winner (P) v. Internal Revenue Service (D)

U.S. Tax Ct., 119 T.C. 1 (2002).

NATURE OF CASE: Action challenging a deficiency based on a determination that amounts claimed as capital gains were ordinary income.

FACT SUMMARY: Davis (P) claimed that amounts he received in exchange for his assignment of his right to receive a portion of annual lottery payments that he had won were capital gains, but the Internal Revenue Service (IRS) (D) determined that they were ordinary income.

RULE OF LAW
Amounts received by a taxpayer in exchange for the assignment of their right to receive a portion of certain future annual lottery payments are ordinary income.

FACTS: Davis (P) won $13,580,000 in the California State Lottery's On-Line LOTTO game and was entitled to receive this only in 20 equal annual payments of $679,000. A few years later, Davis (P) entered into an agreement with Singer Asset Finance Company, LLC (Singer), pursuant to which, in exchange for a lump-sum payment to Davis (P) and his wife by Singer of $1,040,000, the Davises (P) assigned to Singer their right to receive a portion (i.e., $165,000 less certain tax withholding) of each of 11 future annual lottery payments that they were entitled to receive. On their return for that year, the Davises (P) reported their assignment as a sale of a capital asset held for more than one year, a sale price of $1,040,000, a cost basis of $7,009, and a long-term capital gain of $1,032,991. In that return, they also reported as ordinary income the $514,000 payment that they received from California. The IRS (D) determined that the $1,040,000 payment was ordinary income "because rights to future annual lottery payments do not meet the definition of a capital asset." The Davises (P) challenged the Commissioner's (D) determination in tax court.

ISSUE: Are amounts received by a taxpayer in exchange for the assignment of his right to receive a portion of certain future annual lottery payments ordinary income?

HOLDING AND DECISION: (Chiechi, J.) Yes. Amounts received by a taxpayer in exchange for the assignment of his right to receive a portion of certain future annual lottery payments are ordinary income. The issue is whether the right to receive future annual lottery payments constitutes a "capital asset" as defined in Internal Revenue Code (I.R.C.) § 1221. The IRS (D) contends that although the right to receive future annual lottery payments is property in the ordinary sense of the word, such right does not qualify as a capital asset because the lump sum received is in exchange for the future right to receive ordinary income. Precedent does not support the Davises' (P) position. They assigned to Singer their right to receive a portion of certain future annual lottery payments. In exchange for the assignment, they received the discounted value (i.e., $1,040,000) of certain ordinary income that they otherwise would have received. Therefore, Singer paid the Davises (P) $1,040,000 for the right to receive such future ordinary income, and not for an increase in the value of income-producing property. Therefore, the Davises' (P) right to receive future annual lottery payments does not constitute a capital asset within the meaning of § 1221. Decision for the Commissioner (D).

ANALYSIS

This case elucidates the point that while a capital asset is property held by the taxpayer, not everything that can be called property in the ordinary sense, and which is outside the statutory exclusions, qualifies as a capital asset. It is well established that the purpose for capital gains treatment is to afford capital gains treatment only in situations typically involving the realization of appreciation in value accrued over a substantial period of time, and thus to ameliorate the hardship of taxation of the entire gain in one year. Here, the court essentially found the element of appreciation in value to be lacking.

Quicknotes

CAPITAL ASSET The sale or exchange of property that produces capital gain or loss.

CAPITAL GAIN AND LOSS Gain or loss from the sale or exchange of a capital asset.

Kenan v. Commissioner

Testamentary trustee (P) v. Internal Revenue Service (D)

114 F.2d 217 (2d Cir. 1940).

NATURE OF CASE: Cross-petitions on appeal from decision sustaining the Commissioner's (D) determination that capital gain was realized on the distribution of stock to the legatee of a testamentary trust.

FACT SUMMARY: Mrs. Bingham, the testatrix, provided in her will that Louise Wise would receive $5,000,000 when she reached 40. A proviso allowed the substitution of marketable securities of equal value, so part of the $5,000,000 was paid in that manner to Louise by the trustees (P) of Bingham's testamentary trust. The Commissioner (D) determined that such distribution gave rise to a taxable capital gain in the trustees.

🏛 **RULE OF LAW**
While no gain is realized on the transfer by a testamentary trustee of specific securities, or other property bequeathed by will to a legatee, a pro tanto exchange of securities or other property to satisfy the general claim of a legatee is a "sale or disposition" and can result in such a gain.

FACTS: A clause in the will of Mrs. Bingham, in which she left Louise Wise (her niece) an annual income and a $5,000,000 lump sum to be paid when she became 40, permitted the trustees of Mrs. Bingham's testamentary trust to substitute securities of equal value in making certain payments (including that to Louise Wise). Mrs. Bingham's death in 1917 was followed later by the trustees' (P) decision to pay part of Louise's allocation in securities (which they selected and valued in keeping with the will); this occurred when Louise reached 40 in 1935. All of the securities, most of which had been owned by the testatrix and became part of her estate and some of which the trustees (P) had purchased, had appreciated. The Commissioner (D) determined the distribution of same to Louise constituted a sale or exchange of capital assets and resulted in taxable capital gain. The board of tax appeals overruled the trustees' (P) contention that no income of any character was realized and denied a motion by the Commissioner (D) to amend his answer to assert all the gain was ordinary income. From this confirmation of the original deficiency determination of $367,687.12, both sides appealed, with the Commissioner (D) seeking a deficiency of $1,238,841.99. The court of appeals granted review.

ISSUE: While no gain is realized on the transfer by a testamentary trustee of specific securities, or other property bequeathed by will to a legatee, is a pro tanto exchange of securities or other property to satisfy the general claim of a legatee a "sale or disposition" that can result in such a gain?

HOLDING AND DECISION: (Hand, J.) Yes. While no gain is realized on the transfer by a testamentary trustee of specific securities, or other property bequeathed by will to a legatee, is a pro tanto exchange of securities or other property to satisfy the general claim of a legatee a "sale or disposition" that can result in such a gain. A satisfaction of a legatee's general claim against an estate via a pro tanto property exchange is not akin to the donative disposition that occurs via the transfer of specific property bequeathed by will to a legatee. The first is the sale or exchange of a capital asset coming within the rules governing capital gains, while the latter is a donative transfer in which no gain is realized. Unlike a legacy of specific property, the instant legacy did not give title or right to the securities until they were delivered upon exercise of the trustees' (P) option. Furthermore, Louise was not subject to the same chances that a specific property-legatee faces in dealing with the fluctuating value of same. The result was the same as if the securities were sold by the trustees (P) and the $5,000,000 cash derived therefrom was used to pay Louise. In either case, a taxable capital gain is realized. Thus, the board's decision is affirmed and its petition to treat the gain as ordinary gain is denied.

▶ **ANALYSIS**

In this case, the court concluded that the satisfaction of a bequest with appreciated capital assets constituted a "sale of exchange" of those assets, thus triggering a capital gain or loss. While § 1222 requires a "sale or exchange" of capital assets for there to be a capital gain or loss, Congress has effectively eliminated that requirement in specific circumstances. For example, in § 165(g)(1), if a security that is a capital asset becomes worthless, Congress has provided that a resulting loss is to be treated as a loss from the sale or exchange of the asset—without there actually being such a sale or exchange. Similar treatment is also accorded to amounts received on the retirement of a debt instrument (§ 1271(a)); certain involuntary conversions (§ 1231); and the cancellation, lapse, expiration, or other termination of certain property rights or obligations (§ 1234(a)).

Quicknotes

CAPITAL ASSET The sale or exchange of property that produces capital gain or loss.

Continued on next page.

CAPITAL GAIN AND LOSS Gain or loss from the sale or exchange of a capital asset.

PRO TANTO For so much; as far as it goes. Often used in eminent domain cases when a property owner receives partial payment for his land without prejudice to his right to bring suit for the full amount he claims his land to be worth.

■━━■

Assignment of Income

Quick Reference Rules of Law

Lucas v. Earl

Internal Revenue Service (P) v. Joint tenant spouse (D)

281 U.S. 111 (1930).

NATURE OF CASE: Appeal from reversal of board of tax appeals decision upholding Commissioner's (D) imposition of tax.

FACT SUMMARY: The Earls (D) entered into a contract whereby they agreed that whatever each acquired in any way during their marriage would be received and owned by them as joint tenants. Hence Mr. Earl (D) claimed he could be taxed for only half of his income.

> 🏛 **RULE OF LAW**
> An anticipatory contract cannot prevent a salary from vesting, for tax purposes, in the person who earned it.

FACTS: The Earls (D) entered into a contract whereby they agreed that whatever each acquired in any way during their marriage would be received and owned by them as joint tenants. Mr. Earl (D) claimed that due to the contract he could only be taxed for one-half of his income for 1920 and 1921. The validity of the contract was not questioned. The Commissioner (D) imposed a tax on all of Mr. Earl's earnings for those years, and the board of tax appeals sustained the Commissioner (D). The court of appeals reversed, and the United States Supreme Court granted certiorari.

ISSUE: Can an anticipatory contract prevent a salary from vesting, for tax purposes, in the person who earned it?

HOLDING AND DECISION: (Holmes, J.) No. An anticipatory contract cannot prevent a salary from vesting, for tax purposes, in the person who earned it. Section 213(a) imposes a tax upon the net income of every individual including income derived from salaries, wages, or compensation for personal service of whatever kind and in whatever form paid. There is no doubt that the tax act could tax salaries as to those who earned them. The tax could not be escaped by anticipatory arrangements and contracts however skillfully devised to prevent the salary from vesting even for a second in the person who earned it. This is true regardless of whatever the motives for the contract might have been. Reversed.

▌ *ANALYSIS*

The Earls lived in California. Under that state's community property laws the wife did not have a vested interest in the husband's earnings until 1927. In *Commissioner v. Harmon*, 323 U.S. 44 (1945), the Court held a 1939 Oklahoma statute permitting spouses to elect to be governed by a community property system was not effective for federal income taxation. The Court said that the existence of an option resulted in a status similar to that in *Lucas* and distinguished *Poe v.*

Seaborn, 282 U.S. 101 (1930), where "the Court was not dealing with a consensual community, but one made an incident of marriage by the inveterate policy of the state." The dissent argued that *Lucas* and *Poe* state competing theories of income tax liability.

■=■

Helvering v. Horst

Internal Revenue Service (D) v. Bond holder (P)

311 U.S. 112 (1940).

NATURE OF CASE: On writ of certiorari to review a reversal of a tax court decision.

FACT SUMMARY: Shortly before their due date, Horst (P) detached negotiable interest coupons from negotiable bonds and gave them to his son, who in the same year collected them at maturity. The Commissioner (D) ruled that the interest payments were taxable to Horst (P) in the year paid.

🏛 RULE OF LAW
For income tax purposes, the power to dispose of income is the equivalent of ownership of it, so that the exercise of that power to procure payment of the income to another is the equivalent of realization of the income by the one exercising such power.

FACTS: Horst (P) owned some negotiable bonds from which he detached the negotiable interest coupons shortly before their due date and gave them to his son. The son, in the same year, collected them at maturity. The Internal Revenue Service Commissioner (D) claimed that the interest payments were taxable to Horst (P) in the year they were paid. The board of tax appeals sustained the tax, but the court of appeals reversed, finding that as the consideration for the coupons had passed to the obligor, Horst (P) no longer had any control over them and their payments. The United States Supreme Court granted certiorari.

ISSUE: For income tax purposes, is the power to dispose of income the equivalent of ownership of it, so that the exercise of that power to procure payment of the income to another is the equivalent of realization of the income by the one exercising such power?

HOLDING AND DECISION: (Stone, J.) Yes. For income tax purposes, the power to dispose of income the equivalent of ownership of it, so that the exercise of that power to procure payment of the income to another is the equivalent of realization of the income by the one exercising such power. The owner of negotiable bonds stands in the place of the lender. When by the gift of the coupons he separates his right to interest payments, as Horst (P) did here, and procures the payment of the interest to the donee, here, Horst's (P) son, the owner enjoys the economic benefits of the income in the same manner and to the same extent as though the transfer were of earnings, and, in either case, the fruit is not to be attributed to a different tree from that on which it grew. Reversed.

▶ ANALYSIS

If the doctrine of *Horst* were applied literally, a donor who gave Blackacre in 1930 might still be taxed on the income from it in 1960. On the other hand, the doctrine of *Blair*, 300 U.S. 5 (1937), which holds that where ownership of property is transferred the income arising therefrom cannot be taxed to the donor, has been criticized as restricting taxation of the donor too narrowly, since every inchoate right to past or future income may be said to be "property." In *Horst*, the Court distinguished *Blair* on the nature of the gift and the income transferred, frequently a determining issue.

■=■

Helvering v. Eubank

Internal Revenue Service (D) v. Life insurance agent (P)

311 U.S. 122 (1940).

NATURE OF CASE: Appeal from reversal of decision finding renewal commissions to be taxable income.

FACT SUMMARY: The Commissioner (D) contended that that renewal commissions assigned by Eubank (P) were taxable in the year in which they became payable.

> **RULE OF LAW**
> Renewal commissions assigned by the taxpayer are taxable to the taxpayer in the year in which they become payable.

FACTS: Eubank (P) was a life insurance agent and a cash-basis taxpayer. After the termination of his agency contracts and services as an agent, he assigned renewal commissions to become payable for services rendered before his termination. The Commissioner (D) assessed the renewal commissions paid to the assignees as income to Eubank (P) in the year they became payable. Eubank (P) challenged this tax treatment in the board of tax appeals, which sustained the tax. The court of appeals reversed, holding that the commissions assigned by Eubank (P) were not taxable to him in the year they became payable. In a companion case to *Helvering v. Horst*, 311 U.S. 112 (1940), the United States Supreme Court, granted certiorari.

ISSUE: Are renewal commissions assigned by the taxpayer taxable to the taxpayer in the year they become payable?

HOLDING AND DECISION: (Stone, J.) Yes. Renewal commissions assigned by the taxpayer are taxable to the taxpayer in the year in which they become payable. There was no purpose to the assignments other than to confer on the assignees the power to collect the commissions. Based on the rationale of *Helvering v. Horst*, 311 U.S. 112 (1940), the commissions were taxable to Eubank (P) as income in the year they were paid. Reversed.

DISSENT: (McReynolds, J.) Upon assignment of the commissions, Eubank (P) could do nothing further with respect to them. In no sense were they earned or received by him during the taxable year. The court below was correct in stating that when a taxpayer who makes his income tax on a cash basis assigns a right to monies payable in the future for work already performed, he transfers a property right, and the money when paid is not taxable to the taxpayer in the year paid. If Eubank (P) had received consideration for the assignment, that consideration would be taxable to him as income—not the payments made to others under a contract which he transferred in good faith.

▶ **ANALYSIS**

Future commissions such as those involved in the present case involve an element of interest on the amount of the commission earned. Issues can arise as to what amount must be taxed; for example, whether it should be the present value of the commission assigned, or the face value of the amount of the commissions at the time of the assignment.

Quicknotes

CASH BASIS A system of accounting used instead of a system of accrual basis accounting.

Salvatore v. Commissioner

Inheriting widow (P) v. Internal Revenue Service (D)

U.S. Tax Ct., T.C.M. 1970-30 (1970).

NATURE OF CASE: Appeal from notice of deficiency for failure to fully report gain.

FACT SUMMARY: Salvatore (P) conveyed half of her gas station to her children as a gift just prior to selling it. The Commissioner (D) issued a notice of deficiency, asserting that Salvatore (P) should pay capital gains taxes on the entire proceeds of the sale.

RULE OF LAW
The true nature of a transaction, rather than formalisms, determines the tax consequences.

FACTS: Salvatore's (P) husband died and left his gas station to her. Salvatore's (P) children operated the gas station for several years before deciding to sell the property to Texaco for $295,000. The family decided that the proceeds from the sale would first be used to satisfy outstanding liabilities of the property. Then it was decided that Salvatore (P) would need approximately $100,000 to provide income for the rest of her life and that the balance would be divided among the children. Thus, Salvatore (P) conveyed a one-half interest in the property as a gift to her children just prior to the sale. Salvatore (P) reported the gifts on her tax return and paid a gift tax and then paid long-term capital gains taxes on her half of the sale proceeds. Her children paid gains taxes on their portions. The Commissioner (D) issued a notice of deficiency, maintaining that Salvatore (P) should pay capital gains taxes on the entire proceeds. Salvatore (P) challenged the Commissioner's (D) determination in tax court.

ISSUE: Does the true nature of a transaction, rather than formalisms, determine the tax consequences?

HOLDING AND DECISION: (Featherston, J.) Yes. The true nature of a transaction, rather than formalisms, determines the tax consequences. The United States Supreme Court in *Commissioner v. Court Holding Co.*, 324 U.S. 331 (1945), established that taxation depends upon the substance of transactions. Tax consequences that arise from the sale of property are not determined solely by the means employed to transfer title. A sale by one person cannot be transformed into a sale by another by using the latter as a conduit through which to pass title. In the present case, Salvatore (P) owned the property outright. Her subsequent conveyance, unsupported by consideration, was actually only an intermediate step in the sale to Texaco. The children were conduits through which to pass title. The fact that the conveyance was a bona fide gift is immaterial in determining the tax consequences of the sale. Salvatore's (P) tax liabilities cannot be altered by a rearrangement of the legal title after the sale was already contracted. Therefore, all of the gain on the sale was properly taxable to Salvatore (P). Decision is entered for the Commissioner (D).

ANALYSIS

This decision simply means that Salvatore (P) and her children will have to amend their returns. Salvatore (P) will still be liable for the gift tax, but her children will not owe capital gains tax. The principle of this case may prove difficult to apply when more complicated transactions are involved.

■▬■

Quicknotes

CAPITAL GAIN AND LOSS Gain or loss from the sale or exchange of a capital asset.

■▬■

Stranahan v. Commissioner

Decedent stockholder (P) v. Internal Revenue Service (D)

472 F.2d 867 (6th Cir. 1973).

NATURE OF CASE: Action against Commissioner for notice of deficiency of taxes.

FACT SUMMARY: Decedent Stranahan (P) assigned his rights to anticipated dividends to avoid tax liability.

RULE OF LAW

A taxpayer stockholder may assign his rights to anticipated dividends in exchange for the present discounted value of those dividends to avoid tax liability so long as the assignment is a bona fide, good-faith commercial transaction.

FACTS: Decedent Stranahan (P), after paying the Internal Revenue Service more than $750,000 in back taxes, attempted to accelerate his income so that he could take full advantage of the interest deduction. He therefore assigned his rights to anticipated dividends in certain stocks to his son in consideration of $115,000, which he declared as ordinary income and thus was able to deduct the full interest payment from the sum of this payment and his other income. The dividends actually received by the son amounted to around $40,000. The son reported this dividend income on his own return as ordinary income subject to the offset of his basis of $115,000. On these facts, the Commissioner (D) claimed a deficiency of taxes based on the dividends to Stranahan's estate (P). The Commissioner (D) viewed the transaction as merely a temporary shift of funds, with an appropriate interest factor, within the family unit, arguing that no change in the beneficial ownership of the stock was effected and no real risks of ownership were assumed by the son. The estate challenged the deficiency in the tax court, which concluded that Stranahan's (P) assignment of future dividends in exchange for the present discounted value of those dividends, even though conducted in the form of an assignment of a property right, was in reality a loan to Stranahan (P) masquerading as a sale and so lacked any business purpose. Therefore, the tax court ruled that Stranahan (P) realized taxable income when the dividend was declared. The court of appeals granted review.

ISSUE: May a taxpayer stockholder assign his rights to anticipated dividends in exchange for the present discounted value of those dividends to avoid tax liability so long as the assignment is a bona fide, good-faith commercial transaction?

HOLDING AND DECISION: (Peck, J.) Yes. A taxpayer stockholder may assign his rights to anticipated dividends in exchange for the present discounted value of those dividends to avoid tax liability so long as the assign-

ment is a bona fide, good-faith commercial transaction. In this case, the transaction was economically realistic. The facts establish that Stranahan (P) did in fact receive payment from his assignee, the son. Stranahan (P) completely divested himself of any interest in the dividends and vested that interest to his assignee son. The fact that the transaction was a family transaction did not vitiate the transaction but merely subjected it to special scrutiny. Here, both the form and substance of the transaction assigned the right to receive future income. Therefore, the tax court erred in not giving effectiveness to Stranahan's (P) plan. Reversed and remanded.

ANALYSIS

The decision in this case represents a departure from the general rule that income is chargeable to the person rendering the service for which income is paid or owning property from which the income is earned. Note also that the result in the case would have been different if Stranahan (P) had attempted to make a gratuitous assignment or if the court would have felt that the assignment was not a bona fide commercial transaction. The court emphasized that the acceleration of income was not designed to avoid or escape recognition of the dividends but rather to reduce taxation by fully utilizing a substantial interest deduction which was available, and that tax avoidance motives alone will not serve to obviate the tax benefits of a transaction.

May v. Commissioner

Leasing doctor (P) v. Internal Revenue Service (D)

723 F.2d 1434 (9th Cir. 1984).

NATURE OF CASE: Appeal from tax court decision allowing business-expense deductions.

FACT SUMMARY: May (P) deeded property to an irrevocable trust for the benefit of his children and then leased back the property from the trust for use in his medical practice.

🏛 RULE OF LAW

In a gift-leaseback situation, rental payments are deductible as an ordinary business expense if the transfer is irrevocable and the benefits inure to the trust.

FACTS: May (P), a doctor, deeded his entire interest in a parcel of real estate to an irrevocable trust for the benefit of his children. The trust instrument appointed a friend, Gross, as co-trustee. May (P) then rented the property from the trust for $1,000 a month under an oral lease to conduct his medical practice there. About four times a year, Gross checked to see if the rent, which the Commissioner (D) conceded was reasonable, had been paid. May (P) claimed the rent payment as an ordinary and necessary business-expense deduction. The Commissioner (D) maintained that the deduction should be disallowed under the circumstances, but the tax court agreed with May (P). The Commissioner (D) appealed, and the court of appeals granted review.

ISSUE: In a gift-leaseback situation, are rental payments deductible as an ordinary business expense if the transfer is irrevocable and the benefits inure to the trust?

HOLDING AND DECISION: (Pregerson, J.) Yes. In a gift-leaseback situation, rental payments are deductible as an ordinary business expense if the transfer is irrevocable and the benefits inure to the trust. The question of whether rental payments in a gift-leaseback situation are deductible under § 162(a)(3) is a frequently litigated issue. The tax court and the courts of appeals have developed different but similar standards. The Ninth Circuit has established that the fundamental issue is the sufficiency of the property interest transferred. Four factors must be considered in assessing the transfer: (1) the duration of the transfer; (2) controls retained by the donor; (3) use of the property for the benefit of the donor; and (4) independence of the trustee. In the present case, May (P) donated the property to an irrevocable trust, did not retain the same control over the property as before the gift, and used the property only as a lessee. Co-trustee Gross might have devoted more time to supervising the trust, but appeared to be independent of

May (P). Therefore, May (P) is allowed to deduct the rental payment as a business expense. Affirmed.

▶ ANALYSIS

The court noted that some courts of appeals allow the deduction only if there was a business purpose for the entire transaction. Other circuits first look at the validity of the transfer and then examine the business purpose of the leaseback alone. The approach adopted by the Ninth Circuit requires only that the transfer be grounded in economic reality. Here, the transaction met that test because it was not a "sham or a fraud." Rather, it was an irrevocable transfer of real property in trust to provide for the health, care and educational needs of May's (P) children. May (P) did not retain the same control over the property he had before the transfer; for example, the transfer was grounded in economic reality, and the lease-back of the medical property had a business purpose.

Quicknotes

BUSINESS EXPENSE A cost incurred or amounts expended as "ordinary and necessary expenses" in the process of conducting an income-generating activity, currently deductible from a taxpayer's liability.

Tax Consequences of Divorce

Quick Reference Rules of Law

PAGE

1. *United States v. Gilmore.* Litigation costs for resisting a claim are deductible only if the claim arises in connection with the taxpayer's profit-seeking activities. *136*

United States v. Gilmore

Federal government (D) v. Divorcing spouse (P)

372 U.S. 39 (1963).

NATURE OF CASE: Review of allowance of deductions for litigation costs.

FACT SUMMARY: Gilmore (P) sought to deduct the costs of his successful defense against his wife's claims, brought during divorce proceedings, that Gilmore's (P) business interests were community property. The Commissioner (D) determined the litigation expenses were of a "personal" or "family" nature, and denied the deductions.

> **RULE OF LAW**
> Litigation costs for resisting a claim are deductible only if the claim arises in connection with the taxpayer's profit-seeking activities.

FACTS: Gilmore's (P) wife brought a divorce action and claimed that Gilmore's (P) interests in three companies were community property. Gilmore (P) spent around $40,000 successfully defending against his wife's claims. He subsequently sought to deduct the litigation expense from his federal income taxes on the grounds that it was incurred for the conservation of property held for the production of income. The Commissioner (D), finding the expenses were of a "personal" or "family" nature, determined that the expenses were not deductible. The Court of Claims disagreed with the Commissioner (D), and allowed Gilmore (P) to deduct 80 percent of the litigation costs. The Commissioner (D) appealed, and the United States Supreme Court granted certiorari.

ISSUE: Are litigation costs for resisting a claim deductible only if the claim arises in connection with the taxpayer's profit-seeking activities?

HOLDING AND DECISION: (Harlan, J.) Yes. Litigation costs for resisting a claim are deductible only if the claim arises in connection with the taxpayer's profit-seeking activities. Section 212 of the Internal Revenue Code allows for the deductibility of expenses for the conservation of property held for income. However, deductibility of these expenses depends on the origin and nature of the claims themselves, not the consequences of a successful claim. Legal expenses do not become deductible merely because they are paid for services that relieve a taxpayer of a liability. The legal claim must arise in connection with the business at issue. The fact that the claim would affect the taxpayer's income-producing property is not relevant. In the present case, Gilmore (P) was defending against claims of a personal nature. The divorce proceedings had no connection with the business interests of Gilmore (P) other than the consequences. Accordingly, Gilmore's (P)

litigation expenses were not deductible. Reversed and remanded.

► ANALYSIS

This decision resolved a conflict in the lower courts on the issue. The Court decided that § 212 deduction rules should mirror those of § 162 business expenses. Each excludes personal and family expenses. By concluding that Gilmore's (P) litigation expenses were not business expenses, the Court avoided the further question of whether that portion of Gilmore's (P) payments attributable to litigating whether the businesses were community property was a capital expenditure or a personal expense, since in neither event would the payments be deductible from gross income.

Quicknotes

COMMUNITY PROPERTY In community property jurisdictions, refers to all money or property acquired during the term of the marriage in which each spouse has an undivided one-half interest.

Nonrecourse Debt: Basis and Amount Realized Revisited

Quick Reference Rules of Law

Crane v. Commissioner

Property inheritor (P) v. Internal Revenue Service (D)

331 U.S. 1 (1947).

NATURE OF CASE: Appeal from reversal of decision overruling a deficiency based on the basis assigned to property.

FACT SUMMARY: Crane (P) inherited real property subject to an unassumed mortgage. After she sold the property, she claimed income using her equity as the property's basis. The Commissioner (D) levied a deficiency, arguing that her income should have been computed using as a basis the property's fair market value at the date she acquired it.

RULE OF LAW

A taxpayer who sells property encumbered by nonrecourse debt that is less than the property's value must include the unpaid balance of the debt in computing the amount the taxpayer realized on the sale.

FACTS: Crane (P) inherited an apartment building. The building had a $255,000 mortgage on it which, when combined with unpaid interest of $7,042.50, exactly equaled the estate tax appraiser's valuation of the building and property. Crane (P) did not assume the mortgage. She (P) agreed to remit the net rental proceeds after taxes to the mortgagor. Close to seven years later, forced with the threat of foreclosure, Crane (P) sold the property and received $2,500 in cash for it (net), and the purchaser assumed the mortgage. Crane (P) included $1,250 in her income for the year on the theory that the property was a capital asset; her original basis in the property was zero; and, therefore, one-half the profits had to be included as income from the sale of a capital asset. The Commissioner (D) levied a deficiency tax. He claimed that her basis was the fair market price at the time of acquisition less allowable depreciation. Therefore, according to the Commissioner (D), Crane (P) actually realized a gain of $2,500 in cash plus around seven years of depreciation deductions, a total of $23,767.03. Crane (P) argued that only her equity in the property could be considered as her basis; that since it was zero to begin with, no depreciation was allowed, and that since she only realized $2,500 in cash, this was all that could be taxed. The tax court agreed that the building itself was not a capital asset, but otherwise held for Crane (P). The court of appeals reversed, and the United States Supreme Court granted certiorari.

ISSUE: Must a taxpayer who sells property encumbered by nonrecourse debt that is less than the property's value, include the unpaid balance of the debt in computing the amount the taxpayer realized on the sale?

HOLDING AND DECISION: (Vinson, C.J.) Yes. A taxpayer who sells property encumbered by nonrecourse debt that is less than the property's value must include the unpaid balance of the debt in computing the amount the taxpayer realized on the sale. The fair market value of property at the date of acquisition, rather than the owner's equity, determines basis. Section 113(a)(5) states that the basis for property received by inheritance is the fair market value of the property on the date of acquisition. "Value" is nowhere defined or treated as synonymous with "equity." Therefore, petitioner's basis in the apartment was $262,042.50, i.e., its fair market value at date of acquisition. The apartment building was an asset subject to exhaustion through wear and tear used in Crane's (P) trade or business. Section 113(b)(1)(B) requires that proper adjustments to basis shall be made in such cases. Upon sale of the asset, the seller realizes any cash received plus the amount of the indebtedness on the property. This is necessary to compute the selling price that must be subtracted from the taxpayer's adjusted basis to compute a loss or gain on the transaction. Adjusted basis is defined under § 113(b)(1)(B) as the basis less allowance for depreciation of the asset whether or not actual deductions were taken. The difference between the selling price and Crane's (P) adjusted basis is $23,767.03. Crane (P) actually took most of the deductions allowed her by law. Crane (P) used these deductions to reduce her income. Crane (P) cannot now be allowed the benefit of such deductions with no corresponding gain as of the date of sale; otherwise, she could enjoy a double deduction, in effect, on the same loss of assets. Crane (P) actually realized $2,500 in cash plus all her allowable deductions over six years. Affirmed.

ANALYSIS

In determining profit or loss on the disposition of an asset, liens and other indebtedness are not considered. The formula is fair market value at date of acquisition minus depreciation (if allowed) equals adjusted basis. This is subtracted from the selling price. It is immaterial whether the lien has gotten greater or smaller during the interim. If the selling price is greater than the adjusted basis, a profit has been made which is taxable, even if, because of an increase in mortgage indebtedness, the taxpayer receives no money.

■ ▬ ■

Quicknotes

ADJUSTED BASIS The occurrence of events with respect to an asset that require a corresponding increase or decrease in the value a taxpayer assigns to the costs

Continued on next page.

expended in acquiring that asset, to reflect the occurrence of those events.

DEPRECIATION An amount given to a taxpayer as an offset to gross income to account for the reduction in value of the taxpayer's income-producing property due to everyday usage.

LIEN A claim against the property of another in order to secure the payment of a debt.

MORTGAGOR Party who grants an interest in property in order to secure a loan.

■≡■

Commissioner v. Tufts

Internal Revenue Service (D) v. Member of partnership (P)

461 U.S. 300 (1983).

NATURE OF CASE: Appeal from reversal of decision upholding a deficiency assessment.

FACT SUMMARY: Tufts (P) contended that the assumption of a mortgage that exceeded the fair market value of the property by the purchaser was not a taxable event.

RULE OF LAW
A taxpayer who sells property encumbered by nonrecourse debt that is greater than the property's value must include the unpaid balance of the debt in computing the amount the taxpayer realized on the sale.

FACTS: Tufts (P) and others entered into a partnership with Pelt, a builder who had previously entered into an agreement with Farm and Home Savings to transfer a note and deed of trust to the bank in return for a loan to construct an apartment complex in the amount of $1,851,500. The loan was made on a nonrecourse basis in that neither the partnership nor the partners assumed personal responsibility for repayment. A year after construction was completed, the partnership could not make the mortgage payments, and each partner sold his interest to Bayles. The fair market value of the property at the time of the transfer did not exceed $1,400,000. As consideration, Bayles paid each partner's sale expenses and assumed the mortgage. The Internal Revenue Service (D) assessed a deficiency against each partner, contending the assumption of the mortgage constituted the creation of taxable gain to each of them that they failed to report. Tufts (P) and the others sued for a redetermination, contending that no gain was realized because the mortgage exceeded the fair market value of the property. The tax court upheld the deficiencies, and the court of appeals reversed. The United States Supreme Court granted certiorari.

ISSUE: Must a taxpayer who sells property encumbered by nonrecourse debt that is greater than the property's value include the unpaid balance of the debt in computing the amount the taxpayer realized on the sale?

HOLDING AND DECISION: (Blackmun, J.) Yes. A taxpayer who sells property encumbered by nonrecourse debt that is greater than the property's value must include the unpaid balance of the debt in computing the amount the taxpayer realized on the sale. When a mortgage is executed, the amount is included, tax free, in the mortgagor's basis of property. The amount is tax free because of the mortgagor's obligation to repay. Unless the outstanding amount of an assumed mortgage is calculated in the seller's amount realized, the money originally received in the mortgage transaction will forever escape taxation. When the obligation to repay is canceled, the mortgagor is relieved of his responsibility to repay the amount he originally received. Therefore he realizes value to the extent of the relief from debt. When the obligation is assumed, it is as if the mortgagor was paid the amount in cash and then paid the mortgage off. As such it is clearly income and taxable. Reversed.

ANALYSIS

This case, which settled the issue left open by *Crane v. Commissioner*, 331 U.S. 1 (1947), i.e., whether nonrecourse indebtedness can be excluded from the amount realized on a sale where the debt exceeds the fair market value of the property, illustrates that the cost basis of the property under Internal Revenue Code § 1012 is the cost of the property including any amount paid with borrowed funds. These funds must be included regardless of their source. When property is purchased subject to debt, the purchaser is deemed to have received cash in the amount of the debt, and, in turn, to have used it to purchase the property. Relatedly, under Rev. Rul. 91-31, 1991-1 C.B. 19, the reduction of the principal amount of an undersecured nonrecourse debt by the holder of the debt who was not the seller of the property securing the debt results in the realization of discharge of indebtedness income under § 61(a)(12) of the Code.

Quicknotes

MORTGAGE An interest in land created by a written instrument providing security for the payment of a debt or the performance of a duty.

NONRECOURSE Indicates one who holds an instrument giving him no legal right against prior endorsers or the drawer to compel payment if the instrument is dishonored.

Estate of Franklin v. Commissioner

Estate (P) v. Internal Revenue Service (D)

544 F.2d 1045 (9th Cir. 1976).

NATURE OF CASE: Appeal from decision upholding the disallowance of a taxpayer's deductions.

FACT SUMMARY: Estate of Franklin (P) challenged the Commissioner's (D) disallowance of deductions for Franklin's and six other doctors' distributive share of losses reported by a limited partnership with respect to its acquisition of a motel.

RULE OF LAW

Where nonrecourse debt unreasonably exceeds the fair market value of the property securing the debt, the purchaser of the property cannot include the full amount of the debt in basis, given that the taxpayer has no investment in the property and no economic incentive to pay the debt.

FACTS: The Commissioner (D) sought to disallow deductions for the distributive share of losses reported by Twenty-Fourth Property Associates (Associates) (P), a California limited partnership of seven doctors of which decedent Franklin was one, with respect to its acquisition of a motel and related properties. These losses had their origin in deductions for depreciation and interest claimed with respect to these properties. Under a sales agreement, the owners of the Thunderbird Inn, an Arizona motel, agreed that the property would be paid for over a period of ten years, with interest on any unpaid balance of 7½ percent per annum. Prepaid interest in the amount of $75,000 was payable immediately; monthly principal and interest installments of $9,045 would be paid for approximately the first ten years, with Associates (P) required to make a balloon payment at the end of the ten years, forecast as $975,000. The sale was combined with a lease-back of the property by Associates (P) to the owners, so Associates (P) never took physical possession. The owners remained responsible under the mortgages, which they could increase, and could make capital improvements. The tax court, agreeing with the Commissioner (D), held that the transaction more nearly resembled an option than a sale, the benefits and burdens of ownership remaining with the original owners. Associates (P) appealed, and the court of appeals granted review.

ISSUE: Where nonrecourse debt unreasonably exceeds the fair market value of the property securing the debt, can the purchaser of the property include the full amount of the debt in basis, given that the taxpayer has no investment in the property and no economic incentive to pay the debt?

HOLDING AND DECISION: (Sneed, J.) No. Where nonrecourse debt unreasonably exceeds the fair market value of the property securing the debt, the purchaser of the property cannot include the full amount of the debt in basis, given that the taxpayer has no investment in the property and no economic incentive to pay the debt. An acquisition such as that of Associates (P) if at a price approximately equal to the fair market value of the property under ordinary circumstances would rather quickly yield an equity in the property that the purchaser could not prudently abandon. It meshes with the form of the transaction and constitutes a sale. No such meshing occurs when the purchase price exceeds a demonstrably reasonable estimate of the fair market value. It is fundamental that depreciation is not predicated upon ownership of property but, rather, upon an investment in property. No such investment exists when payments of the purchase price in accordance with the design of the parties yield no equity to the purchaser. In the transaction before the court, the purchase price payments by Associates (P) have not been shown to constitute an investment in the property. Depreciation was properly disallowed. For these reasons, interest deductions were also properly disallowed because, under the circumstances, Associates (P) had not secured "the use or forbearance of money." The transaction in economic terms gave rise only to the chance that a genuine debt obligation would arise, but that is not enough to support an interest deduction. To justify such a deduction, the debt must exist; potential existence is insufficient. Having no personal liability, and not being required by the economic realities of the transaction to make a capital investment of the unpaid purchase price, Associates (P) was not entitled to take an interest deduction. Only the original owners had an investment in the property, and only they were entitled to take the deductions. Affirmed.

ANALYSIS

The court points out that its focus on the relationship of the fair market value of the property to the unpaid purchase price should not be read as premised upon the belief that a sale is not a sale if the purchaser pays too much. Bad bargains from the buyer's point of view—as well as sensible bargains from buyer's, but exceptionally good from the seller's point of view—do not thereby cease to be sales. See *Commissioner v. Brown*, 380 U.S. 563 (1965); *Union Bank v. United States*, 285 F.2d 126 (1961). The holding was limited to transactions substantially similar to the one before the court. One question that was not addressed by *Estate of Franklin*, and that has since been answered differently in various decisions, is whether, in

Continued on next page.

such circumstances, the nonrecourse debt may nonetheless be taken into account to the extent of the value of the underlying property, or must be disregarded in its entirety. The Court of Federal Claims, in *Bergstrom v. United States,* 37 Fed. Cl. 164 (1996), held in favor of disregarding the debt in its entirety, thus supporting the disallowance of depreciation and interest deductions attributable to the debt. The court in *Bergstrom* indicated that "when nonrecourse purchase money debt exceeds a reasonable approximation of the property's fair market value, the debt is disregarded in its entirety for the purposes of determining depreciation and interest deductions."

■═■

Quicknotes

DISTRIBUTIVE SHARE Share received by an heir through intestate succession.

■═■

Aizawa v. Commissioner

Property buyer (P) v. Internal Revenue Service (D)

U.S. Tax Ct., 99 T.C. 197 (1992), *aff'd unpublished opinion,* 29 F.3d 630 (9th Cir. 1994).

NATURE OF CASE: Appeal from notice of deficiency.

FACT SUMMARY: Aizawa (P) claimed that the amount realized from a foreclosure sale should be the unpaid mortgage principal less the deficiency judgment.

🏛 RULE OF LAW

The "amount realized" on a foreclosure sale under Internal Revenue Code § 1001 is represented by the proceeds of the sale.

FACTS: Aizawa (P) purchased rental property in 1981 for $120,000 and gave the sellers a $90,000 recourse mortgage note with interest only payable until the entire principal was due in June 1985. Aizawa (P) stopped making interest payments in February 1985 and made no payment on the principal. In 1987, the sellers obtained a deficiency judgment of $133,506 in a foreclosure action, which was subsequently reduced to $60,806 after the property was sold for $72,700. Aizawa (P) claimed that this deficiency judgment should be deducted from the unpaid mortgage principal and that the difference ($29,193) was the amount realized for calculating his loss from the original basis of the property. The Commissioner (D) maintained that the $90,000 unpaid mortgage principal constituted the amount realized on the foreclosure sale resulting in a much smaller loss for Aizawa (P).

ISSUE: Is the "amount realized" on a foreclosure sale under § 1001 represented by the proceeds of the sale?

HOLDING AND DECISION: (Tannenwald, J.) Yes. The "amount realized" on a foreclosure sale under § 1001 is represented by the proceeds of the sale. The position of Aizawa (P) in this matter is clearly wrong since it calculates the amount realized by offsetting against the unpaid principal the total amount of the deficiency judgment. However, this deficiency judgment includes not only the unpaid balance but also amounts representing accrued interest, attorneys' fees, and court costs. Aizawa (P) has not paid these costs. Still, the Commissioner's (D) position would require Aizawa (P) to treat as money received an amount of his unpaid mortgage principal obligation that has not yet been discharged. If Aizawa (P) is later relieved of the obligation, the usual rules of income from discharge will be difficult to apply. Thus, the Commissioner's (D) position also does not present an acceptable resolution of the issue. Where the discharge of recourse liability is separated from the foreclosure, as in this case, the amount of the proceeds from the sale becomes significant. Thus, the true amount realized under

§ 1001(a) here is simply $72,700; that is, the amount the property sold for, which can be deducted from Aizawa's (P) original basis to determine his loss. It must be understood that this approach allows Aizawa (P) to deduct a loss that represents borrowed funds that he might not repay and on which he has not yet paid a tax, but the basic rules of cash-basis accounting mandate this result. Therefore, Aizawa's (P) loss is $27,391, representing the difference between his original basis ($100,091) and the $72,700 received in foreclosure.

▶ ANALYSIS

The court also noted its conclusion was supported by the fact that the result would have been the same under a different scenario. If Aizawa (P) had had the opportunity to sell the property to a third party for $72,700 and the sellers had released the mortgage, the tax consequences would have been the same. In both situations, the mortgage disappears as security and Aizawa's (P) personal obligation to pay the balance of his recourse obligation survives.

Quicknotes

BASIS The value assigned to a taxpayer's costs incurred as the result of acquiring an asset, and used to compute tax amounts toward the transactions in which that asset is involved.

Like-Kind Exchanges

Quick Reference Rules of Law

Bolker v. Commissioner

Property owner (P) v. Internal Revenue Service (D)

760 F.2d 1039 (9th Cir. 1985).

NATURE OF CASE: Appeal from rejection of notice of deficiency for invalid like-kind exchange.

FACT SUMMARY: Bolker (P), through his corporation, exchanged his property for other property and reported no gain on the transaction, asserting that it qualified for nonrecognition. The Commissioner (D) asserted that because the property was not held for productive use in trade or for investment, it did not qualify for nonrecognition treatment.

RULE OF LAW

Taxpayers satisfy the holding requirement for like-kind exchanges by a lack of intent to liquidate the investment or to use it for personal pursuits.

FACTS: Bolker (P) was the sole shareholder of Crosby Corporation, the owner of the Montebello property. When Bolker (P) was unable to develop the property himself, he decided to liquidate Crosby and to exchange the Montebello property for other like-kind investment property owned by Southern California Savings & Loan (SCS). On the same day, Crosby transferred all of its assets, including the deed to Montebello, and liabilities to Bolker (P), in redemption for the stock. Bolker (P) then contracted with SCS to convey Montebello for certain designated properties. Bolker (P) reported no gain on the transaction, asserting that it qualified for nonrecognition treatment under Internal Revenue Code (I.R.C.) § 1031(a). The Commissioner (D) maintained that Bolker (P) did not hold Montebello for productive use in trade or for investment and could not qualify under § 1031. The tax court agreed with Bolker (P), and the Commissioner (D) appealed. The court of appeals granted review.

ISSUE: Do taxpayers satisfy the holding requirement for like-kind exchanges by a lack of intent to liquidate the investment or to use it for personal pursuits?

HOLDING AND DECISION: (Boochever, J.) Yes. Taxpayers satisfy the holding requirement for like-kind exchanges by a lack of intent to liquidate the investment or to use it for personal pursuits. Section 1031(a) of the I.R.C. allows for the nonrecognition of property exchange transactions. Nonrecognition is allowed where the taxpayer holds the property for use in business or investment. The continuity of investment is the principle underlying § 1031(a). There appears to be no controlling precedent on this precise issue, so the plain language of the statute must govern. The statute requires that property be "held for productive use in trade or business or for investment." Given the ordinary meaning of § 1031, taxpayers satisfy the holding requirement by owning the property and the remaining trade, business, or investment requirement by their lack of intent to liquidate the investment or to use it for personal pursuits. These two requirements are also essentially those placed on the property acquired in a § 1031(a) exchange. Bolker (P) acquired the Montebello property with the intent to exchange it for like-kind property. Therefore, he held Montebello for investment under § 1031(a) and is entitled to nonrecognition. Affirmed.

ANALYSIS

The Commissioner (D) had cited two revenue rulings in support of his position—Rev. Rul. 77-337, 1977 C.B. 305, and Rev. Rul. 77-297. The court noted, however, that revenue rulings are not controlling. Furthermore, the court pointed out that the revenue rulings were distinguishable since they did not deal with taxpayers who actually owned and held the property, as did Bolker (P). Further, the court rejected the Commissioner's (D) position, which would read into the statute the requirement that the taxpayer, prior to forming the intent to exchange one piece of property for a second, have an intent to keep the first piece of property indefinitely.

Quicknotes

LIKE-KIND EXCHANGE Exchange of business or investment property solely for business or investment property of a like kind.

Bell Lines, Inc. v. United States

Interstate trucking company (P) v. Federal government (D)

480 F.2d 710 (4th Cir. 1973).

NATURE OF CASE: Appeal from refund of taxes paid.

FACT SUMMARY: Bell Lines, Inc. (Bell) (P) sold their old trucks, purchased new trucks, and then claimed depreciation at the full purchase price of the new trucks. The Commissioner (D) asserted the transaction was a nontaxable exchange of old trucks for new trucks and adjusted the basis of the new trucks downward, which reduced Bell's (P) claimed depreciation deductions.

🏛 RULE OF LAW
Independent sales of old equipment and the purchase of new equipment do not give rise to a like-kind exchange.

FACTS: Bell Lines, Inc. (Bell) (P) operated an interstate trucking line. In 1959, Bell (P) decided to replace its trucks. Mack Trucks, Inc. (Mack) submitted the most competitive bid, and Bell (P) decided to purchase 148 new Mack trucks. Bell (P) then sold its old trucks to Horner Service Corp. (Horner). Unknown to Bell (P), Horner agreed to buy the trucks pursuant to an agreement with Mack whereby Horner could try to make a profit on resale but Mack guaranteed no losses. Ultimately, Mack ended up with title to most of the old trucks and treated the transactions as a trade-in. However, Bell (P) treated the transactions as a purchase and sale and paid capital gains tax on the old trucks and depreciated the new trucks from their full purchase price. The Commissioner (D) maintained that the transactions were a nontaxable exchange of trucks, and accordingly made a downward adjustment to the basis for the new trucks, which reduced Bell's (P) claimed depreciation deductions. The tax court ruled for Bell (P), and the Commissioner (D) appealed. The court of appeals granted review.

ISSUE: Do independent sales of old equipment and the purchase of new equipment give rise to a like-kind exchange?

HOLDING AND DECISION: (Craven, J.) No. Independent sales of old equipment and the purchase of new equipment do not give rise to a like-kind exchange. Section 1031(a) of the I.R.C. provides for nonrecognition of like-kind exchanges of property. The purpose of this provision is to defer recognition of gain or loss when there is a direct exchange of property. A sale for cash does not qualify even if the money is immediately reinvested in like property. The distinction between an exchange and two separate transactions depends on whether they are mutually dependent transactions. In the present case, Bell's (P) agreement to buy the new trucks was a legal obligation without regard to Horner's purchase of the old trucks. Additionally, there is no evidence that Bell (P) had any knowledge of the Mack-Horner agreement or would not have bought the new trucks without selling the old trucks to Horner. Accordingly, the transactions were independent and do not give rise to the application of § 1031(a). Affirmed.

▶ ANALYSIS

The court distinguished the Fifth Circuit's decision in *Redwing Carriers, Inc. v. Tomlinson*, 399 F.2d 652 (1968). In that case, the taxpayer would not have purchased new equipment without a concurrent and binding agreement to sell its old equipment. Revenue Ruling 90-34 shows how a transfer may qualify for nonrecognition as to a transferor even where the transferee never holds legal title to the like kind property received by the transferor.

Quicknotes

ADJUSTED BASIS The occurrence of events with respect to an asset, that requires a corresponding increase or decrease in the value a taxpayer assigns to the costs expended in acquiring that asset, to reflect the occurrence of those events.

LIKE-KIND EXCHANGE Exchange of business or investment property solely for business or investment property of a like kind.

CHAPTER 40

Involuntary Conversions

Quick Reference Rules of Law

Liant Record, Inc. v. Commissioner

Building owner (P) v. Internal Revenue Service (D)

303 F.2d 326 (2d Cir. 1962).

NATURE OF CASE: Appeal from affirmance of notice of deficiency for alleged unreported capital gains.

FACT SUMMARY: Liant (P) took the proceeds from a forced sale of a commercial building and acquired three residential apartment buildings. The Commissioner (D) maintained that the new buildings were not similar or related in service or use to the condemned office building, and asserted that capital gains should have been reported.

🏛 RULE OF LAW
In determining whether replacement property acquired by an investor is similar in use to involuntarily converted property, a comparison of the service or use that the properties have to the taxpayer-owner is critical.

FACTS: Liant (P) owned a 25-story building in Manhattan, New York. The building was leased to 82 commercial tenants. In 1953, New York City forced the sale of the building pursuant to condemnation proceedings. Liant (P) received payments for the building in 1954 and 1955 and acquired three pieces of real estate, each containing residential apartment buildings. Liant (P) contended that the gain on the involuntary conversion of the original building was nontaxable under Internal Revenue Code (I.R.C.) § 1033. The Commissioner (D) maintained that the new apartments were not similar or related in service or use to the condemned office building, and asserted that capital gains should have been reported. The tax court upheld the Commissioner's (D) deficiency on the ground that the actual, physical end use of the offices differed from the end use of the apartments, and Liant (P) appealed. The court of appeals granted review.

ISSUE: In determining whether replacement property acquired by an investor is similar in use to involuntarily converted property, is a comparison of the service or use that the properties have to the taxpayer-owner critical?

HOLDING AND DECISION: (Lumbard, C.J.) Yes. In determining whether replacement property acquired by an investor is similar in use to involuntarily converted property, a comparison of the service or use that the properties have to the taxpayer-owner is critical. Section 1033 of the I.R.C. provides that gains from involuntary conversions of property may be postponed if the taxpayer immediately spends the money in replacing the property. The replacement property must be similar or related in service or use to the converted property. Section 1033 does not allow the taxpayer an opportunity to alter the nature of the investment tax-free. The tax court in this case applied a literal "functional test" whereby the physical end use of the properties by the tenants was examined. However, if the taxpayer-owner is an investor rather than a user, it is not the tenant's use but the nature of the lessor's relation to the property that is properly at issue. In the present case, Liant (P) was invested as the owner-lessor of real estate. The tax court should have examined the extent and type of Liant's (P) management activity, the amount and kind of services rendered by him to the tenants, and the nature of his business risks connected with the properties. Reversed and remanded.

▶ *ANALYSIS*

The standard of § 1033 is similar to that of § 1031 and like-kind principles. In 1958, Congress decided that § 1033 was being interpreted too narrowly and amended it to provide for the broader like-kind standard. The Internal Revenue Service, in Revenue Ruling 64-237, adopted the position of the *Liant Record* decision by rejecting the functional-use test in favor of the service-or-use-relationship test.

Quicknotes

LIKE-KIND EXCHANGE Exchange of business or investment property solely for business or investment property of a like kind.

Willamette Industries, Inc. v. Commissioner

Timber-processing company (P) v. Internal Revenue Service (D)

U.S. Tax Ct., 118 T.C. 126 (2002).

NATURE OF CASE: Cross-motions for partial summary judgment in action to determine whether taxpayer was entitled to defer gain resulting from the salvage (processing and sale) of damaged trees under Internal Revenue Code (I.R.C.) § 1033.

FACT SUMMARY: Willamette Industries, Inc. (Willamette) (P), which owned and processed timber, suffered damage to some of its standing trees from various natural causes. Willamette (P) salvaged the trees, processed them, and then sought to defer that portion of the gain attributable to the difference between its basis and the fair market value of the trees at the time salvage began. The Internal Revenue Service (IRS) (D) determined that Willamette (P) improperly deferred this gain.

> ### RULE OF LAW
> A taxpayer is not disqualified from electing deferral of gain under I.R.C. § 1033 because it is able to salvage and process damaged raw materials into finished products rather than being forced to sell the damaged property to a third party.

FACTS: Willamette Industries, Inc. (Willamette) (P) operated a vertically integrated forest products manufacturing business, meaning that it owned trees and also processed them (as well as those from other sources) into finished products. Over several years, it suffered damage to some of its standing trees caused by wind, ice storms, wildfires, or insect infestations. The damage left part of Willamette's (P) damaged trees standing and part of them fallen. The intended use of the trees was continued growth and cultivation until maturity, at which time the trees would have been systematically and efficiently harvested. The damage occurred prior to the intended time for harvest. Willamette (P) chose to salvage the trees (process and sell them) rather than sell them to a third party. Willamette (P) did not realize income from harvesting and processing the damaged trees until it sold the products it manufactured from the damaged trees. On its tax returns for the years in question, Willamette (P) relied on I.R.C. § 1033 for involuntary conversion treatment (deferral of gain). It sought to defer only that portion of the gain attributable to the difference between its basis and the fair market value of the damaged trees as of the time its salvage of them began; that is, the value Willamette (P) contended would have been recognized if it had sold the damaged trees on the open market instead of further processing and/or milling the damaged trees into finished products. Willamette (P) further contended that it was not attempting to defer any portion of the gain attributable to the processing, milling,

or finishing of products. The IRS (D) determined that Willamette (P) understated income by improperly deferring gain from the sale of the end product of the damaged trees. Willamette (P) challenged the Commissioner's determination in tax court.

ISSUE: Is a taxpayer disqualified from electing deferral of gain under I.R.C. § 1033 because it is able to salvage and process damaged raw materials into finished products rather than being forced to sell the damaged property to a third party?

HOLDING AND DECISION: (Gerber, J.) No. A taxpayer is not disqualified from electing deferral of gain under I.R.C. § 1033 because it is able to salvage and process damaged raw materials into finished products rather than being forced to sell the damaged property to a third party. The IRS (D) claims that the conversion here was not involuntary because damaged trees were processed into end products in the ordinary course of Willamette's (P) business in the same manner as undamaged trees. Willamette (P) counters that it was compelled, involuntarily, to salvage the damaged trees before they were scheduled to be harvested to avoid further loss. It argues that its choices for salvaging the damaged trees should not preclude deferral of the portion of the gain that it was compelled to realize on account of the damage to its trees and emphasizes that it is not attempting to defer gain from processing and/or milling the damaged trees. Under § 1033, relief is intended only where the conversion is involuntary. Case-law deferral of gain falls under § 1033. First, a taxpayer's property must be involuntarily damaged, and, second, the property must no longer be available for the taxpayer's intended business purposes for the property. Under Rev. Rul. 80-175, 1980-2 C.B. 230, there is no requirement that the damage-causing event convert the property directly into cash or other property. Willamette (P) argues that a taxpayer may not have a choice as to whether to dispose of damaged property, but a taxpayer may have a choice as to how to dispose of damaged property. The IRS (D), which is arguing that a taxpayer should not be entitled to such deferral because of its choice to further process the property, contrary to Rev. Rul. 80-175, would require that the conversion be the direct result of the damage-causing event. The critical factor here is that Willamette (P) was compelled to harvest the damaged trees prior to the time it had intended. The possibility that the partial damage to its trees might have been relatively small or resulted in a nominal amount of reduction in gain is not a reason to

Continued on next page.

deny relief. Thus, here, the statutory purpose and intent are fulfilled, given that there was unanticipated tax liability due to various casualties that damaged the trees, and that Willamette (P) was forced to salvage the trees or suffer a total loss. Section 1033 simply requires that property be involuntarily converted into money or property. There is no requirement, as argued by the IRS (D), that the deferred gain be derived in a particular manner; i.e., only from a distress sale. Based on the holding of Rev. Rul. 80-175, it is unlikely that the IRS (D) would have questioned the deferral of gain if Willamette (P) had been forced to sell the damaged trees in place. Also, § 1033 does not have a quantitative threshold as to how much damage there has to be. Here, Willamette (P) is not seeking a windfall or to take advantage of the unexpected circumstances to get tax-free gain. It is seeking to defer the unexpected gain that resided in trees that it had not, at the time of the damage, intended to harvest and to reinvest that gain in trees that will fulfill its intended purpose; such deferral is the objective of § 1033. The IRS (D) argues that the purpose of § 1033 would be better served where a taxpayer is unable to process damaged property into the taxpayer's usual product(s). But that disability is not a threshold for relief or a requirement of the statute. Finally, had Willamette (P) only grown trees, under the IRS's (D) position, it would have been entitled to relief. Merely because it was also a processor of trees, and had choices of what to do with the damaged trees, the IRS (D) would deny it relief. This would require the court to impose its own judgment as to which taxpayer deserves relief; such line drawing is "illusive and a matter of conjecture." Willamette's (P) motion is granted.

▶ *ANALYSIS*

Section 1033, being a relief provision, is construed liberally to provide taxpayers the benefit of nonrecognition of gain in circumstances where recognition could create severe hardship. Given that there is very little legislative history regarding the use of damaged assets in a taxpayer's business under this statute, the court in this case seems to be giving effect to the statute's purpose.

■≡■

Quicknotes

GAIN Refers to situation where amount realized exceeds the basis of an asset.

■≡■

Installment Sales

Quick Reference Rules of Law

Burnet v. Logan

Commissioner, Internal Revenue Service (D) v. Shareholder (P)

283 U.S. 404 (1931).

NATURE OF CASE: Appeal from reversal of decision upholding deficiencies on an alleged closed sale.

FACT SUMMARY: When Youngstown Sheet and Pipe purchased their shares in Andrews and Hitchcock Co., Logan (P) and the other shareholders received, among other things, 60 cents per ton of ore mined each year from a particular leased mine. The Commissioner (D) found this was an ascertainable value and characterized it as a closed transaction, making payments subject to allocation between return of capital and income.

> ### 🏛 RULE OF LAW
> Where the compensation received for a sale is partly or totally indeterminate and speculative, it is an open transaction whereby the seller has no tax assessed on the same until her basis in the property sold is recovered.

FACTS: The shareholders of Andrews and Hitchcock Iron, including Logan (P), sold their shares to Youngstown Sheet and Pipe for a sum less than fair market value and an agreement to pay them 60 cents per ton for ore mined each year under a 97-year lease covering a specific mine. The lease did not require any minimum or maximum amount of ore to be mined each year. Logan (P) owned 250 of the 4,000 shares in Andrews and Hitchcock, for which she received the aforementioned compensation. She also was paid one-half of the payments accruing to her mother's estate, as such was the mandate of the will. This was valued for estate purposes at $277,000. Because she had not yet recovered her basis in her own stock or the assessed value on her mother's stock, Logan (P) did not pay taxes on the amounts she received. The Commissioner (D) held that the iron ore payments to be made by Youngstown had an ascertainable value, the sale constituted a closed transaction, and each payment had to be allocated between income and a return of capital. The court of appeals overruled the board of tax appeals' affirmance of the Commissioner's (D) position and allowed Logan (P) to escape assessments until she recovered her basis, holding the transaction was an open one. The United States Supreme Court granted certiorari.

ISSUE: Where the compensation received for a sale is partly or totally indeterminate and speculative, is it an open transaction whereby the seller has no tax assessed on the same until her basis in the property sold is recovered?

HOLDING AND DECISION: (McReynolds, J.) Yes. Where the compensation received for a sale is partly or totally indeterminate and speculative, it is an open transaction whereby the seller has no tax assessed on the same

until her basis in the property sold is recovered. Where the value of the compensation cannot be determined, as in this case, there exists an open transaction. It is obvious that nobody can ascertain what 60 cents per ton will be worth or is worth when there is no minimum or maximum amount to be mined under the lease, Youngstown's future needs are unpredictable, and the value of the ore left in the mine is uncertain. Thus, in this open transaction, the compensation payments are not subject to tax until if and when Logan (P) recovers her basis therein. Thereafter, any payments constitute gain and are taxable as such. This basis, insofar as Logan's (P) inheritance from her mother's estate, is equal to her mother's basis. Therefore, the Commissioner's (D) position is unsound. Affirmed.

ANALYSIS

Had there been a method to estimate the value of the ore payment, the court would probably have accepted it readily. It is, after all, a predisposition on the part of the courts to value property whenever possible to provide a basis, even a rough one. This arises from the desire to subject all property to tax when it is first proper to do so, avoiding deferral of revenue collection beyond the necessary time.

■━■

Quicknotes

BASIS The value assigned to a taxpayer's costs incurred as the result of acquiring an asset, and used to compute tax amounts toward the transactions in which that asset is involved.

■━■

Sale of a Business and Sale-Leasebacks

Quick Reference Rules of Law

Williams v. McGowan

Member of partnership (P) v. Collector, Internal Revenue (D)

152 F.2d 570 (2d Cir. 1945).

NATURE OF CASE: Appeal from reversal of deficiency on sale of a business.

FACT SUMMARY: Williams (P) sold his going business after buying out his deceased partner's interest in it. The Commissioner (D) determined that tax should have been determined on separate elements of the business, some as ordinary, some as capital, and accordingly issued a deficiency.

> ## 🏛 RULE OF LAW
> The assets of a business must be separately treated to determine if income from their sales is capital or ordinary based on § 1221.

FACTS: Williams (P) and Reynolds formed a partnership. When Reynolds died, Williams (P) purchased Reynolds's interest from the estate. Williams (P) then sold the assets of the business to a third party. Williams (P) reported the sale as an ordinary loss on his tax return. The Commissioner (D) determined that tax should have been determined on separate elements of the business, some as ordinary, some as capital, and accordingly issued a deficiency. The district court, finding that the business as a whole was a capital asset, reversed the deficiency. The court of appeals granted review.

ISSUE: Must the assets of a business be separately treated to determine if income from their sales is capital or ordinary based on § 1221?

HOLDING AND DECISION: (Hand, J.) Yes. The assets of a business must be separately treated to determine if income from their sales is capital or ordinary based on § 1221. While it has been held that a partner's interest in a going concern should be treated as a capital asset, when Williams (P) bought Reynolds's share, the business became a sole proprietorship. There is no suggestion of a tax-avoidance scheme, and the business must be treated as a sole proprietorship. Since there is no special treatment designated for a sole proprietorship, we § 1221 must be interpreted to determine the appropriate tax treatment. Section 1221 requires that all assets be treated as capital ones unless they fit within three exceptions, i.e., stock in trade, property held primarily for resale to customers, and depreciable business property. Williams (P) transferred cash, receivables, fixtures, and inventory. Fixtures are depreciable, and inventory is primarily held for customer resale. Therefore, neither of these assets is subject to capital gains treatment. Cash transfers cannot result in gains or losses. Therefore, the only asset that might be deemed capital in nature is the receivables. However, it had not been argued whether they are subject to

depreciation. Therefore, that point is left open for the district court if the parties cannot agree. All other assets should be treated as yielding ordinary income. Reversed.

DISSENT IN PART: (Frank, J.) The parties, in their contract, stated that Williams (P) was to transfer his "rights, title and interest . . . in, and to, the hardware business." Congress did not intend to carve the sale of a business into separate distinct sales. The parties transacted for the sale and purchase of the business as a whole. There does not seem to be any rationale to support the majority's decision either on a contract theory or on the purpose of § 1221. What was sold was the business, not the individual assets.

▌ANALYSIS

Goodwill is considered a capital asset when a business is sold. Rev. Rul. 57-480, 1957-2 C.B. 47; Regs. § 1.167(a)-3. On the other hand, accounts receivable acquired on the sale of inventory property will be deemed noncapital assets, § 1221(4). Since most businesses are on the accrual basis, the receivables will already have been reported as income so that § 1221(4) will have little effect on them. It may be more significant for cash-basis taxpayers.

◼▬◼

Quicknotes

ACCOUNTS RECEIVABLE Amounts that are owed pursuant to an open account and that arise in the normal course of business dealings.

CAPITAL ASSET The sale or exchange of property that produces capital gain or loss.

CAPITAL GAIN AND LOSS Gain or loss from the sale or exchange of a capital asset.

FIXTURE An item of personal property that has become so attached to the real property that it is considered a part of the real property.

◼▬◼

Annabelle Candy Co. v. Commissioner

Corporation (P) v. Internal Revenue Service (D)

314 F.2d 1 (9th Cir. 1962).

NATURE OF CASE: Appeal from affirmance of disallowance of deductions for the amortized cost of a restrictive covenant.

FACT SUMMARY: After Sommers left the Annabelle Candy Company (P), the company claimed that a portion of the buyout price for his share of the business was for a covenant not to compete that supported deductions for the amortized cost of the covenant. The Commissioner (D) denied the deduction, finding that the entire payment was for payment of Sommers's share, with none allocable to a restrictive covenant.

RULE OF LAW

The intent of the parties at the time a business interest is bought out determines whether a portion of the buyout price was allocated for a covenant not to compete that would support a deduction for the amortized cost of the covenant.

FACTS: Altshuler and Sommers were equal shareholders in Annabelle Candy Company (P). They had a distinctive method of making Rocky Road candy. When differences between them surfaced, a negotiated buyout of Sommers was arranged. The agreement provided for total consideration of $115,000 to be paid to him in installments. Sommers also agreed not to compete or engage in any activities that might be prejudicial to the business, such as disclosing the company's unique way of making Rocky Road, for a period of five years. These restrictive covenants were discussed after the price was agreed upon, but were a critical part of the contract. On its tax return, Annabelle Candy (P) allocated around $80,000 of the total purchase price to the covenant not to compete and began to deduct the amortized cost of the allocated portion over the five years of the covenant. The Commissioner (D) disallowed this deduction, maintaining that the entire buyout price was for Sommers's share of the business rather than for a restrictive covenant. The tax court sustained the Commissioner's (D) deficiency notice, and Annabelle Candy (P) appealed.

ISSUE: Does the intent of the parties at the time a business interest is bought out determine whether a portion of the buyout price was allocated for a covenant not to compete that would support a deduction for the amortized cost of the covenant?

HOLDING AND DECISION: (Barnes, J.) Yes. The intent of the parties at the time a business interest is bought out determines whether a portion of the buyout price was allocated for a covenant not to compete that would support a deduction for the amortized cost of the

covenant. Section 167(a)(1) authorizes taxpayers to use a depreciation deduction for property used in trade or business. There is no question that a covenant not to compete for a definite term qualifies under this section. However, in order to amortize a payment for a restrictive covenant there must be an actual payment for the covenant. To determine whether the covenant has been paid for, the terms of the contract should be examined. Additionally, it is proper to look behind the contract to the intentions of the parties. In the present case, the buyout agreement does not contain any allocation of consideration for the covenant. However, the tax court did not strictly determine whether there was an intention, at the time the parties signed the agreement, to allocate a portion of the price to the covenant. The parties were entitled to such a determination. Therefore, the case must be remanded for this determination. Remanded.

ANALYSIS

In 1993, Congress significantly altered the way business intangibles, such as covenants not to compete, goodwill, going concern value, etc., were treated by enacting § 197. This provision permits the amortization of such intangibles over a 15-year period. Thus, for example, if § 197 applied in this case, rather than being able to take amortization over the five-year life of the covenant, Annabelle Candy (P) would have to take it over the longer 15-year period, thus making the deductions less attractive. Certain intangibles, such as patents and copyrights, are expressly excluded by § 197 from the 15-year period.

Quicknotes

AMORTIZATION The satisfaction of a debt by the tendering of regular, equal payments over a period of time.

DEPRECIATION An amount given to a taxpayer as an offset to gross income to account for the reduction in value of the taxpayer's income-producing property due to everyday usage.

RESTRICTIVE COVENANT A promise contained in a deed to limit the uses to which the property will be made.

Frank Lyon Co. v. United States

Property buyer and lessor (P) v. Federal government (D)

435 U.S. 561 (1978).

NATURE OF CASE: Appeal from denial of a tax refund.

FACT SUMMARY: A bank entered into a sale-leaseback arrangement with Frank Lyon Co. (P).

🏛 RULE OF LAW
Where there is a genuine multiple-party transaction with economic substance that is compelled or encouraged by business or regulatory realities, imbued with tax-independent considerations, and not shaped solely by tax-avoidance features that have meaningless labels attached, the form of the transaction adopted by the parties should govern for tax purposes.

FACTS: When the Federal Reserve System nixed Worthen Bank's (Worthen's) plan to finance its own building, because state and federal banking laws and regulations precluded it from doing so, Worthen sought other financing and entered into a sale-and-leaseback arrangement with Frank Lyon Co. (Lyon) (P). Under the arrangement, Lyon (P), whose principal stockholder was a bank director, would buy the building as Worthen constructed it and lease it back to Worthen. Lyon (P) obtained both a construction loan and permanent mortgage financing. The primary lease term was 25 years with options to extend for 40 more years. These options were at prices equal to the then unpaid balance of Lyon's (P) mortgage and initial $ 500,000 investment. Lyon (P) was the sole party directly liable on the permanent mortgage loan from an insurance company. Worthen was to take care of the expenses usually associated with maintaining a building, and the rent was set at just enough to cover interest and principal on the mortgage loan. Lyon (P) obtained both a construction loan and permanent mortgage financing. On its federal income tax return for the year in which the building was completed and the bank took possession, Lyon (P) accrued rent from Worthen and claimed as deductions depreciation on the building, interest on its construction loan and mortgage, and other expenses related to the sale-and-leaseback transaction. The Commissioner (D) disallowed the deductions on the ground that Lyon (P) was not the owner of the building for tax purposes but that the sale-and-leaseback arrangement was a financing transaction in which Lyon (P) loaned Worthen $ 500,000 and acted as a conduit for the transmission of principal and interest to Lyon's (P) mortgagee. This resulted in a deficiency and Lyon (P) brought suit in the district court to recover the deficiency amount. The district court held that the claimed deductions were allowable, but the court of appeals reversed. The United States Supreme Court granted certiorari.

ISSUE: Where there is a genuine multiple-party transaction with economic substance that is compelled or encouraged by business or regulatory realities, imbued with tax-independent considerations, and not shaped solely by tax-avoidance features that have meaningless labels attached, should the form of the transaction adopted by the parties govern for tax purposes?

HOLDING AND DECISION: (Blackmun J.) Yes. Where there is a genuine multiple-party transaction with economic substance that is compelled or encouraged by business or regulatory realities, imbued with tax-independent considerations, and not shaped solely by tax-avoidance features that have meaningless labels attached, the form of the transaction adopted by the parties should govern for tax purposes. In this case the presence of a third-party lender distinguishes this from many two-party sale-leaseback cases where the form was merely a tax-avoidance device. Here Lyon (P) was liable on the mortgage loan and exposed its business well-being to a real and substantial risk. The form was not a sham and is to be respected. While it is clear that none of the parties to the sale-and-leaseback agreements is the owner of the building in any simple sense, it is equally clear that Lyon (P) is the one whose capital was invested in the building and is therefore the party entitled to claim depreciation for the consumption of that capital under § 167 of the Code. Reversed.

DISSENT: (Stevens J.) The controlling issue in this case is the economic relationship between Worthen and Lyon (P), and matters given great weight by the majority, such as the number of parties, their reasons for structuring the transaction in a particular way, and the tax benefits that may result, are largely irrelevant. The question whether a leasehold has been created should be answered by examining the character and value of the purported lessor's (here, Lyon's (P)) reversionary estate. Since Worthen has at present the unrestricted right to control the residual value of the property for a price not exceeding the cost of its unamortized financing, it is the owner as a matter of law. Lyon (P) is in the role of a lender, and as such, has assumed the risk—as most lenders do—of Worthen's insolvency and that Worthen might not exercise its option to purchase at or before the end of the original 25-year term.

▶ ANALYSIS

The majority relied heavily on the fact that a regulatory agency prohibited Worthen from financing its own building in reaching its conclusion that the transaction was com-

Continued on next page.

prised of a genuine sale, followed by a leaseback. Alternatively, however, this transaction could have been viewed, as Justice Stevens indicates in his dissent, as merely a financing arrangement akin to a mortgage. In cases such as these, the factual evidence, such as whether the parties understood the transaction to be a financing arrangement or a sale-leaseback, or whether rental payments were viewed as simply constituting interest payments, will ordinarily be determinative of the outcome.

■══■

Quicknotes

DEPRECIATION An amount given to a taxpayer as an offset to gross income to account for the reduction in value of the taxpayer's income-producing property due to everyday usage.

MORTGAGE An interest in land created by a written instrument providing security for the payment of a debt or the performance of a duty.

■══■

Leslie Co. v. Commissioner

Financing-seeking company (P) v. Internal Revenue Service (D)

539 F.2d 943 (3d Cir. 1976).

NATURE OF CASE: Appeal from the reversal of a denial of a loss deduction.

FACT SUMMARY: In order to obtain financing for a new plant, to be built on property it already owned, Leslie Co. (P) entered into a sale and leaseback arrangement with Prudential Insurance Company (Prudential). The cost of construction was greater than the purchase price, and Leslie (P) took the difference as a deduction for the loss on the sale. The Commissioner (D) treated the difference as Leslie's (P) cost in obtaining the lease, and amortized the sum over the life of the lease, which resulted in tax deficiencies being assessed against Leslie (P).

RULE OF LAW

Where property is sold for its approximate fair market value, the presence of a long-term leaseback will not render the sale an exchange.

FACTS: Leslie Co. (P) wished to construct a new plant. Leslie (P) was unable to obtain financing. Prudential agreed to advance $2,400,000 for the construction of the plant. After construction, Leslie (P) was to sell Prudential the plant for $2,400,000 or its actual construction cost, whichever was less. Leslie (P) then would sign a 30-year lease with two ten-year options. The plant cost $3,187,000 to build. Upon completion, Leslie (P) "sold" the building to Prudential for $2,400,000, as required by their agreement. A loss of $787,000 was reported from the "sale." The Commissioner (D) denied the loss based on the rationale in *Century Electric Co. v. Commissioner*, 192 F.2d 155 (8th Cir. 1951), alleging that this was an exchange of like-kind properties, on which no loss is recognized under § 1031. The tax court, on petition for redetermination, found that the fair market value of the property was approximately $2,400,000 and that the transaction was a sale with a concurrent condition requiring a lease. Since the sale was for the full market value of the plant, the lease had no capital value, there was no exchange of like-kind properties, and Leslie (P) was entitled to deduct the entire amount under the general recognition provision of the Code. The court of appeals granted review.

ISSUE: Where property is sold for its approximate fair market value, will the presence of a long-term leaseback render the transaction an exchange?

HOLDING AND DECISION: (Garth, J.) No. Where property is sold for its approximate fair market value, the presence of a long-term leaseback will not render the sale an exchange. Regulation 1.1002(d) states that an exchange must involve the reciprocal transfer of property.

If the sale is for the fair market value of the asset/property, the lease has no separate value, but is merely a condition of sale. Under this regulation, the transaction cannot be deemed an exchange. Valuation of the property is the key to determining whether such transactions are to be characterized as sales or exchanges for tax purposes. Congress did not intend § 1002 to require taxes on paper gains. Correspondingly, paper losses should also not be recognized. However, where there is a transfer of property for cash, which is the equivalent of the property's fair market value, the transaction is a sale, and a loss may be taken on it. Affirmed.

ANALYSIS

An essential difference between *Century* and *Leslie* is the courts' respective view on the need for valuation. In *Century,* the court viewed the legislative enactment as one to relieve the administrative burden of valuation, and therefore regarded the value of the properties involved as irrelevant. By contrast, in *Leslie,* the court viewed the congressional purpose behind the non-recognition provision as one of avoiding taxation of paper gains and losses, and therefore required valuation of the properties involved to determine whether the requirements of an "exchange" had been met. The interpretation of congressional intent is more convincing in *Leslie,* since, if Congress had intended to obviate the need to conduct difficult valuations, it would have provided for nonrecognition of gains and losses in all exchanges, regardless of whether the property received was of a like kind, or not of a like kind.

Quicknotes

CONCURRENT CONDITIONS Dependent conditions that are to be performed at the same time.

CHAPTER 43

Original Issue Discount

Quick Reference Rules of Law

United States v. Midland-Ross Corporation

Federal government (D) v. Note-holding company (P)

381 U.S. 54 (1965).

NATURE OF CASE: Appeal from affirmance of reversal of deficiency notice for failure to treat gains as ordinary income.

FACT SUMMARY: Midland-Ross Corporation (P) sought to treat earned original issue discount as capital gains, but the Commissioner (D), finding this to be the equivalent of interest, determined that the gains should be taxed as ordinary income.

RULE OF LAW
Under the Internal Revenue Code (I.R.C.) of 1939, earned original issue discount is not entitled to capital gains treatment.

FACTS: Midland-Ross Corporation (P) bought non-interest-bearing promissory notes from the issuers at prices discounted below the face amounts. Midland-Ross (P) held these notes for over six months and then sold them for more than the issue price, but still less than the face amount. Midland-Ross (P) sought capital gains treatment for its profit rather than declaring the gain as ordinary income. The Commissioner (D) issued a notice of deficiency, but Midland-Ross (P) prevailed on its suit for a refund in the district court and court of appeals. The United States Supreme Court granted certiorari to resolve a split among the circuits.

ISSUE: Under the I.R.C. of 1939, is earned original issue discount entitled to capital gains treatment?

HOLDING AND DECISION: (Brennan, J.) No. Under the I.R.C. of 1939, earned original issue discount is not entitled to capital gains treatment. Capital gains treatment applies only to situations in which appreciation in value accrues over a substantial period of time. Capital gains treatment applies only to gains on the sale or exchange of a capital asset. However, not everything that is called property in the ordinary sense qualifies as a capital asset. The term "capital asset" must be construed narrowly in accordance with the purpose of Congress to give capital gains treatment only for appreciations in value accrued over a long period of time. Earned original-issue discount serves the same function as stated interest; it is the equivalent of compensation for the use of money to the date of sale. Unlike typical capital appreciations, the earning of discount to maturity is predictable and measurable. Therefore, since earned original issue discount is so similar to stated interest income, it must be treated as ordinary income. In other words, it cannot be regarded as typically involving the realization of appreciation in value accrued over a substantial period of time which is given capital-

gains treatment to ameliorate the hardship of taxation of the entire gain in one year. Thus, Midland-Ross (P) should have reported its gain from the purchase and sale of discounted notes as ordinary income. Reversed.

▶ ANALYSIS

This decision resolved a conflict between the courts of appeals on this issue. In the instant case, Midland-Ross (P) sold the notes in the same year of purchase. Thus, the Court did not reach the question of whether accrual-basis taxpayers would be required to report discount earned before final disposition of the obligation. The decision also was subsequently confirmed and codified by the original issue discount (OID) statutory provisions.

Quicknotes

ACCRUAL BASIS A method of calculating taxable income based on the time at which certain events have become fixed, including the right to receive that income, the deductions to which the taxpayer has been subject, and the obligation to pay tax owed, regardless of when the taxpayer actually earned the income.

CAPITAL ASSET The sale or exchange of property that produces capital gain or loss.

CAPITAL GAIN AND LOSS Gain or loss from the sale or exchange of a capital asset.

Note: There are no principal cases in Chapter 44 of the casebook.

CHAPTER

45

The Alternative Minimum Tax

Quick Reference Rules of Law

Klaassen v. Commissioner

Parent with many dependent children (D) v. Internal Revenue Service (P)

182 F.3d 932 (10th Cir. 1999).

NATURE OF CASE: Appeal from affirmance of determination of deficiency.

FACT SUMMARY: The Internal Revenue Service (IRS) (D) issued the Klaassens (P) a notice of deficiency for the taxable year 1994, determining they were liable for the alternative minimum tax (AMT).

🏛 RULE OF LAW

The alternative minimum tax (AMT) imposes a tax whenever the sum of specified percentages of the excess of AMT income over the applicable exemption amount exceeds the regular tax for the taxable year.

FACTS: The Klaassens (P) had ten dependent children in 1994, the taxable year in issue. They filed a joint federal income tax return for 1994, claiming a total of twelve exemptions, two for themselves and ten for their children, as well as itemized deductions for medical and dental expenses and state and local taxes. The Commissioner (D) issued a notice of deficiency determining that the Klaassens (P) were liable for the AMT. The tax court upheld the Commissioner's (D) position, and the court of appeals granted review.

ISSUE: Does the AMT impose a tax whenever the sum of specified percentages of the excess of AMT income over the applicable exemption amount exceeds the regular tax for the taxable year?

HOLDING AND DECISION: [Judge not stated in casebook excerpt.] Yes. The AMT imposes a tax whenever the sum of specified percentages of the excess of AMT income over the applicable exemption amount exceeds the regular tax for the taxable year. The alternative minimum tax imposed by § 55 is in addition to the regular tax. The alternative minimum tax is equal to the difference between the tentative minimum tax and the regular tax. The tentative minimum tax is 26 percent of the excess of the taxpayer's alternative minimum taxable income over an exemption amount of $45,000. The term "alternative minimum taxable income" is the taxpayer's taxable income for the taxable year determined with the adjustments of § 56 and increased by the items of tax preference of § 57. Here, the Klaassens (P) had no items of tax preference in 1994. The adjustments in § 56 include the following: (1) no itemized deduction is allowed for state and local taxes; (2) in determining the amount allowable as a deduction for medical expenses, a 10 percent floor must be applied; and (3) no personal exemptions are permitted. Taking such factors into account, the Klaassens (P) are liable for $6,196.43. Because this amount exceeds the Klaassens' reg-

ular tax of $5,111, they are liable for the difference. Affirmed.

CONCURRENCE: (Kelly, J.) The legislative history of the AMT supports an argument that the original purpose of the AMT was to ensure that taxpayers with substantial economic income pay a minimum amount of tax on it. However, now, many middle-income taxpayers who have not utilized Internal Revenue Code (I.R.C.) § 57 preferences to reduce regular taxable income are caught by the AMT's original attempt to impose fairness. That is the case here. The regular tax already reduces or phases out itemized deductions and personal exemptions based upon income; surely Congress never intended a family of 12 that still qualified for these items under the regular tax to partly forfeit them under the AMT. Notwithstanding these concerns, which may only be addressed by Congress, an interpretation of the existing statute requires imposing the tax on the Klaassens (P), no matter how inequitable it is to do so.

▶ ANALYSIS

The Klaassens (P) challenged the application of the AMT on the basis that such tax was solely intended to limit items of tax preference. The court, reading the plain language of the statute, construed the AMT to mean the taxpayer's taxable income for the taxable year determined with the adjustments of § 56 and increased by the tax preferences of § 57. While the tax preferences were significant, they did not constitute an indispensable component of the equation. Thus, the AMT may apply even when there are no items of tax preference. Congress has not acted generally to adjust or "index" the AMT triggers for inflation to ensure the tax applies only to the highest-income taxpayers, but has only provided occasional one- or two-year "patches" to prevent a return to lower exemption amounts. Accordingly, as judge Kelly points out in his concurrence, more and more taxpayers end up paying the AMT, contrary to Congress's original intent, resulting in increased tax inequity.

■━■

Quicknotes

ALTERNATIVE MINIMUM TAX Tax designed to guarantee that those whose source of income is given preferential treatment and exceeds a certain amount pay at least a minimum amount of tax.

EXEMPTION Colloquial term usually used to refer to a deduction not keyed to actual expenditures.

■━■

Glossary

Common Latin Words and Phrases Encountered in the Law

A FORTIORI: Because one fact exists or has been proven, therefore a second fact that is related to the first fact must also exist.

A PRIORI: From the cause to the effect. A term of logic used to denote that when one generally accepted truth is shown to be a cause, another particular effect must necessarily follow.

AB INITIO: From the beginning; a condition which has existed throughout, as in a marriage which was void ab initio.

ACTUS REUS: The wrongful act; in criminal law, such action sufficient to trigger criminal liability.

AD VALOREM: According to value; an ad valorem tax is imposed upon an item located within the taxing jurisdiction calculated by the value of such item.

AMICUS CURIAE: Friend of the court. Its most common usage takes the form of an amicus curiae brief, filed by a person who is not a party to an action but is nonetheless allowed to offer an argument supporting his legal interests.

ARGUENDO: In arguing. A statement, possibly hypothetical, made for the purpose of argument, is one made arguendo.

BILL QUIA TIMET: A bill to quiet title (establish ownership) to real property.

BONA FIDE: True, honest, or genuine. May refer to a person's legal position based on good faith or lacking notice of fraud (such as a bona fide purchaser for value) or to the authenticity of a particular document (such as a bona fide last will and testament).

CAUSA MORTIS: With approaching death in mind. A gift causa mortis is a gift given by a party who feels certain that death is imminent.

CAVEAT EMPTOR: Let the buyer beware. This maxim is reflected in the rule of law that a buyer purchases at his own risk because it is his responsibility to examine, judge, test, and otherwise inspect what he is buying.

CERTIORARI: A writ of review. Petitions for review of a case by the United States Supreme Court are most often done by means of a writ of certiorari.

CONTRA: On the other hand. Opposite. Contrary to.

CORAM NOBIS: Before us; writs of error directed to the court that originally rendered the judgment.

CORAM VOBIS: Before you; writs of error directed by an appellate court to a lower court to correct a factual error.

CORPUS DELICTI: The body of the crime; the requisite elements of a crime amounting to objective proof that a crime has been committed.

CUM TESTAMENTO ANNEXO, ADMINISTRATOR (ADMINISTRATOR C.T.A.): With will annexed; an administrator c.t.a. settles an estate pursuant to a will in which he is not appointed.

DE BONIS NON, ADMINISTRATOR (ADMINISTRATOR D.B.N.): Of goods not administered; an administrator d.b.n. settles a partially settled estate.

DE FACTO: In fact; in reality; actually. Existing in fact but not officially approved or engendered.

DE JURE: By right; lawful. Describes a condition that is legitimate "as a matter of law," in contrast to the term "de facto," which connotes something existing in fact but not legally sanctioned or authorized. For example, de facto segregation refers to segregation brought about by housing patterns, etc., whereas de jure segregation refers to segregation created by law.

DE MINIMIS: Of minimal importance; insignificant; a trifle; not worth bothering about.

DE NOVO: Anew; a second time; afresh. A trial de novo is a new trial held at the appellate level as if the case originated there and the trial at a lower level had not taken place.

DICTA: Generally used as an abbreviated form of obiter dicta, a term describing those portions of a judicial opinion incidental or not necessary to resolution of the specific question before the court. Such nonessential statements and remarks are not considered to be binding precedent.

DUCES TECUM: Refers to a particular type of writ or subpoena requesting a party or organization to produce certain documents in their possession.

EN BANC: Full bench. Where a court sits with all justices present rather than the usual quorum.

EX PARTE: For one side or one party only. An ex parte proceeding is one undertaken for the benefit of only one party, without notice to, or an appearance by, an adverse party.

EX POST FACTO: After the fact. An ex post facto law is a law that retroactively changes the consequences of a prior act.

EX REL.: Abbreviated form of the term "ex relatione," meaning upon relation or information. When the state brings an action in which it has no interest against an individual at the instigation of one who has a private interest in the matter.

FORUM NON CONVENIENS: Inconvenient forum. Although a court may have jurisdiction over the case, the action should be tried in a more conveniently located court, one to which parties and witnesses may more easily travel, for example.

GUARDIAN AD LITEM: A guardian of an infant as to litigation, appointed to represent the infant and pursue his/her rights.

HABEAS CORPUS: You have the body. The modern writ of habeas corpus is a writ directing that a person (body) being detained (such as a prisoner) be brought before the court so that the legality of his detention can be judicially ascertained.

IN CAMERA: In private, in chambers. When a hearing is held before a judge in his chambers or when all spectators are excluded from the courtroom.

IN FORMA PAUPERIS: In the manner of a pauper. A party who proceeds in forma pauperis because of his poverty is one who is allowed to bring suit without liability for costs.

INFRA: Below, under. A word referring the reader to a later part of a book. (The opposite of supra.)

IN LOCO PARENTIS: In the place of a parent.

IN PARI DELICTO: Equally wrong; a court of equity will not grant requested relief to an applicant who is in pari delicto, or as much at fault in the transactions giving rise to the controversy as is the opponent of the applicant.

IN PARI MATERIA: On like subject matter or upon the same matter. Statutes relating to the same person or things are said to be in pari materia. It is a general rule of statutory construction that such statutes should be construed together, i.e., looked at as if they together constituted one law.

IN PERSONAM: Against the person. Jurisdiction over the person of an individual.

IN RE: In the matter of. Used to designate a proceeding involving an estate or other property.

IN REM: A term that signifies an action against the res, or thing. An action in rem is basically one that is taken directly against property, as distinguished from an action in personam, i.e., against the person.

INTER ALIA: Among other things. Used to show that the whole of a statement, pleading, list, statute, etc., has not been set forth in its entirety.

INTER PARTES: Between the parties. May refer to contracts, conveyances or other transactions having legal significance.

INTER VIVOS: Between the living. An inter vivos gift is a gift made by a living grantor, as distinguished from bequests contained in a will, which pass upon the death of the testator.

IPSO FACTO: By the mere fact itself.

JUS: Law or the entire body of law.

LEX LOCI: The law of the place; the notion that the rights of parties to a legal proceeding are governed by the law of the place where those rights arose.

MALUM IN SE: Evil or wrong in and of itself; inherently wrong. This term describes an act that is wrong by its very nature, as opposed to one which would not be wrong but for the fact that there is a specific legal prohibition against it (malum prohibitum).

MALUM PROHIBITUM: Wrong because prohibited, but not inherently evil. Used to describe something that is wrong because it is expressly forbidden by law but that is not in and of itself evil, e.g., speeding.

MANDAMUS: We command. A writ directing an official to take a certain action.

MENS REA: A guilty mind; a criminal intent. A term used to signify the mental state that accompanies a crime or other prohibited act. Some crimes require only a general mens rea (general intent to do the prohibited act), but others, like assault with intent to murder, require the existence of a specific mens rea.

MODUS OPERANDI: Method of operating; generally refers to the manner or style of a criminal in committing crimes, admissible in appropriate cases as evidence of the identity of a defendant.

NEXUS: A connection to.

NISI PRIUS: A court of first impression. A nisi prius court is one where issues of fact are tried before a judge or jury.

N.O.V. (NON OBSTANTE VEREDICTO): Notwithstanding the verdict. A judgment n.o.v. is a judgment given in favor of one party despite the fact that a verdict was returned in favor of the other party, the justification being that the verdict either had no reasonable support in fact or was contrary to law.

NUNC PRO TUNC: Now for then. This phrase refers to actions that may be taken and will then have full retroactive effect.

PENDENTE LITE: Pending the suit; pending litigation under way.

PER CAPITA: By head; beneficiaries of an estate, if they take in equal shares, take per capita.

PER CURIAM: By the court; signifies an opinion ostensibly written "by the whole court" and with no identified author.

PER SE: By itself, in itself; inherently.

PER STIRPES: By representation. Used primarily in the law of wills to describe the method of distribution where a person, generally because of death, is unable to take that which is left to him by the will of another, and therefore his heirs divide such property between them rather than take under the will individually.

PRIMA FACIE: On its face, at first sight. A prima facie case is one that is sufficient on its face, meaning that the evidence supporting it is adequate to establish the case until contradicted or overcome by other evidence.

PRO TANTO: For so much; as far as it goes. Often used in eminent domain cases when a property owner receives partial payment for his land without prejudice to his right to bring suit for the full amount he claims his land to be worth.

QUANTUM MERUIT: As much as he deserves. Refers to recovery based on the doctrine of unjust enrichment in those cases in which a party has rendered valuable services or furnished materials that were accepted and enjoyed by another under circumstances that would reasonably notify the recipient that the rendering party expected to be paid. In essence, the law implies a contract to pay the reasonable value of the services or materials furnished.

QUASI: Almost like; as if; nearly. This term is essentially used to signify that one subject or thing is almost analogous to another but that material differences between them do exist. For example, a quasi-criminal proceeding is one that is not strictly criminal but shares enough of the same characteristics to require some of the same safeguards (e.g., procedural due process must be followed in a parole hearing).

QUID PRO QUO: Something for something. In contract law, the consideration, something of value, passed between the parties to render the contract binding.

RES GESTAE: Things done; in evidence law, this principle justifies the admission of a statement that would otherwise be hearsay when it is made so closely to the event in question as to be said to be a part of it, or with such spontaneity as not to have the possibility of falsehood.

RES IPSA LOQUITUR: The thing speaks for itself. This doctrine gives rise to a rebuttable presumption of negligence when the instrumentality causing the injury was within the exclusive control of the defendant, and the injury was one that does not normally occur unless a person has been negligent.

RES JUDICATA: A matter adjudged. Doctrine which provides that once a court of competent jurisdiction has rendered a final judgment or decree on the merits, that judgment or decree is conclusive upon the parties to the case and prevents them from engaging in any other litigation on the points and issues determined therein.

RESPONDEAT SUPERIOR: Let the master reply. This doctrine holds the master liable for the wrongful acts of his servant (or the principal for his agent) in those cases in which the servant (or agent) was acting within the scope of his authority at the time of the injury.

STARE DECISIS: To stand by or adhere to that which has been decided. The common law doctrine of stare decisis attempts to give security and certainty to the law by following the policy that once a principle of law as applicable to a certain set of facts has been set forth in a decision, it forms a precedent which will subsequently be followed, even though a different decision might be made were it the first time the question had arisen. Of course, stare decisis is not an inviolable principle and is departed from in instances where there is good cause (e.g., considerations of public policy led the Supreme Court to disregard prior decisions sanctioning segregation).

SUPRA: Above. A word referring a reader to an earlier part of a book.

ULTRA VIRES: Beyond the power. This phrase is most commonly used to refer to actions taken by a corporation that are beyond the power or legal authority of the corporation.

Addendum of French Derivatives

IN PAIS: Not pursuant to legal proceedings.

CHATTEL: Tangible personal property.

CY PRES: Doctrine permitting courts to apply trust funds to purposes not expressed in the trust but necessary to carry out the settlor's intent.

PER AUTRE VIE: For another's life; during another's life. In property law, an estate may be granted that will terminate upon the death of someone other than the grantee.

PROFIT A PRENDRE: A license to remove minerals or other produce from land.

VOIR DIRE: Process of questioning jurors as to their predispositions about the case or parties to a proceeding in order to identify those jurors displaying bias or prejudice.

Casenote® Legal Briefs